CW00672525

THE
RISING
TIDE

AMONG THE ISLANDS
AND ATOLLS
OF THE PACIFIC OCEAN

PRAISE FOR *DEEP FIELD: DISPATCHES FROM THE FRONTLINES OF AID RELIEF*

'He's also one hell of a storyteller and wordsmith: astute, descriptive, ironic, funny and philosophical. As Australians argue over the reductive logic of "Stopping the Boats", Bamforth illuminates the intricacies and entanglements of history, politics and self-interest and introduces us to the eccentrics who keep ploughing through it all for a better world. Verdict: Astonishing.'

Herald Sun

'It reads as if Don Delillo had been sent to Darfur.'

John Freeman, Granta

THE
RISING
TIDE

AMONG THE ISLANDS
AND ATOLLS
OF THE PACIFIC OCEAN

TOM BAMFORTH

Hardie Grant

BOOKS

Published in 2019 by Hardie Grant Books,
an imprint of Hardie Grant Publishing

Hardie Grant Books (Melbourne)
Building 1, 658 Church Street
Richmond, Victoria 3121

Hardie Grant Books (London)
5th & 6th Floors
52–54 Southwark Street
London SE1 1UN

hardiegrantbooks.com

All rights reserved. No part of this publication may be reproduced, stored in a retrieval
system or transmitted in any form by any means, electronic, mechanical, photocopying,
recording or otherwise, without the prior written permission of the publishers and
copyright holders.

The moral rights of the author have been asserted.

Copyright text © Tom Bamforth 2019

Earlier versions of some of the chapters appeared in the following publications:
- 'Charged with banana leaves and sea shells: impressions of Tuvalu',
  Island Magazine 149, 2017.
- 'Port Moresby Revisited', *Island Magazine* 156, 2019.
- 'The Men in Green: encounters with populism in the Pacific',
  Griffith Review 57, 2017.
- 'Adventures in the nuclear Pacific', *Meanjin*, 78/1, 2019.

Every effort has been made to trace and acknowledge all copyright holders. Please contact
the publisher with any information on errors or omissions.

 A catalogue record for this
book is available from the
National Library of Australia

The Rising Tide
ISBN 978 1 74379 307 7

Cover design by Josh Durham, Design by Committee
Typeset in 10.75/16 pt Sabon LT Std by Post Pre-Press Group
Printed by McPherson's Printing Group, Maryborough, Victoria

 The paper this book is printed on is certified against the
Forest Stewardship Council® Standards. FSC promotes
environmentally responsible, socially beneficial and
economically viable management of the world's forests.

Contents

Introduction

From above, Kiribati looked spectacular: the image of a Pacific paradise sold in tourist brochures and on package holiday websites. The main atoll of Tarawa was a thin, L-shaped sliver of bone-white sand lined by a blur of coconut palms and surrounded by the green and turquoise waters of the lagoon. It resembled a place of honeymoons, winter escapes, family adventures and seclusion from the pressures of life and work.

As the plane descended through a cloudless sky, I dreamed of running straight from the landing strip to the ocean and diving into its cool, glinting colours. Once and for all, the stale air conditioning of the previous twelve hours in planes and airport lounges would be left behind. Many have had this dream. In the early 1990s, a British student called Dan Wilson found himself doing a holiday job on the Polish–German border during a particularly harsh winter of climatic and economic malaise. With few financial resources available and only his imagination to rely on, Wilson had a stroke of genius. He wrote to the government of Kiribati and suggested that they appoint him poet laureate, offering his services in verse:

I'd like to live in Kiribati
I feel it's the country for me
Writing poems for all the people
Under a coconut tree.

Surprised, but not entirely taken in by the charms of Wilson's doggerel, the government accepted his proposal and appointed him to the position. Wilson was given a hut to live in but, so that he would not be too much of a nuisance to anyone, the government ensured that it was 'conveniently located on one of the outer islands'.

From the air, the beaches, palms and crystal waters of the Tarawa lagoon made it seem the perfect place to write poems under a coconut tree, but on the ground the reality was different. By the time of my first visit in 2009, the southern part of Tarawa was densely populated. Including its water territories, Kiribati occupied an area about half the size of Australia and was the biggest of the Pacific's 'large ocean states'. Yet the majority of the country's one hundred thousand people have moved from outer islands to the atoll of South Tarawa in search of jobs. As with other archipelago states in the Pacific, the country's population was initially dispersed across the islands, but in the years following independence in 1979 this changed with the concentration of economic activity and state resources in the capital. The introduction of a money economy and changes in occupation and lifestyle led to accelerated migration from the outer islands to Tarawa. Similar urbanisation had occurred throughout the Pacific as nuclear testing, climate change, the power of cash, the possibility of overseas migration and the increasing difficulty, unpredictability and unfashionability of agricultural life caused a gradual decline in the traditions of communal and subsistence living elsewhere. Growing yams and fishing as a way of life in the villages had given way to purchasing instant noodles, Fanta Orange and spam at the local store in the capital. These stores were often run by recently arrived Chinese migrants who, reflecting broader geopolitical unease about the growing influence of China in the region, were sometimes subjected to varying degrees of racial denigration. In Tonga, for example, I was always directed to 'the Chinese shop' whenever I needed anything, as if the hundreds of Chinese-run enterprises in the capital were all one and the same. In some areas of the Pacific, especially Kiribati, the Marshall Islands and French Polynesia, traditional lives and livelihoods were no longer even possible on islands that had been 'vaporised' by nuclear testing.

Densely populated urban life in the Pacific has brought additional concerns. Traditionally, the ocean was the great sanitiser of island life, particularly for those living on atolls. With small populations scattered among the islands, waste, effluence and excreta were borne away instantly in the vast currents of the Pacific Ocean. In Kiribati, with most of the population now crowded onto one small atoll, the local environmental balance had begun to shift. This was especially true in the shallower waters of the lagoon, which, during my visits, were contaminated with sewage. I was under strict instructions not to eat the fish, for fear of ciguatera poisoning. More alarming still, the atoll states of the Pacific were dependent on rainwater, which percolated through holes in the dead coral of the atoll into a freshwater lens that floated on the heavier saltwater of the ocean beneath. Sea level rise and the increasing number, unpredictability and severity of droughts had begun to alter the balance of saltwater and freshwater in the lens, with the result that existing freshwater sources were becoming saline. This problem was compounded by additional water pumping to meet the needs of the growing population, whose waste and effluence were disposed back into the lagoon and sometimes into the freshwater lens itself. By 2014, the twin processes of development and climate change led the government of Kiribati under former president Anote Tong to buy land more than 2000 kilometres away in Fiji to sustain future settlement.

There has been substantial investment in climate change adaptation since I first visited Kiribati in 2009, when the country presented a grim image of the future. Surrounded by collapsing seawalls and the wreckage of mitigation projects that had fallen apart through lack of maintenance and the remorseless pressures of the sea, I met with an international aid official who managed large-scale infrastructure investment programs. 'We fully support Kiribati', she said, 'but informally we recognise that, in the longer term, we promote migration with dignity.'

If climate change, urbanisation and migration had brought great changes to life in the Pacific, the region was also remarkable for its ingenuity, resilience and independence. South Tarawa may have been overcrowded, but Kiribati – like many of the Pacific island states – had achieved the extraordinary. It is a viable, stable country with well-managed finances that had preserved its language and culture on the islands and atolls of the largest ocean on earth. The small island states Kiribati, Tuvalu, Fiji and the Marshall Islands have played leading roles in some of the most pressing, urgent and complex global debates, among them climate change, environmental sustainability, nuclear disarmament and the future of the world's oceans. In a sign of their confidence, these so-called micro-states have, like Tuvalu (population 11,000), rejected the view that population size or landmass matter. They have embraced the seagoing boldness of their ancestors, preferring to be known as 'large ocean states'. Despite the experience of colonialism, nuclear testing, resource exploitation and great power rivalry, language, custom and identity have been preserved, often providing the basis for forms of resistance. The revival of the ancient art of canoe building in the Marshall Islands and the revolution in Bougainville that was – in part – a reaction to the environmental destruction caused by mining were ways in which islanders chose their own futures, sometimes at great cost. While traditional Pacific societies survived against the odds, migration to cities has seen the development of newer urban cultures with their own evolving dynamic across the region.

This book brings together some of these threads of contemporary Pacific experience. It is based on my personal travels and encounters, as well as my involvement in disaster response as an aid worker in the region between 2008 and 2019. While most of the stories here are based on my experiences of independent travel, a number reflect on the circumstances and characters I worked with in the aftermath of natural disasters. At times, in order to get a better understanding of the countries beyond their official circles, non-government organisations (NGOs) and the complexities of aid and emergencies, I revisited places where I had previously worked. At other times, I visited parts of the Pacific that were new to me and there I relied on the generosity of strangers who shared their stories and invited me into their homes. I have not sought to visit every country, island or isolated community. Instead, I often spent my time in urban areas, following relatively well-trodden paths. My aim was to capture states of contemporaneity and flux, rather than embarking on the investigation of remote societies that marks so much writing about the region.

In 2014, when I first contemplated writing this book, I attended a speech, given by the then Australian foreign minister in Canberra, which announced a 'new aid paradigm' that dismantled the well-regarded national aid program. What remained was slashed to an all-time low and subordinated to narrowly defined Australian economic and strategic interests in the Pacific. In an unfortunate phrase, given the likely impact of sea-level rise in the Pacific, the 'new aid paradigm' would 'lift all boats on a rising economic tide'. I knew then that I had a working title for my book. What followed became an attempt to present the region not as a series of economic, environmental and strategic systems to be navigated but as complex, ancient and changing societies in their own right.

At the time of the foreign minister's speech, my exposure to life in the Pacific had mainly been through my work with an aid agency based in Melbourne, Australia. As a result, I tended to see the region through the calibrated language, often passed down by government, that tended to frame the work of international development institutions. This was sometimes a weird mix of technical jargon, military diction, and 1990s business school rhetoric. The term 'background noise' was sometimes used to describe history, politics, personalities and cultures that could interfere with the otherwise smooth operation of an aid program. Important as those aid programs were, I was fascinated by Pacific societies in their own terms. Here, between the cracks of aid and development programs, were great realms of experience, covering a third of the surface area of the globe, that I became aware of.

This book is about the background noise. I have largely screened out discussion of aid and development, which were the main subjects of my earlier book, *Deep Field: Dispatches from the Frontlines of Aid Relief*. Instead, this book is about interaction, race, colonisation, climate change, nuclear testing, resistance, cultural preservation, urban life, the tastiness of well-roasted pig and the pleasures of canoeing at dusk.

I hope that the stories here – from eleven countries, written about different times and different contexts – will depict elements that are true of the Pacific region as a whole. There are 25,000 islands in the Pacific. Inevitably many places, cultures and societies, which could make for many entirely different trajectories, are not included here. This is a personal account based on multiple visits, interactions and conversations over more than a decade rather than a single journey. It is inherently biased and partisan and it charts, through random encounters and points of contact, my own evolving course in trying to know and understand the region.

It is sometimes said that the Pacific is to the contemporary world what the Mediterranean was to the ancients and what the Atlantic was to the twentieth century. *The Rising Tide*, then, is a journey into the ocean of the future.

Prologue

ISLAND SONG

TUVALU BY MOTOR SCOOTER

I opened the throttle and tore down the tarmac, pushing the rusty motor scooter as fast as it could go. The warm night air, thick with salt, flowed around me as the scooter cranked out its top speed and I headed for the edge of the island. The atoll narrowed and the houses thinned. Within a few minutes of what seemed like flight, I had arrived at the isthmus of the Funafuti lagoon; a metre-wide strip of land separating the moonlit mercury of the lagoon from the crashing waves of the great Pacific Ocean. Tuvalu is one of the smallest countries on earth, and the trip from end to end of its largest atoll took just twenty minutes on a clapped-out motor scooter. But that short journey into the vast night of sky and ocean, sand and stars – a unity of the elements – made Tuvalu much greater than the sum of its minute islands. During the day, there was the risk of 'island fever' – a sense of being trapped forever on this tiny coral atoll. But at night, as everyone went to bed, the country seemed to expand with space and freedom and I urged my scooter faster into the encroaching dusk, past the parliament buildings and the shanties at the edge of town, and on into the roar of the ocean and the sonorous grunting of the local pigs.

*

'You're never helpful, Randal', erupted an annoyed parent to the aircraft cabin at large. From the back of the plane the objection 'We didn't have to come here, you know' floated up from the growing din as holiday-makers on family tours started to squabble under the stress of the journey. Young lovers, clad in singlets and shorts in anticipation of a holiday in the Pacific sun, were by now freezing in the plane's arctic air conditioning. Babies cried with the turbulence and air pressure, while exasperated parents lost their cool after several hours constraining the airborne boredom of their teenage children. This desperation intensified as the mildewed cold of the cabin gave way to airless morning heat on the tarmac as we transited through the tourist destination of Fiji.

Then the plane grew quiet as we flew on, three hours north, towards Tuvalu. The squabbling families were left behind to their resorts, tinned cries of '*Bula*' – 'good health' – and an idealised Pacific experience of neatly planted rows of frangipani, golf courses and artificial white-sand beaches that have been hermetically sealed from military coups, urban sprawl and the toughness of village life. Fiji worked in the resorts as it didn't in reality. Beaming, handsome Fijians set the Pacific tone while, behind the reception counters and in back offices, Indo–Fijian clerks and accountants laboured industriously, turning profits and making sure their guests wanted for neither sun nor smiles nor beer. Bar the tourists clad in singlets and thongs, this must have been what pre-resort Fiji looked like in 1960: an immaculate pre-independence European playground of instantly met needs and exotically pliant locals.

As we flew further from Fiji, there was nothing now beyond the hum of the engines and the distant white tips of the breaking waves below – the white-on-blue mirror of the clouds that thinly strafed the sky above. A pale outline of a lagoon surrounded by coral atolls appeared – a vast bleached semicircle, like the jawbone of an ancient sea-monster – and hinted at more habitable atolls to come.

The resemblance of some of the atolls to ancient sea monsters clearly struck early Tuvaluans, who considered the eel and the flounder to be the creators of the land. Having been friends, the creatures fell out and started to fight over who could carry a heavy stone in a test of strength. Hit in the stomach and badly injured, the eel magically cursed the flounder, whose crushed body became thin and flat and formed the land of Tuvalu. The eel then became round as a coconut as it feasted on the flounder's body, explaining the presence of coconut trees on Tuvalu. Having consumed the flounder, the eel went back to collect the stone they had been carrying together and noticed its three colours: blue, black and white. He threw it in the air, and the blue piece got stuck and did not come back to land. Angrily, he threw the stone again, and this time the black piece became stuck as well. Having thus created day and night, the eel uttered some magic words, and the white part of the stone fell, creating light. A small part of the blue stone still remained, so the eel broke this into eight parts and created the main atolls of Tuvalu.

If Tuvalu's atolls have inspired myth and folklore, they have also been significant to Western science. It was on the main atoll, Funafuti, that Charles Darwin's theory about the origins of coral atolls was demonstrated. To answer the question as to why coral atolls appear in the middle of the ocean while coral itself occurred only in shallow water, Darwin proposed that it grew on the slowly subsiding craters of ancient volcanoes. The growth of the coral kept pace with the subsidence, eventually forming a habitable landmass that outlined the volcano's rim. Geological expeditions organised by the Royal Society in London in the 1930s drilled into the Funafuti atoll and found at great depths traces of fossilised shallow-water organisms, proving Darwin correct.

I was visiting Tuvalu to manage an international development program and there had been some problems with the project:

delays, a lack of reports, budgets that had begun to go slightly awry. Alarm bells had started ringing when I could not get through on the phone from Melbourne. For some reason, the Tuvalu connection was rerouted to the Midwest of the United States, and my afternoon calls to the Tuvalu office of my organisation were diverted to hardware store owners in Ohio and evangelical churches in Wyoming in the middle of their night. When I eventually did get through to my colleagues in Funafuti, their concerns were entirely different from mine. Instead of talking about the aid program, there was much discussion on the arrival of an outer-island choir for its centenary celebrations. Days, even weeks, had been declared choral holidays. It had become clear that the only way of discovering what was happening on this archipelago of coral atolls, home to a sovereign nation of 11,000 people and at a deep remove from the aid agency's Australian headquarters, was to get on a plane and see for myself.

The plane circled above Tuvalu's capital, Funafuti, and eventually glided down, the atoll becoming less bone-like and more like a living, breathing human settlement as we approached. I stumbled out of the air-conditioned insularity of the cabin, blinded by the sudden light and heat of the runway. The weekly arrival of the plane was a major event on Funafuti, most of whose land was taken over by the airstrip built by the Americans during World War Two. The short supply of land meant that it had also become the main playground for children during the day. At night, young lovers and those seeking to escape from their extended families camped there to catch the sea breeze and listen to the roar of the ocean. A fire truck had been dispatched shortly before our landing to clear away the last of the children, and excited relatives had gathered nearby, carrying shell necklaces and floral headdress as gifts of welcome. Market stalls were conducting a gentle trade. Some locals had taken the opportunity for a lunchtime doze under the shade of a breadfruit tree – an afternoon somnolence that daily overcame the island and stretched on into the early evening.

In Funafuti (whose international airport code was 'FUN'), everything seemed in miniature. The Development Bank of Tuvalu was a one-room building a few metres from the airport, and the parliament house was a small open-sided meeting hall that was used by children to watch the arrival of the weekly flight from Fiji. The towering government administrative office, built by Taiwan in exchange for diplomatic recognition, was the only structure on the atoll more than two storeys high, while the Tuvalu campus of the grandly named University of the South Pacific was a small classroom and an outdoor meeting table. Between the landing strip, the main road and the government buildings was a maze of paths and side roads leading to built-up settlements where extended families, sometimes up to thirty people, packed into small, tin-roofed houses.

While the airstrip was the hub of social life, however, its construction had come at a cost. During World War Two, at each narrow tip of the croissant-shaped island, coral had been cut out of the atoll and used to surface the runway, leaving deep trenches on either side. As the population of Funafuti gradually increased with migration from the outer islands, communities sprang up on the only land available to them – the trenches. The communities grew, building stilt houses in the trenches, and these slowly filled with rubbish and waste. Every time there were heavy rains or strong winds, damage was caused to the unstable houses. During drought, the opposite problem occurred. The absence of water and the rubbish strewn around the area posed sanitation and hygiene risks. For all its charm, even this miniature nation was beginning to struggle with the pressures of urbanisation.

If the settlements were not enough, the Tuvaluans' relation to the sea was one of palm-tingling precariousness. Each year, during the king tides, a third of Funafuti was submerged as water bubbled up through the porous coral. More alarmingly still, while Tuvalu was generally said to be outside the cyclone belt, cyclones were not completely unknown. Bebe, which struck in 1972, caused the total inundation of Funafuti and destroyed all the island's buildings. When I visited Tuvalu's meteorological office, old pictures on the walls showed scientific staff bravely carrying on their work knee deep in water.

*

'We'll collect you at nine this evening', said one of my Tuvaluan colleagues, who was eager to be left alone to make preparations for the night's entertainment. I had unwittingly arrived during the centenary celebrations of Tuvalu's island choirs and these were now at their height. There was, unusually for Funafuti, an excited anxiety in the air. The choirs, founded by missionaries in 1914, were coming together like a great gathering of the tribes. The finest singers and community elders had made sea voyages from the remotest of the atolls, taking days to reach the capital, where each island had its own local community whose centre was an open-sided meeting hall, or *maneapa*.

That evening, dressed in floral shirts and crowns of frangipani, we made our way to the *maneapa*. I followed gingerly, aware that this was a serious business and no mere tourist attraction. I was there on sufferance as a cordially invited guest but felt that I could not have walked in on my own. We processed slowly on ancient motor scooters – a floral chugging that was both stately and faintly comical as enormous Tuvaluans festooned in flowers balanced delicately on their tiny mechanised transports, knees turned out for balance.

The *maneapa* was surrounded by concentric circles of community members organised, it seemed, hierarchically, watching the performances from outside in the cool of the night. Inside, groups of men and women, organised by island, gave competing performances that rose in tempo, volume and drumming as they sought to outperform each other. Supporting the *maneapa*'s enormous roof were eight columns, one for every island of Tuvalu. The leader of each community sat with his back against one of the columns and together they formed an inner circle of wizened elders deep in contemplation who lent gravitas to the proceedings.

Troupe after troupe stood to perform. The young girls started first; bedecked in flowers and pandanus fronds they danced from a sitting position. Theirs was a slow dance, classically Polynesian, with a gentle swaying of shoulders and choreographed arm movements – the calm of the lagoon – before the older women stood to the increased beat of the drums, building on the swaying arms below with fuller undulations. As the drumming resonated, deep Pacific male voices sang, and the tempo grew, before the men too were on their feet, moving with still greater freedom as the drumming and singing reached a crescendo. Around the edge, the crowds cheered and laughed with ever-greater volume and hilarity as jokes were introduced into the routine: a sudden frenetic paddling of imaginary canoes, a mock amorous proposal and rebuff. Before long all were up in a general mêlée of noise, flowers and whirling pandanus. Round and round this ritual went, growing louder and more intoxicating with each repetition as the dancers sought to outdo each other. Unhappy with just one crescendo, some performers repeated the best and loudest bits. In the confusion, old women armed with spray bottles of lemon-scented cologne pumped thick wafts into the energetic dancers as they worked themselves into a fragrant island ecstasy.

Behind the *maneapa*, feasts were prepared by women for the performers and spectators. Multiple roast pigs turned slowly on spits, fresh tuna sashimi was cut into mouth-watering slices and doused with seawater. There were buckets of lightly salted flying fish, sweet pandanus desserts and great mounds of taro and breadfruit. This was proper feasting – food prepared for the entire contingent of hundreds of people every night. And each night was a new celebration that lasted till dawn as more boats arrived from the islands and as the official choral ceremonies took place. The feasts then continued as the representatives from each outer island were farewelled back to their boats for the long journey home. For three weeks, the singing, dancing and feasting continued till dawn, stopping all other activities beyond preparing food, training voices and picking fresh flowers for that evening's crowns.

As the food was consumed, each of the hitherto silent elders stood to speak, offering advice, humour, religious instruction and formal greetings from their island to the world. But a concern for the old ways had now crept into the proceedings. At length, the elders shared their knowledge about the world in which they had grown up and which was rapidly transforming around them. They gave details about how to set fish traps in the traditional way, the multiple uses of the pandanus tree, the art of making canoes. These ancient skills of Pacific life and survival were solemnly and formally recited. There was also a quiz – a stoic attempt to engage the younger Tuvaluans in elements of their culture that the elders deemed important.

'Which island in Tuvalu first converted to Christianity?'

'Funafuti!'

'Who was the Roman general who denied that Christ was the son of God?'

'Chuck Norris!' called out an irreverent youth from the back of the *maneapa*.

'How do you know who you are?'

The answer to the last question was convoluted and it involved references to faith, biblical study and island life. But in a way it was also crucial to the proceedings: the frantic vigour of the performances was the reinforcement of collective identity in the face of the country's unknown future.

Leaving the *maneapa* at midnight, I set off on a late-night motor scooter ride exploring the nocturnal world of Funafuti. I was no longer a guest seated in the charmed inner ring of the *maneapa* but a distant spectator, lurking on the outskirts as other *maneapas* in different parts of the island went through the same rituals. I had been at one of the great *maneapas* – a place that occasionally doubled as the country's parliament. It was made of concrete – a sign of wealth – and its walls bore elaborately woven pandanus mats spelling out the names of all the islands of Tuvalu in perfect missionary copperplate. The other *maneapas* were small and more modest wooden buildings with corrugated-iron roofs, but the noise was just as great, the concentric circles were smaller and tighter, and the performances took on a greater level of intensity. No one here called out 'Chuck Norris' irreverently to strange questions from local elders. The music continued, hundreds of bodies swaying, singing, drumming in a driven unison that was at once celebration and preservation. The solution to rising sea levels, migration, urbanisation and the decline of outer island life, it seemed, was to drum louder. Here, the edge was harder, more visceral, the dancing defiant. The effect was of a musical centrifuge whose forces ever magnified and tended inwards – the focus was the disappearing point at the centre.

For all the intensity of the outer island choirs, this was not the chosen entertainment of Funafuti's young. As the singing and drumming in the *maneapas* continued into the night, young people crept away, taking off their floral crowns and pandanus skirts. They put on shorts and tight-fitting t-shirts and set out for the 'chicken shed' for some 'twisting' – the local term for modern dancing that seemed to conjure the presence of long-departed American GIs. The 'chicken shed' was a large wire construction on the other side of the runway, well away from the houses, where Funafuti's massed youth sweated out the night with beer, and with hip-hop blasting from the club's massive speakers, before they crashed out on the tarmac.

Eventually, I headed back to my hotel, where the house band was in action. As I fell asleep, a Tuvaluan-Fijian reggae ensemble crooned, 'I'll give you fish and chips if you swing your hips.'

The next morning, I left the hotel early and joined some friends from the night before. We crammed into a small motorboat for the islet of Funafala, in the Funafuti lagoon. For the Tuvaluans, this was an opportunity to 'get away from it all' and escape the megalopolis of Funafuti for the island life they had known as children, before roads, shops, flights and a money economy had changed their society forever. For forty-five minutes we skimmed across the waves of the relatively calm lagoon. With each passing minute, the water turned an ever more brilliant shade of turquoise. Ahead, the beaches gleamed, and the coconut and pandanus trees swelled with burgeoning fruit. We landed, and the children with us instantly disappeared, pursuing startled crabs along the beach. One of the adults produced a sharp knife and an enormous whole tuna – it was time for a Pacific hangover cure. For the next hour we sat in the shallows carving exquisite buttery slivers, lightly doused in saltwater, before ripping pandanus fruit from the trees and gnawing on the sweet, fibrous husks.

'You know, I'm thinking about migrating to New Zealand', said Atiu, a colleague, between bites. Most of his family had already left Tuvalu, and his children were at school in Auckland.

I suggested we could swap – Melbourne for Funafuti.

He laughed. 'It's not the paradise we remember', he said. 'It is difficult to get a good education, and there are few opportunities for our children.' Of his extended family, only he and his wife, who worked in the bank, had jobs with wages, and the social expectations were endless. At any one time there were around thirty people staying at his house, all of whom had to be provided for. And then there was illness, which was increasingly common across the Pacific, where changes in diet and lifestyle had led to epidemic proportions of diabetes and heart disease. Fully one-third of young Tuvaluans were diagnosed with what was locally called 'gout' – a catch-all description for what were, most likely, the early signs of diabetes. Those who could afford it went to New Zealand where proper treatment was available for diseases that were a death sentence in Tuvalu.

'But then I think', Atiu continued, 'if island life was good enough for me, why should it not be good for my children?' We reflected on the differences between the sunlit freedom of the islet and long school days in cold, suburban Auckland. 'Maybe I could ultimately migrate to Mackay in central Queensland', he said. 'From the pictures it looks most like Tuvalu.'

As we left the islet, speeding back towards the urban centre of Funafuti to return to jobs and a flight home, I saw a message scrawled by one of the children in the sand. The words 'Funafala is very good' appeared just beyond the line of the rising tide.

Part 1

EMPIRE OF THE ELEMENTS:
CYCLONES, TSUNAMIS AND
THE SPACES IN BETWEEN

1

THE GREEN MEN OF VANUATU

Hunched against the incessant rain and strong winds that followed in the wake of Tropical Cyclone Pam, which struck Vanuatu in 2015, I made my way slowly towards the National Emergency Management Office. The capital's buses shot by, one after the next splattering me with water and mud. From one eye I caught their eerie and incongruous mottos: 'Rasta never die', 'Facebook', 'Happiness is free' and 'Paris shopping'. The turnoff to the government offices was marked by an Eezy Kill Pest Control shop that displayed a large picture of a stricken rat, while near the shore further on there was *Tru Blu II*, a wrecked fishing boat, its name adorning a shattered gunwale. Nearby, its sister ship, *Felicity*, listed dangerously on the foreshore.

'Don't stand in the puddle', shouted a well-dressed aid worker hurrying past as I stood dripping wet in front of the building. 'You'll ruin your boots.' He handed me an immense multicoloured umbrella, and, brandishing this, I entered the National Emergency Management Office and was led to a small, glass-sided room known as the 'fishbowl'. This was where I would spend almost every waking hour for the next three months, working as an aid coordinator with the international humanitarian response to the cyclone.

In 2015, Cyclone Pam was the strongest cyclone ever to have hit the South Pacific, a record that lasted only briefly until Cyclone Winston struck Fiji a year later. Cyclone Pam crashed through twenty-three of the Vanuatu's sixty-five inhabited islands at 280 kilometres an hour. More than 30,000 houses were destroyed and there was major damage to crops. At least eleven people lost their lives.

The number of deaths was strikingly low. Many of the aid workers had flown in from the Philippines, where Typhoon Haiyan – the most recent super-typhoon – had smashed cities and killed more than 6000 people. And this was the point of comparison for arriving aid workers. 'It's not Tacloban' was a common observation made by those arriving in the Pacific for the first time, Tacloban being a destroyed city in the Philippines province of Leyte. The low death toll was a testament to the work done by the government of Vanuatu and long-term development agencies over the preceding years. In the fishbowl, near where I sat, there was as poster in Bislama (the Vanuatu pidgin) announcing, '*Yumi save stanap agansem disasta*' – We know how to stand up against disasters. It depicted two scenes: one before and the other after a cyclone. In the first scene, a Ni-Vanuatu man stood proudly to attention in front of a carefully prepared house with neat grounds and a thatched roof that was weighed down with heavy palm fronds to prevent it from being blown away. 'Preparded', announced the poster with a satisfied flourish. In the second, an absence of such vigilance was evident. The beautiful thatched house had been destroyed, a Ni-Vanuatu woman stood crying out the front, and a middle-aged European man with a floppy white hat, short shorts, protuberant belly and a backpack was standing nearby with his hands on his hips. 'Unpreparded', read the caption sternly.

Fearing the worst following the cyclone, the government of Vanuatu had called for international assistance, and aid agencies had poured in, accompanied by the military assets of six governments:

Australia, New Zealand, France, the United States, the United Kingdom and Tonga. In the fishbowl, civil–military coordination officers jostled with sprightly French naval logisticians in green jumpsuits and NGO representatives clad, like racing drivers, in emblem-encrusted gilets that announced a parade of funding agencies and partners. This was a near-compulsory sartorial item, known more colloquially as the 'wanker jacket'. Australian aid officials took their place, apologetically sporting their own aid program's newly designed jacket. These featured the red kangaroos – or the 'red rat', as they were known to those obliged to wear them. While they didn't resemble the ogres of international disaster relief clad in short shorts and terry-towelling hats envisaged by Vanuatu's disaster preparedness authorities, the internationals had arrived and taken up residence in the fishbowl. The relaxed pace of life in Port Vila had been replaced by military briskness, shouted instructions and a propensity to bellow 'Yes, sir' at anyone potentially in any position of authority.

Every now and again the clamour in the fishbowl would be interrupted as someone from the prime minister's office appeared and tried to remind the assembled militaries and aid agencies that the government still existed. The policy expert from the prime minister's office, Ben Shing, would come and read the riot act. With his clipped English accent, army boots, Afro and full beard, he looked like a 1970s political agitator rather than a high-level bureaucrat. Unlike the more retiring public servants, he was a 'big man' in the Melanesian tradition: a relation of the prime minister and an influential figure with licence to alternate between the charming and incisive and the grandiose and overbearing modes of political expression. Staring over his steel-rimmed glasses, he would inform the fishbowl inhabitants that any deviation from the highest standards of humanitarian assistance as expected by the government would result in expulsion.

'I can make any of you persona non grata!' he roared one day, particularly incensed by some out-of-date food supplies that had been brought in by the World Food Programme.

'Yes, sir!' shouted the various militaries, while NGO representatives cowered at the back of the room.

I had been invited by the National Emergency Management Office to help coordinate the response and so I needed to identify someone in government as my official counterpart. Who this might be was not immediately obvious. Over the next few days I visited all the offices in and around the fishbowl. Gradually, a whole apparatus of invisible local administration emerged. From corridors and back offices, from behind photocopiers and bookshelves stuffed with development reports, the state's representatives, softly spoken, courteous and deeply knowledgeable, appeared. It was a world entirely different from the assertiveness of much of the rest of the response community. I asked one government employee if she minded being kicked out of her office by the arrival of international response. 'No', she replied. 'In a couple of weeks the men in green will have left and things will be back to normal.'

But for the first few weeks, there was intense activity. It was a fast, hectic and impressive display of military cooperation and prowess – a logistician's paradise – as the men in green jumpsuits developed elaborate plans to integrate the assets of six different military forces. In Port Vila harbour the usual parade of cruise ships had been replaced by equally vast naval assets, HMAS *Tobruk* and HMNZS *Canterbury*, which steamed around the islands delivering assistance, accompanied by Tongan patrol boats that darted into narrower straits to reach areas inaccessible to the larger vessels. Black Hawk helicopters flew constant sorties to the outer islands, while massive military transport planes overshadowed the local airport as they arrived with fresh supplies. With incredible precision, the French military's Puma helicopters would intersect with the

Tongan patrol boats via Australian and New Zealand cruisers at distant islands and on schedules planned down to the last minute.

The activity also seemed excessive and I wondered if there was something else at play. A delay in items being shipped from Australia meant that many of the military assets flew around with relatively little to deliver. Commercial transport companies quickly resumed operations, and NGOs quietly and efficiently went about their work, chartering civilian ferries, trucks and banana boats to deliver aid while rendering much of the high-volume military effort redundant. Amid fears of a rising China beginning to assert itself in the Pacific, Cyclone Pam seemed the perfect cover under which to flex combined military might and test the strength of the FRANZ Arrangement, in which France, Australia and New Zealand agreed to cooperate in disaster responses in the Pacific, presumably with a view to wider geopolitical realities.

The cyclone also presented opportunities for tourists. Outside the fishbowl, I met a young visitor who had just been on an assessment mission and had spent the day hurtling over Vanuatu's airspace in a Black Hawk. His previous experience in humanitarian assessment had consisted of a brief stint at a local resort during the school break. He had nonetheless volunteered to help and had made it onto one of the assessment teams headed for the outer islands. I asked what he had seen. 'Lots of needs out there', he said without elaboration. 'But what a way to end the holiday. I can't wait to tell Mum I've just flown in four Black Hawks.'

Some days later I too was in a helicopter, trying to get a sense of the damage to housing on some of the outer islands. I had jumped on board with a Red Cross delegate who was managing a program trying to restore family links. Concerned relatives from New Zealand and Australia had contacted him to discover the fate of their distant cousins and long-lost aunts. He had been unable to contact five of them, and the only way of ascertaining their situation was to track them down in person. For hours, we flew over the deep blue of the Pacific, gazing out at the distant islands and listening to the drone of the rotor blades as the pilot navigated towards their remote villages.

This was no fast-paced Black Hawk or snarling Puma but a small commercial helicopter that more closely resembled a mechanised mosquito. We scanned the horizon and studied maps, searching for the coordinates of villages and possible landing sites. The pilot descended slowly on unsuspecting hamlets, places where there was no electricity or running water, circling before finding a clear patch to put down the sophisticated machine. Children usually spotted us first and swarmed towards the helicopter, excited but trepidatious. Some had seen war films and had observed the flight of powerful military craft charging across the sky. They assumed, they told us, that we would leap out with guns blazing to start a war.

In one village, the elders approached cautiously and we announced our purpose: we were looking for missing people and had received a report that an elderly woman in the village had not been heard from since the cyclone. Did she live here? Maybe we could talk. The elders smiled and showed us to a small thatched hut. Producing a satphone, we stood at a discreet distance as, perplexed at first but then delighted, she spoke at length with her worried relative in New Zealand, packing ten years of life since they had last seen each other into the twenty short minutes allowed for the call. She was well, unharmed by the cyclone. With that, we walked back to the helicopter. It was a moving scene. We were no longer part of the impersonal apparatus of planning and management that characterised the response coordination epicentre of the fishbowl; we were searching for specific individuals about whom relatives had expressed concern.

What mattered was not reports and spreadsheets and the myriad administrative tasks to keep donors and headquarters happy but the wellbeing of specific individuals who were not necessarily the most powerful, influential or well known in their communities. As we strapped ourselves in and the pilot started the rotor blades once more, I couldn't help noticing that some of the elders were clutching mobile phones and could possibly have communicated the news themselves. It was unclear if the phones worked, or whether they were symbols of status and authority but technologically defunct. I said nothing, and we flew on to the next village, searching once more for the missing.

That evening, back in Port Vila, I visited a *nakamal* with some colleagues. This was a dark and secluded establishment under a tree that was also an important cultural centre for traditional life in Vanuatu. Here, evenings were whiled away in conversation fuelled by a mildly sedative drink made from the crushed root of the kava plant. We joined a group of American Peace Corps volunteers and I found myself sitting on an uncomfortable wooden log drinking barely palatable local kava next to Bree, an Australian volunteer, with large, doleful eyes and fragile, bird-like features.

'You will have seen the news about me and Troy?' she asked.

I confessed I hadn't, so she launched into her history. She had come to Vanuatu to escape the pressures of a relationship.

'Well, we're on again, off again. When we met I thought this one would last. We got on so well and we're really in tune. The first time we met he said, "Nice rack", and I said, "Yeah, thanks. You're a babe-a-tron". And we were on for a while, but then it all got too much, and because there were other contestants and I thought I could win. But I didn't win, so we got back together again.'

I was struggling to make head or tail of this until one of the Americans came over and helped me out, translating as Bree continued with her story. 'Baby bird was a semifinalist on the Australian *Bachelorette*', he explained. 'She's been telling us all, and it's your turn to hear all about it. Good job. You're taking one for the team, and if it wasn't you, it'd be me.'

I looked around and found that I had been abandoned to the tale of Bree and Troy. The Americans were laughing and enjoying themselves a few metres away, and I was trapped.

'So, I'm thinking about starting my own health and wellbeing TV show or maybe going into acting, and my promoter says I could have a really large audience who want to be a part of Team Bree, so I've got to be careful with my personal brand and not rush into anything.'

Fortunately, the kava was beginning to take its famed numbing effect, and I quickly lost track of the television show and baby bird's brand dilemmas, which, after a while, merged with the soft breeze and the washing of the ocean waves against the shore.

*

It rained like I'd never seen it rain before. A lucky break in the weather had allowed some of the disaster response coordinators to catch a flight from Port Vila to Whitegrass Airport on Tanna, Vanuatu's southern island. The island had also been badly hit by Pam and debates about the equity of assistance had become increasingly contentious in the capital, playing into old rivalries between the main island of Efate and Tanna itself. Many of the country's leading politicians were from Tanna, and the word on the street and the rumours circulating in the capital's buses was that 'man Tanna' was getting it all. But other reports suggested a different story. The lack of paved roads and the intense rain had meant that, while relief items had been shipped to the main port and the airfield, actually getting them out into rural areas had been difficult if not impossible. One of the ministers had even called for the establishment of what he called a 'tented city' in order to house people who had lost everything in the cyclone. Agencies had set up operations, only to find themselves stuck, unable to move as the dirt roads turned to rivers of thick, rich mud that swallowed up truck tyres and brought operations to a halt. To try to head off an even more politicised response and to prevent the establishment of another miserable camp, I went with a couple of colleagues to see directly what was happening.

This was not easy. Despite a brief break in the weather that had allowed our flight to land, the rain resumed harder than before. We hired a car at the airport – a clapped-out pick-up truck belonging to Stephen, the uncle of one of my colleagues – and, standing in the back, were quickly getting soaked as the truck made its painful way back to town from the airport. After a few kilometres we stopped outside a small tin shack and the truck's engine spluttered out. 'No benzene', said Stephen and he made his way into the shack where a wizened man appeared, dragging plastic fuel containers behind him. At twenty dollars a litre, it was hideously expensive and I wondered if, having managed to get there, we would ever be able to afford to leave the immediate precinct of the airport.

Very quickly we abandoned more formal clothes and I put on my swimming shorts – anything else seemed impractical in the torrential downpour – and we half drove, half pushed the car to a largely abandoned hotel near the town. The rain seemed only to intensify, making any further exploration impossible. We decided to wait in the hotel until it eased.

But the sky darkened further and the rain continued to pound with persistent intensity. All through the night it poured and poured, and on again into the next day and the next. So we waited, and after the fourth day of unceasing downpour, it appeared that something almost biblical was happening. I'd never seen a deluge like this. As what remained of our hotel started to fall apart under the intensity of the aquatic barrage, I took refuge in what had once been the restaurant. It seemed like building some kind of raft might not be the maddest use of our time. The forced inactivity, the complete severance from any kind of communications, and the inability to go anywhere had demoralising effects. The persistent heavy drumming of the post-cyclone rain produced a great lethargy and our heavy-limbed movements were marked by an incredible slowness. Everyone slept, becoming comatose with tiredness and the incessant rhythmic hammering of the rain.

I tried to work, to catch up on documents, occupy myself somehow, but after a few hours my computer lost power and I was in the dark. Looking around the hotel, I found a candle and then, to my surprise, an unopened carton of red wine that had been left over by a long-departed French official. Vanuatu, it has been joked, was fortunate. It had been ruled jointly, as a condominium, by the British and the French until the country became independent in 1980. When the colonial powers left the country, they bequeathed to it a combination French cuisine and British justice, but it could just as easily have been the other way round. For a fourth and a fifth day, I sat and slowly drank the red wine, looking out into a bleak landscape of storm clouds, sodden fields, and sheet after grey sheet of relentless and unending rain.

On the sixth day, although it was still raining heavily, a chink in the cloud cover emerged. We did the only thing now open to us. We walked out, barefoot and clad in swimming shorts, and followed the road North in what we hoped was the direction of a camp run by the French Red Cross. Knee-deep in mud, we picked our way along the road, little more than a cut in red mud looking like a cruel, meandering scar. At one point, we passed a food distribution centre where people had lined up waiting for trucks to arrive with sacks of rice, grimly contemplating the prospect of a monthly ration of acrid calcium-enriched sorghum, delivered by the World Food Programme. But the road was impassable and the delivery had been cancelled. Word reached the distribution centre, patience ran out, and the crowd shouted and gestured angrily at my colleague, who was wearing a Vanuatu government t-shirt.

We continued on our way, passing more forlorn sights. A group of men stood in their traditional *nakamal*, its deep canopy of leaves and branches providing a few moments of shelter from the rain. Their community had initially taken refuge in a house that had recently been constructed from concrete blocks by one of the wealthier members of the village. He had a job in Port Vila and could afford what he considered to be modern materials that appeared heavy, sturdy and potentially cyclone proof. The villagers had thought they were safe until the cyclonic winds picked up speed, and then the men had needed to use their collective weight to hold down the roof. But the walls had started to collapse, and the community took the quick but agonising decision in the middle of the night to make a run for it to the nearest traditional cyclone shelter. They had been unable to see clearly and feared being struck by the debris flying around them at nearly 300 kilometres an hour.

It was the traditional structures that had survived; made of sticks and twine, they were light but immensely strong. Twenty or thirty people holding down the roof could keep these buildings from blowing apart, and the low design, with deep eaves all the way to the ground, had an aerodynamic effect, conducting the intense winds over the top of the house rather than causing a 'box explosion' as the walls and roof simultaneously blew apart from within. The traditional buildings were simple, beautiful and effective and yet, as the area had gradually changed, as money had flowed in, and as status dictated that expensive concrete was a more desirable building material, the houses too had changed. Where the newer houses and the schools had collapsed, the older buildings, kept together with bush twine that over the years hardened to have the tensile strength of steel, stood proud. The high-vaulted roofs, made from local *nipa*, or palm thatch, were the cathedrals of the Pacific. 'We came to Tanna expecting to have to teach building techniques', a colleague told me, 'but when we got there we found that we had nothing to teach. What we could do was help people remember.'

*

The sun finally came out as we crested a hill and arrived at the French camp. '*Salut et bienvenue*', said a warm but surprised voice as we appeared from nowhere, unannounced and covered in mud. 'Would you like some coffee? Tanna coffee is the best.'

Later that night, I sat with the French aid workers and some local volunteers in a *nakamal* drinking strong kava. The night was clear, and we listened to the sound of the waves as the powerful drink began to have its effect. In that penumbral setting, as the sun sank and the evening breeze picked up, relieving us of the heat and intensity of the day, there was also a constant, almost symphonic, hawking, hacking and spluttering. Vanuatu kava, lightly infused with hibiscus leaf, is among the strongest in the Pacific. Even for regular drinkers, the initial taste is so gut-wrenching that many *nakamals* have designated areas for their customers to drink and spit before returning to their shaded seats beneath trees or thatched huts to resume their conversations. The depth and auditory variety of the hawking that night spoke of a deeply musical society whose best singing voices were trained on the production of copious quantities of phlegm. Between shells of kava and protracted bouts of expectoration, we talked long into the night.

I had recently been attacked in the Australian right-wing media for 'scaring children with climate change alarmism'. This came in response to a small role I had played in promoting a cartoon that tried to advocate greater disaster preparedness measures among Pacific island communities. Slightly unsure, I tried raising the subject in the *nakamal* with local volunteers, avoiding the combination of words that were so polarising at home. 'Do you think the environment is changing?' I asked.

'You mean climate change?' came a chorus of replies. 'Of course! It is here with us now. We see it all the time. There are few in Tanna who do not believe that this is what's happening to them.'

The impacts initially were slow. Traditional farming patterns were disrupted, and cropping and planting seasons occurred later. Already dry and wet seasons had been exacerbated by El Niño and La Niña weather patterns which, while naturally occurring, made those seasons more extreme and more unpredictable. Harvests of taro and coconuts were affected by rising sea levels as saltwater gradually intruded into agricultural lands. And then there were the cyclones, whose strength and unpredictability had shocked everyone. In addition, the cyclone season appeared to have become longer.

The islanders could not predict what the future held. Many had already left the island, migrating to cities to find paid work and to escape the growing instability of traditional life. But the money coming back to the island had also changed it. There were new, less secure but more expensive buildings, more fast food and fewer indigenous crops, and immensely high rates of diabetes and heart disease. In silent protest, tarpaulins delivered by aid agencies and emblazoned on one side with red kangaroos (to ensure there could be no mistake as to whom the beneficiaries owed their gratitude) were turned inside out so the islanders' own houses would not be branded by increasingly assertive donors.

As we talked, and my lips grew numb with the kava, the ground under the tree seemed to soften and the hushed yet resonant tones of the islanders reflecting on their societies and place in the world drifted out on the evening breeze and into the stars and the night.

*

When I returned to Australia after three months working on the cyclone response, I found I had received a surprising letter. I had been nominated, along with a number of colleagues, for an award. I was honoured but regretted that, owing to prior commitments, I couldn't attend the ceremony in person.

Like politicians everywhere, Vanuatu's leaders existed in an unstable, cut-throat environment a long way removed from the subtleties of quiet evening reflection in the *nakamal*. Shortly before the awards ceremony was to take place, the prime minister of Vanuatu left the country on official business, and members of his cabinet decided it was a perfect opportunity to instigate a coup. In a rage, the premier got on the next flight back to Port Vila, stormed into the government buildings and accused the coup makers of corruption. With the police on his side, he ordered that the mutinous politicians be thrown into a shipping container on the wharf, accompanied by their lawyers for good measure.

Meanwhile, in a balmy afternoon breeze at the outdoor arena where the awards ceremony was to be held, excited guests, dressed in their finest attire, waited to receive their decorations. But they waited in vain. In the midst of the coup and counter-coup, the awards were forgotten, and the deflated humanitarians returned home gong-less. Some months later, by way of compensation, another letter arrived for me containing a certificate of participation to which the label of a Granny Smith apple had mysteriously become attached. Recognition of my involvement in the disaster response was lent additional gravitas by the words *fresh and tasty* on the small green sticker in the corner.

2

FIJI: TWO CAPITALS AND A CYCLONE

Against the deep and ominous glow of sunset over Suva Harbour, the Grand Pacific Hotel shone brilliantly in its newly restored grandeur. For over twenty years it had been a run-down barracks for the Republic of the Fiji Military Forces, but in its heyday the hotel, known simply as GPH, had presided over an insular colonial society in the nation's capital. The army trucks, barbed-wire fences and soldiers' cots had only recently been removed when I first visited in 2011 and the resurrected GPH stood, resplendent once more, in the palm-fronded lee of Suva Harbour. The building seemed to view the surrounding changes to the capital's urban fabric with regal disregard, passing an unspoken comment on the neighbouring Holiday Inn, once Suva's main business hotel, whose more mercantile squat concrete construction lacked GPH's resurgent glamour. Over the road, the Piccadilly Taxis Service, run out of a deferential tin shack, offered battered yellow cabs to the GPH's discerning customers twenty-four hours a day. In the hotel, long-armed ceiling fans turned languidly to catch the evening breeze, heels clipped on the polished wooden floorboards, and glasses chinked above the laughter and murmur of sunset conversations held around the pool.

If it felt, strangely, as though the prewar world of the great ocean liners had undergone a ghostly resuscitation in the South Pacific, this was because, quite literally, they had. Built in 1914 by the Union Steam Ship Company, the GPH was designed to make guests feel as if they hadn't actually left the boat. The building's first-class staterooms, wrought-iron portico, long galley halls and curved bow replicated on land the design of luxury liners at sea; the era of Cunard and the White Star Line, of quoits and canapés. Sepia images of old Suva lined the walls: Europeans in white suits and broad sunhats taking refuge from the heat on the hotel's balcony, surrounded by attentive Fijian staff and embalming their livers in oceans of gin; a young Queen Elizabeth visiting her loyal subjects in 1953, when, from the hotel's balcony, she addressed a crowd gathered opposite, in Albert Park. It all seemed like yesterday in this grandly fossilised world.

Restored, the GPH now catered for a new elite. Gone were the leather-skinned planters, suited traders and linen-clad colonial administrators. In their place were officials from diplomatic missions, staff of development agencies, construction subcontractors and representatives of Pacific regional conglomerates working in banking, hardware and mobile phones. They watched rugby on the televisions in the bar or lounged outside, sipping from cool tankards of Fiji Bitter and Fiji Gold. Earnest groups, sitting in twos and threes, sat outside in the shade, and the talk was of annual reports, official visits and budget arrangements in view of the pending end of the financial year – conversations that maintained their intensity despite the balmy weather, torpid sunshine and glistening possibilities offered by the nearby pool. If GPH's immediate resemblance was to first class on the Cunard line, on closer inspection it was more akin to the muted world of an airport lounge.

Fiji's capital held much of the charm of an English village by the sea. Warm waves lapped its secluded harbour overlooked by the GPH and a nearby lawn bowls club. The centre was dominated by a large and brilliantly green maidan, the aforementioned Albert Park, while the street names echoed its imperial past as a distant yet loyal outpost of British rule. Victoria Parade is near Disraeli Road and Gladstone Street, while boulevards named after colonial administrators and grand chiefs added to the capital's diminutive yet stately air. The queen's head still featured on banknotes, despite Fiji having become a republic, and the Union Jack flew high in a corner of the sky-blue national flag. Neat rows of weatherboard houses with immaculate tropical gardens lined the harbour and the hilly streets around the town. They remained resolute in their domestic ordinariness while, at the far extremities of the town, new American and Chinese embassies had sprung up bristling with satellite dishes, antennae and razor-wire fences. The solid, squat and ghostly white structures of the evangelising Mormon Church marked the latest player in the conquest of souls, just as the Americans and the Chinese increasingly sought dominance of the Pacific high seas.

*

European trading and religious encounter with the Fijian islands did not start well. In the national Fiji Museum, alongside relics of great ocean-going canoes, there was a small glass case that celebrated the first missionary contact with the country. Inside were a Bible and a pair of spectacles that had once belonged to the Methodist missionary Thomas Baker, who arrived in Fiji in the 1860s. In the adjacent case were the pot and ceremonial fork with which he was subsequently devoured. This regrettable misunderstanding continued for over a century until 2003, when descendants of the Baker family and those of the local chief met in Fiji's (by that time deeply Methodist) capital and, in a jovial encounter, agreed not to repeat the mistake.

But the fuel of colonialism, religion and the newly emerging politics of independence caused flickering tensions that undermined the nation's cosy image as both a half-forgotten imperial outpost and a cheap tourist suntrap. The role of the 'Great Chiefs', of relative importance today, was a product of European, Indian and Fijian claims to cultural and political dominance – a fusion of tradition, invention and attempts to balance ethnic power in the colonies. It was sometimes said of Fiji that its political turbulence resulted from competition between two particularly mismatched peoples – Fijians and Indo-Fijians – who were forced to cohabit on a small group of islands while living in mutually exclusive worlds where, it was claimed, 'even the prostitutes are ethnically divided'. Indo-Fijians, in this view, were the opposite of Fijians: a polytheistic community set against evangelical monotheism, urbanites against rural labourers, Indian entrepreneurialism against the Fijian status quo. Disputes were, above all, about land and political power, with land viewed by Indo-Fijians as something to be bought and sold and used for cash crops but by Fijians as inalienable and collectively owned. More importantly, the demographic rise of the Indo-Fijians was increasingly perceived as a threat, initially by Europeans concerned that they might harbour links with India's own independence movements and later by Fijians worried that an Indo-Fijian demographic advantage might translate into electoral power under the post-independence Westminster system. Fiji's 'coup culture' (two coups were staged in 1987, one happened in 2000 and a fourth in 2006) was in large part caused by the politics of ethnicity.

If the political fault lines of modern Fiji were a product of a colonial legacy, so too were some of the country's main institutions and cultural concepts. The Great Council of Chiefs was not an ancient assembly of 'big men' but an institution established under colonial rule as a means, in part, of placating Fijians worried about the growing influence of the recently arrived Indians. It was suspended by Prime Minister Frank Bainimarama (the 2006 coup leader), then abolished in order to relieve the pressures of ethnic antagonism. 'Traditional' Fijian values about land tenure, which recognise collective ownership and ancestral connections, or *vanua*, were equally recent. In this view, possession of land and traditions of indigenous government were conflated and land came to refer to the more emotive concept of 'ancestral homeland' in which, 'chiefs were a bulwark of security for all and custodians of Fijian identity, land and culture'. This idea was reinforced by the newly introduced religious enthusiasms of the Pacific. Christianity was fused with the existing social order, and chiefly hierarchies came to be seen as both the embodiment of cultural traditions and divinely ordained: 'Fijian paramounts [chiefs] are believed ... to hold their position because their right has been prescribed. To prove this the Bible may be quoted: "For there is no authority except from God, and those that exist have been instituted by God."' The consequences of colonialism, conversion and migration from the subcontinent combined to change and entrench ethnicised perceptions of the political, economic and cultural sources of authority in Fiji.

*

One evening I was taken with some colleagues from the Red Cross to a large, imposing colonial mansion in Suva that had been converted into a Chinese restaurant advertising the nation's finest sizzling Angus steak. While rapidly losing interest in my food, I learned from one of my companions that it had been the family home of John Scott, a former head of the Fiji Red Cross, and that he, along with his partner Greg Scrivener, had been killed in the house with a cane knife after the military coup in 2000. The tragic, brutal murders revealed the depth of change and social tension that lay behind the country's sunny facade.

The Scott family had arrived in Fiji as Methodist missionaries in the mid-1800s and rose to prominence as jurists and colonial administrators in the century that followed, owning islands, holding sunset cocktail parties on the balcony of the GPH overlooking Suva Harbour and receiving knighthoods and acclamations from the queen during the royal tour of her palm-clad Pacific dominions. Theirs was a Pacific of the old colonial elite, which, with its medals, uniforms, hierarchies and titles, saw itself as a modern European incarnation of the 'traditional' Fijian nobility that it had done so much to create. The Scott family was the first in the country to own a Rolls-Royce.

While most of the European residents, administrators and traders left Fiji after independence in 1970, the Scott family, along with a handful of other European settler families, stayed on, alternating between life in Fiji and careers in the United Kingdom and New Zealand. John Scott, a grandson of the early missionaries, eventually returned permanently to Fiji for the Fiji Red Cross – an institution that, while serving the greater good, also closely replicated local social hierarchies. As a talented administrator and a member of the much-diminished European elite, Scott gained in the Red Cross an institution of both social status and influence that matched his family's traditional prominence in Fijian society. The annual Fiji Red Cross Ball was the social event and fundraiser of the year; like the former colonial socialites, men in uniforms and women in ball gowns and tiaras danced through the evening, presided over by the country's new elite.

The military coup of 2000 was triggered by the unprecedented election of a prime minister of Indo-Fijian descent. It was led by the Fijian ultranationalist former army officer George Speight. The coup led the Red Cross and its director to play a prominent humanitarian role. Using his personal standing and the internationally mandated humanitarian responsibilities of the Red Cross in times of conflict, John Scott became in many ways the media image of the political chaos in Fiji. He was able to cross the rebel lines surrounding the parliament and deliver medical supplies and assistance to the parliamentarians locked inside. Wearing a white tabard with the Red Cross emblem on it, he was seen daily going alone between masked gunmen, who surrounded the government buildings, to assist and monitor the conditions of those inside – a nerve-racking undertaking that was filmed and broadcast around the world and which earned him the nickname 'Angel of Mercy'.

But John Scott stood out in other ways. Possibly still inhabiting the world of his parents and grandparents, in which membership of the governing elite precluded censure, Scott was known for his good looks and wealthy lifestyle, and for being openly gay in a culturally conservative, evangelically Christian country that viewed homosexuality as sin. Initially, the murders were thought to have been a direct consequence of Scott's role during the coup, but the real causes went deeper. Scott's former gardener, a deeply devout rugby player, had learned the evangelical lessons too well. He was possibly also gay – he was thought to have had an affair with Scott or his partner – and was mentally unstable. Seeing Scott on television depicted as the 'Angel of Mercy' seems to have set off a toxic mix of sexuality, politics and an overzealous interpretation of scripture. Having hacked his former employers to death, the murderer turned himself in a few days later.

This story, told to me in the Scott family's former home, seemed to capture both the tragedy and the change in Fiji. It contained a lethal mix of postcolonial influences: ethnic politics, invented traditions and cultural confusion. The victim was a member of a European elite who may not have fully realised that the days of untouchability in Fiji were over. The perpetrator, misguided by a set of religious, social and cultural norms brought to the Fiji Islands by early European settlers and missionaries (including the Scott family), was also, in some senses, a victim of the country's mutating politics and traditions.

*

In 2016, Tropical Cyclone Winston smashed into the Fiji Islands with wind speeds of 285 kilometres an hour, cutting a path through the two main islands of Viti Levu and Vanua Levu and pulverising many of the smaller islands in between. Just a year after records had been broken by Cyclone Pam, in Vanuatu, immense destruction had once more been caused in the South Pacific by another record-breaking cyclone. Winston killed forty-four people, destroyed more than 30,000 homes, and blew apart schools, roads, farms and lives along the way. In community after community, what remained were twisted iron, splintered wood and the mangled wreckage of houses and lives.

In one village I visited, a house that had been built to be cyclone resistant after the devastation caused by Cyclone Evan in 2012 had simply exploded in the wind, just as houses had done during Cyclone Pam a year earlier in Vanuatu. Its four walls and roof, all intact, lay at different ends of the village, while the roofing irons were wrapped around a tree on top of a nearby hill. Elsewhere, there were signs of a former stability and prosperity now cruelly destroyed. Toys and battered cooking utensils that had been retrieved sat forlornly in lean-tos and shanties, salvaged from the rubble of the villagers' former homes. One family had completely cleared the concrete base of their house so that there was nothing more than a cleanly swept slab, on which they had neatly stacked their now-defunct household items. A rice cooker, a microwave, a stove and a refrigerator sat on top of each other, forming a kind of totemic assemblage of redundant white goods that had once offered domestic comfort and conferred status. It would be years before such items could be acquired again. Life had, in the pace of forty-eight hours during which the cyclone passed, returned to a world without electricity or running water, a world not seen in the village since the 1950s. In place of the familiar predictability of village life, there were now just mud and ruin.

Families had hidden under their houses as the cyclone passed, hoping that the foundations would be strong enough to protect them from the winds but fearing the rapidly rising waters and unpredictable mudslides from the hills around them. Since then, men, women and children became terrified whenever the wind picked up and they heard the sinister clanking of iron sheets. This was the noise that had immediately preceded the destruction of their homes, as powerful winds had pulled insistently at roofs, walls and foundations.

One woman I met had recurrent nightmares and ran for shelter whenever she heard any sudden sounds. She offered me a cup of sweet tea next to the wreckage of her home and stoked a small fire that smoked out the 'kitchen', a hovel made from twisted iron sheets, not 3 metres from her old electric stove, which was now just more rubble to be cleared away. The inhabitants of her village were not insured and never had been. Their lives and houses were the products of gradual acquisition and hard work – sometimes in the fields, growing root crops to sell; sometimes in the town, labouring, cleaning, mending roads, and building – sometimes paid, sometimes not. Over the course of thirty years they had built their lives and the village, the school and homes, installed electricity, gradually constructing a life less hard, less demanding and potentially longer than that of their parents and grandparents. But all this had gone in minutes. We stared silently into the ashes of the fire as the ancient kettle slowly came to the boil, our eyes stinging in the smoke.

*

After the 2006 military coup led by the then commander of the Fijian armed forces, and now prime minister, Frank Bainimarama, the Australian government had imposed sanctions on Fiji and denounced another blow to local democracy. However, times had changed. Bainimarama had organised constitutional reforms and held elections designed in such a way as to offer the illusion of choice while effectively precluding all other political competitors. On the basis of a quick change of clothes – from his naval commodore's uniform to a dark civilian suit – diplomatic and commercial relations between Australia and Fiji had been restored. The ever-pliant Fijian press now carried puff pieces about Bainimarama 'the family man', complete with sunny pictures of the strongman in avuncular mode, patting puppies, playing with children and smiling benignly in the middle of a suburban garden while wearing a soft-pink shirt.

Cyclone Winston provided the moment for Australia to demonstrate that all was forgotten and to lend a helping hand. This came in the form of assistance to which the commodore would readily respond: military toys on loan from Australia. In a return to the good old days, civilian decision-making was swept aside, and, following a declaration of emergency, the men in green jumpsuits arrived once more to manage the show.

'It's amazing', confessed a colleague who worked in the restricted operations centre that controlled the cyclone response, 'to see just how much the Australians have been told to grovel.' He continued, 'Our soldiers are not generally known for being sycophants, but here everything's "Yes, sir", "How far should I bend over, sir?" to any order, no matter how ridiculous. They've clearly been told to suck it up.'

'We will not be another Vanuatu', the Fijians had declared when Cyclone Winston hit land. The Fijian government had learned from the experience of its neighbouring Pacific island nation when the latter responded to a devastating cyclone a year earlier. An influx of ships, helicopters and NGOs had suggested that the government of Vanuatu lacked resources and capacity, and this was an image that could not be allowed to take hold in Bainimarama's military-dominated Fiji. But the offer of foreign military assistance was too tempting for an old soldier, and rather than keeping the foreign troops out, the Fijian government had instead heavily restricted the presence of NGOs, cracking down on the very civil society organisations that had expertise and capacity in managing disaster response.

I had been dispatched to Fiji to help coordinate this civil society response and, after much searching for someone in government with whom I could discuss the situation, I was introduced to a liaison officer in the operations centre. He was not in uniform but sported a sharp polo shirt with a picture of a handgun and the words 'Glock Perfection'. I concluded fairly quickly that he wasn't with an NGO and seemed uninterested in anything that my colleagues and I were planning. Our conversation was brief. So the on-loan Black Hawks flew reconnaissance missions, the navy ships sailed around the outer islands, and the men in green postured with their swagger sticks inside the operations centre in the capital, while precious little assistance actually made it out.

At one point, the military liaison officer with the Australian contingent asked to speak with me confidentially. 'Look', he said, 'we've got all these helicopters and all this lift capacity, but we haven't got much stuff to move. Can you help?'

I shrugged to reply. The answer was political and completely beyond my control. Without access, influence or cash, there was little by way of relief items, or 'stuff', for the NGOs to lift using military assets. In any case, commercial transport had not been significantly affected by the cyclone. As in Vanuatu during Cyclone Pam, those few relief items that were going out were being transported cheaply and quickly by humble trucks and cargo ships rather than by air.

A few days later, visiting a community on a small island near Suva, I was amazed to hear the sound of a Black Hawk bearing down on the village. I cowered, listening to the thunderous drone of the rotor blades, and watched as it touched down briefly to unload a small consignment of tents – a relief item that, in the context of the island, was hot, expensive, and almost totally unnecessary as villagers were quick to assemble their own emergency shelters. Rather than tents, what people wanted were funds and supplies to start rebuilding their homes. The liaison officer had clearly found some 'stuff', although, having taken the short ferry ride over to the island that morning, I wondered how necessary this display of airborne prowess really was.

Australia's foreign minister was in town and that evening the Grand Pacific Hotel was suddenly packed. A flight of helicopters was returning from another island where Winston had caused great devastation, and a crowd of onlookers had gathered. The minister's aids and departmental staff, adorned with the red kangaroo, rushed around clutching papers. In the dark the helicopters moved slowly, like drugged wasps, buzzing towards the dazzling light of the GPH, and circled slowly before dropping out of sight to land at the helipad next door. The crowds began to disburse and the kangaroo-clad bureaucrats made their way towards the helipad. 'Buy us a drink, Skippy', called someone from the bar as one particularly ponytailed staffer strutted by.

Later that night, I was due to give an interview with rural Queensland radio from the bowels of the budget motor inn where I was staying. They had heard about the foreign minister's visit and wanted to follow up on the response to the cyclone. I had prepared my advocacy in advance, and as I waited on hold for my slot, I ran through what I was going to say: The response had been too slow. The Fijian government's overreliance on foreign military assistance meant that relief items were not getting out quickly enough to those who needed them the most. There was much visibility but little action, and the only organisations capable of working quickly and at scale – local and international NGOs – had been marginalised. A modest redirection of resources away from helicopters charging around and towards relief agencies would make a significant and immediate difference. The foreign minister's visit was all very well, but her refusal to meet, and to discuss the response with members of the humanitarian community, and specifically with the chief humanitarian officer for the Pacific, a special representative of the United Nations' secretary general, was inexplicable. For the response to be efficient and effective, civil society needed to play its role, especially in a state that was ostensibly transitioning away from military rule.

'So, mate', intoned the deep voice from the deep north on the other end of the phone when I finally went to air, 'I've just seen your photo. Jeez, just look at that chin.'

I was outwitted by this verbal googly and completely forgot my lines. 'We're here to help', I heard myself say.

*

'Don't over-panic', said Viliame, as we stood together the following day in the crumbling offices of the Ministry of Infrastructure.

Viliame, the department's permanent administrative officer, would have been managing the emergency response to Cyclone Winston had the army not taken virtually all his responsibilities away, leaving him with only the most vestigial influence. Far from being downbeat about this, Viliame was aware of the remaining authority vested in him by the state and approached his role with gravitas and deliberation. He occupied a small cubicle that was stuffed with the trappings of administrative office. Development reports were stacked by their dozens on overcrowded bookcases whose shelves sagged under the great weight of the yellowing tomes. Reports, newspapers and official files stood in vast tottering piles on the floor, entwined in official pink ribbon. A Bakelite phone was apparently still in use, and behind this was something that resembled a computer, but since it lacked a keyboard and was half hidden by administrative detritus, it was hard to say exactly what kind of machine it was. In this ministry, one of the least important and most neglected organisations to which Fijian sovereign power had devolved, the rubber stamp, the signature and the yellow highlighter reigned supreme, and Viliame was the proud custodian of these bureaucratic rites.

Importantly, Viliame's desk lay at the entrance to a corridor and just below the office of the department's permanent secretary. He thus occupied a position of unique prominence. He knew the exact movements of all the senior staff including when and with whom, and for how long, they were out to lunch. More importantly still, from his cubicle could be heard the footsteps in the permanent secretary's office above. Over the years, Viliame had become adept at interpreting their rhythms and patterns. A slow, heavy tread slightly before lunch indicated the arrival of the permanent secretary himself, while a softer, more plodding tread suggested visitors from inside the department. A staccato quickstep indicated that the minister's secretary was delivering a message from on high, and the faster the quickstep, the more urgent the message. If it was very fast, it meant that the minister wanted to see the permanent secretary immediately on matters of state. The step that Viliame dreaded, however, was slow, heavy and articulated. It meant a military visitation, possibly from the prime minister's office, and that meant the department was in the spotlight.

Viliame had called me in as a matter of urgency, and I found him pacing around the unread development reports in some agitation. There was a problem, a considerable problem. But in all his years in the department, Viliame had learned to handle similar situations. The key, he informed me as my gentle mentor in the affairs of state bureaucracy, was to not over-panic.

'Everyone is looking for Viliame', he said, with a mixture of pride and terror. The staccato quickstep of the secretary's heels on the floor above had alerted him to a problem. Sure enough, a command had been received from the top. The minister was outraged and needed the department to respond urgently, or heads would roll.

Was it, I asked, to do with how the emergency response to the cyclone was going? Was there any information I could provide? Viliame had been kind to me, helping me steer my way through the internal dynamics of the national government, so I offered any assistance I could give. If there was a crisis, I said, I would do my best to help.

The minister had been watching the news on television the previous evening. He had seen the visit of the Australian foreign minister and had listened to the Fijian prime minister's briefing with journalists. He had listened to the weather, the finance and the sport. Everything had appeared to be going on as usual. But then he had watched an entire story devoted to the education minister, who had been filmed and interviewed at the airport, meeting an incoming flight of relief items and looking very much in control. Clearly, this would not do.

Could I, asked Viliame, with the look of a man under intense pressure, help to organise a news story at the airport for his minister too? Fortuitously, I knew of an expected flight containing more relief items: clothes, tarpaulins, chainsaws and construction equipment. It didn't matter to whom they belonged or how they were going to be used; the minister could pose with them as much as he liked and look in control. That evening, both Viliame and the minister were on national television, shown while they were at the airport. They were more than a match for their arch rival in education.

The following morning, I visited Viliame again. He was leaning back in his chair with a look of satisfaction. 'You know, Tom', he observed languidly, 'round here, you've got to set the pace.' And with that he smiled and slowly reached for a digestive biscuit and a cup of lukewarm tea, basking in the wisdom, gained from long years as the department's permanent administrative officer, never to 'over-panic' in a crisis.

3

FRIZZLED MERRIMENT
IN THE TROPIC SUN

Before leaving Fiji, I decided to visit the country's first capital, Levuka, on the island of Ovalau. This was an old whaling station where the Deed of Cession was signed in 1874, formally establishing the British colony of Fiji. If Fijians had sought to resist this development, feuding between two rival chiefs, Cakobau and Ma'afu, divided any potential opposition and Cakobau sided with the British in order to gain an advantage over his old Tongan rival. Any doubts he may have had about the beneficence of British rule were quickly put aside when the British commander of HMS *Dido*, Sir Hercules Robinson, fired a 21-gun salute in Cakobau's honour – a gesture of friendship and a reminder of military potency that led rapidly to the signing of the Deed of Cession and to ninety-six years of formal British dominion in the Fiji Islands.

Australian author Katharine Susannah Prichard was born in Levuka, where her father, Thomas Henry Prichard, had been a trader, a soldier and editor of the *Fiji Times* for fifteen years between 1867 and 1882. Writing in the *Melbourne Leader* in the 1880s, he described the town in its colonial heyday:

Levuka was a merry, bustling and busy a place then as any of the island centres of white population south of the line: not the decayed, deserted fishing village it had since become under the benign influence of British rule, with its dwellings down, their tenants passed away and the sites upon which they stood lapsed again into their original state of bush and scrub.

Then there was no form of government. Law and order existed in fact, but not in name. Three thousand adventurous spirits from the Australian colonies, with a large percentage of the waifs and strays of the Pacific, were congregated there, attracted by cotton growing. Every man did what was right in his own eyes, always provided it did not happen to be wrong in the eyes of his stronger neighbour. The harbour was alive with coastal craft and sea-going vessels, and the people traded, paid their debts, drank, made merry and socially frizzled together under the torrid tropic sun in a spirit of genuine camaraderie, and with an absence of serious crime that was remarkable.

But it was not all frizzled merriment in the tropic sun. An early diary entry, quoted by Katharine Suzannah Prichard in her memoir *Child of the Hurricane*, records hard work and testing physical challenges for early settlers on Levuka. On 9 April 1876, her father wrote: 'Went with two boys to stake out Na Sara Waga passage. Arm in sling. Rotten old canoes. Got swamped. Canoes adrift. Devil of a job. Wet gun, powder, matches and lost knife. Swore.'

The presence of Europeans with aspirations for land acquisition, commercial agriculture and the possession of firearms caused grievances between Fijian tribes as well as altering the local power balance. Reflecting the prejudices of his time, subsequent debates about land use, and traditions of communal land ownership that continue in Fiji to this day, TH Prichard wrote that Fijians were the 'aristocrats of the Pacific, dignified, and conservative in their ways, slow to accept even the white man's tools, preferring their own digging sticks to a plough' and were prey to 'planters, officials, beachcombers and miscellaneous white vagabonds' who were thirsty for land, money and influence. Recruited to edit the *Fiji Times* for his 'judicious and manly prose', TH Prichard was clear eyed about the inequity and impact of this early contact between Europeans and Fijians: 'it was a most difficult matter owing to the unprincipled ways in which sales and purchases had been made on both sides. Europeans had bought from the chiefs large and valuable tracts of land for the most inadequate considerations – a few cases of gin, a few muskets with powder and ball, and a few bolts of cheap print, with a miscellany of assortment of "brummagem" cutlery and showy trinkets. Needless to say, in such transactions the gun was the chief inducement and principal article of barter.'

The power imbalance was caused by the introduction of firearms by which 'an aggressive chief held the tribes without them completely at his mercy', wrote TH Prichard in the *Melbourne Age*. 'The patriarchal head of his people developed into the military dictator and absolute lord of life and death, bound by no other law than that of his own.' An ensuing rebellion caused by the relinquishing of lands led to the formation of a random army of European administrators, adventurers, beachcombers and profiteers to defend him.

Witnessing these events as a soldier in Cakobau's army and later as a translator, TH Prichard described the cruel and lawless atmosphere of the times in the *Sydney Bulletin*:

Cakobau, by the grace of George Austen Woods, Sydney Charles Burt and James Stewart Butters, was king of Fiji and its dependencies. Cotton was the other king, and 'blackbirding' was one of the native industries which flourished under the joint sway. The harbour was seldom without two or three labour vessels, and ructions among the 'recruits' were of frequent occurrence. The Marion Rennie, a top-sail schooner of about 200-tons, was perhaps the unluckiest craft engaged in that most humane a civilising traffic. There was scarcely a plank in her deck that had not been baptised in blood; hardly a trenail in the planks which might not have stood for a man's life.

On 4 December 1883, amid the exploitation of the early colonial encounter, a hurricane bore down on Levuka. In her memoir Katharine Susannah Prichard wrote of the moment of her birth:

Through the thick darkness and fury of the hurricane a light glimmered all night in the bungalow on the steep hillside above Levuka.

After the full blast of the wind struck the island, wrecking the township, smashing frail native huts to the ground, hurling sheets of iron through the air like paper, uprooting trees, the rain poured down in torrents ... Dawn threw wan light on the devastation caused by the hurricane; the township bashed and battered as though by a bombardment, the sea-wall washed away, the sea breaking through the main street, ships in the harbour blown ashore or on to the reef, coconut plantations beaten to the ground. But in that bungalow on the hillside, natives gazed with awe at the baby the hurricane had left in its wake.

'Na Luve ni Cava', they exclaimed, 'she is the child of the hurricane.'

*

If the Grand Pacific Hotel marked a restoration of Fiji's former colonial glory and was the symbolic centre of Fiji's new elites,

Katharine Suzannah Prichard's birthplace of Levuka was the previous century of colonial dominance embalmed. It was the old trading and whaling centre that, through economic change and commercial neglect, appeared largely unchanged since the late nineteenth-century when it had been the country's main trading post. Now the ghosts of traders past lingered in the town's weatherboard shops lining the sea-front. A nearby branch of the Australia and New Zealand Banking Corporation occupied the same building as the town's original bank – the Bank of New South Wales – and featured a large sign with colonial imagery. On a busy main street, the image captured a dashing moustachioed European on horseback, reins in one hand and cigar in the other, as he cantered along the street, basking in his authority and prosperity.

If the European traders had gone, the faded awnings and verandas of their stores shaded the passers-by from the midday sun. Ivan's Hot Bread was the last shop before an expanse of clipped lawn and the gothic tower of the Sacred Heart Church cast an incongruous shadow across the South Pacific island. Indian and Chinese traders, too, had set up shop. RK Singh ('RK the price fighter') was a general store, and down the road a snack shop enticingly offered 'slice fish' and 'pounded grog' along with a shipping schedule for ferries to Suva. The restaurant, in the absence of competition, simply called itself 'Restaurant'. Its intimate, wood-panelled interior and pot-bellied stove must once have heaved with fishermen and salty tales and it appeared to have just been vacated by a crowd of whalers. Dark stains along the walls and near the windows overlooking the street suggested the lingering presence of whale blubber. The menu was unpromising, despite a sign that indicated the availability of cocktails called Sweet Lips and Bamboo Sunset.

'We've run out of food and we don't serve drinks', the waitress told me before catching sight of a passing fisherman who had just speared a brightly coloured coral trout. With a quick shout to the kitchen, she confirmed that they could cook this up if I ran out and bought it. Nearby, a rusty cannery just about kept the town alive with jobs and commerce, but the good times in Levuka had long since passed.

A few hundred meters away from the town stood the Royal Inn, sagging in ever dustier decay. If the whalers and administrators of the last century had dined on freshly speared coral trout at the Restaurant, then they had also stayed at Levuka's Royal Inn whose atrophy was infused with nostalgia. The billiard room housed an immense, slate-topped table complete with a 'wonderful Stanfast cushion' produced by Thurston & Co that had made its way by sailing ship to Levuka in the 1890s and would once have been the pride and joy of the island. Even now, more than a century later, the battered billiards and warped cues were straight and true amid the surrounding atmosphere of collapse.

The walls documented a history of decline, with photographs of visiting cricket teams from the United Kingdom in blazers and ties who had come annually to Levuka to compete against local colonial teams. Chaps in club ties and crested blazers, with names like Woolford, Lancaster, Balfour and Bacon, had played hard-fought innings in the tropics and doubtless retired to the billiard room afterwards. The outline of the cricket pitch and an elegant wooden stand could still be viewed from the back room of the Royal Inn while ancient cricket bats gathered dust in the corner. The fading Angus McDonald Trophy still hung victoriously on the wall above the billiard table, commemorating a forgotten competition in an undisclosed sport between 'Royal v Garrick', two clubs that would once have been the centre of European life in Fiji. World War Two had seen a boom, with servicemen on leave taking up residence at the Royal Inn. A plaque immortalising Buster, Shorty, Sandy, Ross, Jim and Bill of the 'RNZAF Levuka rest camp, first draft' gazed down in jaunty perpetuity on the billiard table. I listened for a second, sensing that I might catch a distant echo of their airman's banter from 1940 rebounding from the panelled walls of the billiard room. But the intimate, Anglo world of gentleman's sporting recreation had come to an end along with the war, and the memorabilia of the ensuing period marked a slow decline. By the late 1960s the cricketers' blazers had gone and open-necked shirts were now being worn. Sideburns had made an appearance in the photos and one or two of the younger players wore longer hair. They all squinted into the camera, eyebrows raised, as if aware that what had once been a way of life for a trading and administrative elite was, by the late 1960s and early 70s, an anachronism. And by 1971, the last time the Albion Cricket Club toured the Fiji Islands, this world had vanished forever.

*

On Sunday afternoon I went for one final walk down Beach Street and around the Levuka township. Even for a Sunday in the Pacific, that Sabbath morning seemed especially silent. All the shops were firmly closed and shuttered, and no children played on the outside. There had been some singing earlier in the day as the communities had all gone to church, but even this had now ended, the churches had closed their doors and there was only stillness in the town. I reflected on Tonga, where, each Sunday, the whole island was awash with song coming from churches and under trees that lasted well into the evening. But here, apart from the old buildings with their air of abandonment, there was only the breeze blowing in from the harbour; the occasional clanking of an ancient shop sign, its peeling paint advertising Kodak film processing; and the gathering storm clouds that added to the sense of melancholic abandonment. I continued down the street, past the Kodak sign and RK Singh 'the price fighter', and on past the draper and the grog shop. Looming on the left, a wide, low building with the enormous letters Morris Hedstrom Ltd announced, in the typeface of a nineteenth century newspaper, a long-defunct trading enterprise. The former traders' store dominated one end of Beach Street and had now been turned into a museum whose dusty artefacts – ancient farming equipment, fragments of European pottery, yellowed photos of old Levuka life – clung on to the detritus of a vanished world as the times had moved on. In a way it was a sad sight. UNESCO World Heritage Status had promised a bright future for Levuka, which had fallen on unprosperous times, and had provided a hope that it would become a tourist magnet like other parts of Fiji and would bring about a revival. But this had not happened. The tourists were few and didn't stay long, disappointed by the lack of 'sites', nightlife – or any kind of life, really – and the crumbling hotels. Instead, in the absence of options, local residents lived alongside the decaying remnants of a vanished past even as the old buildings and remnants of a European highlife that was never theirs collapsed slowly and inexorably around them.

Continuing past Morris Hedstrom Ltd and past the port, I followed the road as it clung to the coast, moving beyond the town and the settlements. After some time, I came to an area that was neatly cordoned off by an immaculate white picket fence around a clipped lawn, with a white flagpole surrounded by three large rocks elevated on white plinths. Opposite was a flight of white-washed stairs, leading up to a grand chiefly house clad in palm leaves, with a vertiginous roof that sat above the main frame of the building like an immense crown. This was Prince Charles House and in 1970, nearly one hundred years after Cakobau had ceded the lands of Fiji to Britain, independence was proclaimed on the very same spot as the last shadows of empire slipped away. It was a solemn monument, simple yet profound: flagpole, rocks, thatched house and picket fence, all on a small promontory looking over the bay – all that remained of the bustling port, the trading centres and old power struggles of the Fiji Islands.

Escaping the long-dead world of Fiji's Europeans, I followed a path behind the hotel, passed an old ornamental bridge and the gutted remains of the masonic lodge and went on into the settlements that had sprung up in hills behind the town over the decades since independence. I walked past the neat lawns of the Levuka Bowling Club and the sky-blue coziness of the Levuka Sailors' Home, past the steep-roofed weatherboard houses of the European traders with their shuttered verandas and the Levuka Public School (established 1879). Soon the lingering presence of old Levuka gave way to newer, more informal settlements of tin and cement, crowded on the hillside. Tropical Cyclone Winston had been devastating here. If the old town had largely survived, the squatter settlements had not, and the surrounding hills were strewn with the wreckage of houses and belongings. Everywhere I looked, twisted tin sheets were piled up with household appliances and shattered timber frames.

'We will rise again' proclaimed a sign painted in white on the one remaining wall of one of the houses. Watching me walk amid the wreckage, one couple invited me in and we sat on the floor eating warm coconut cake and sipping hot, sweet tea. Very little assistance had been received by anyone in the settlement, they told me. It was not their land; they had just come to live there to be closer to the town and jobs. However, the government had allowed them to draw on their pension funds and, at the cost of any retirement savings they might have had, they had been able to buy materials with which to rebuild their house. Outside, although it was a Sunday, the valley echoed with the cheery sound of hammering, the occasional revving of a chainsaw and the clang of tin sheets being straightened for re-use.

The house had a neat, clipped lawn and the humid air carried the scent of heliconias in the afternoon breeze. But rather than linger on the present, the couple wanted to talk instead about the past – about Cakobau and Ma'afu and the conflict of more than a century before.

'We were on the losing side', one family member said, smiling. 'Our families supported Ma'afu and that is why we are here and not on our own land.' After the cyclone, they had rebuilt quickly. The new dwelling was smaller than before but adequate and comfortable, and at least they could remain on the land. Sione, who had invited me in, had been a sailor. Once he finished working on his house, he would return to the sea to raise money now that his retirement savings had been depleted. But he seemed in no hurry and as we talked, the sun began to set over the horizon. His wife joined us after refilling vases with fresh flowers. 'There's too much fighting', she continued. And, after a silence, 'It's strange, animals only fight for survival but humans, they fight to be supreme.' With that, she passed around another cake and another strong and sugary cup of tea.

I continued my walk, this time following Beach Street and the foreshore as far I could go. Aid had reached the more formal settlements along the shore and there were signs of tarpaulins and tents and the gradual process of rebuilding. A few kilometres along I heard a loud clanking and I looked up to see the enormous hull of a battered ferry that had run aground in the cyclone. It was surrounded by teams of men with ropes and pulleys, clambering across the hold and on the bridge, salvaging what they could of the ship that was now little more than scrap metal.

I was waved over to a house in the adjacent village and the local chief asked me what I was doing and where I was from. Some of his relatives had travelled to Australia as part of a school rugby team and I mentioned that I had met them along the road as I walked to the village and we had taken selfies together. As the night gathered in, I joined a group of men and women sitting under a tarpaulin outside a damaged house. The evening ritual of kava had started and they offered me a cup, its acrid taste quickly replaced by a warm, numb feeling that was so conducive to conversation. As the gentle hum of talk continued I felt humbled, in this wrecked village, by the Fijian's courtly welcome and generosity. The school had collapsed and an old man in the village had died during the cyclone. The group quietly told me that they were repairing the school before their homes so their children could resume their education. They asked how I thought the response was going. It was a difficult question to answer in the village, a million miles away from the debates and arguments of the capital, its government offices, United Nations headquarters and stylish hotels where meetings were held and where policy was set. The achievements, limitations and setbacks of that world seemed almost irrelevant to the realities of village life and recovery. I hesitated and tried to turn the question around.

'What would help you?' I asked.

'Tools and hardware' was the reply. After some thought, 'These are difficult to get and expensive to import. We farm for a living and can feed ourselves, but we do not have much money to rebuild.'

As I left, the chief turned to me and said, 'We must apologise we have turned this tarpaulin upside down. There is a red kangaroo on it and we felt that we didn't want to be branded.' Memories of Vanuatu! I reflected on the meetings I'd attended, the priorities of donors and the inevitable quest by relief agencies throughout the Pacific Islands for visibility, for being seen to be doing something. Somewhere in all of this, the question of human dignity seemed to have been forgotten.

Before dawn the following morning I packed my bags and said goodbye to the Royal Inn. It was raining heavily and the pre-dawn bus service to the ferry and back to Suva was about to leave. After the quiet melancholy of the night before, the attempt to catch the bus was riotous. One of Fiji's best girls' schools, run by local nuns, was on the island and the mothers had just dropped off their daughters for the new term and were now getting the bus back to the capital.

In the rain and the excitement of the early morning, crowds of Fijian mothers were beginning to make their way to the bus stop. As the rain intensified, so too did the urgency of the maternal desire to get on the bus and head home. It was a sprint finish with no prisoners taken. Amid good tempered but determined shouts and jostles, I ran from one bus to another only to be beaten to it each time by more nimble-footed women, scrambling for their seats. Finally, I squeezed in and, as dawn broke in the pouring rain, I found a seat at the back of the bus next to a smartly attired man who was also dripping wet. We exchanged glances and he reached into his pocket and handed me his business card.

'I'm the Minister of Education', he said as we braced ourselves for the potholed ride back to Suva.

4

TONGA: A KINGDOM OF TSUNAMIS AND SELF-IMPROVEMENT

In the inauspicious environs of the Royal Suva Yacht Club – a decaying colonial dive in the Fijian capital – I was taken aside to be 'briefed' on Tonga. Inside, exhibits of rope knots used in sailing filled cracked glass display cabinets while pictures of sleek yachts and line honours winners from decades past faded slowly on the walls. Even in the club's current decay and torpor, social traditions of caste-based exclusivity clung on. Aspiring members, I was told, had to be nominated by a current member, who wrote the aspirant's name in the visitors' book at the entrance to the club. The book stayed open for the next two weeks and existing members were given ample opportunity to view who the new aspirants were. Should they not like what they saw, they were entitled to place an anonymous dot next to the name to signify disapproval. Two such dots over a fortnight led to rejection – and presumably, in colonial days, pariah status and social ostracism. However, while the grand old traditions remained, the dots were clearly no longer much in force. Dominating the scene were a few old Europeans. Some had lingered on since Fijian independence, but most had washed up on their yachts some years ago and had decided to stay and decay together at the bar, taking permanent advantage of cheap mooring and cheaper beer. These denizens of the Suva Yacht Club were known collectively as the shipwrecks; they grew daily more gaunt, gnarly and cancerously sun-tanned in preparation for the evening assault on their livers. In these less-than-salubrious confines, Mafua, a friend who had held a minor administrative post attached to the royal household, told me about the inner workings of the Tongan political and regal establishment.

Ringing him late one night, the King of Tonga was by turns aggrieved and apoplectic.

'Pip has been ravaged by that mongrel next door and is in a delicate condition', he shouted down the phone, threatening avenues for revenge sadly no longer available to a constitutional monarch. On the verge of calling the police, Mafua had the good sense to enquire who Pip was and where he or she was currently located.

'My bloody dog. My angel', roared a tired and emotional monarch. 'She's in the throne room.' The beast, a Jack Russell terrier, had escaped the watchful eyes of royal courtiers and the palace guard and had got out through the front fence where she had been set upon by a local stray. At two in the morning, there was nothing for it but to call the vet and gently remind the king, bent on revenge, of the legal limits to his powers.

'Catch', shouted Sione as we parted ways in the car park 'here's a souvenir for you.' Reaching out at a blurry, flying object in the dark, my fingers closed around a dirty polystyrene stubby holder with the words 'Royal Suva Yacht Club' gouged in blue biro into the side.

Despite significant political agitation for democratic reform and growing scepticism among the 'commoners' about the desirability of a monarchical system, official Tonga was still very much in thrall to the idea of royalty. In the offices of the local organisation I was working for, the walls were lined with King George Tupou V coronation wine whose labels showed the regal presence in his full majesty. He was wearing a high-collared red coat, gold braid epaulettes, a full chest of medals, monocle and cascading ermine cloak and carrying a plumed white helmet nestled in the crook of his arm. It looked as if the very model of the modern Major General had just walked off the stage of a Gilbert and Sullivan musical and into power in the Pacific. Ancient staff members at the office, who owed their irrevocable positions to long-defunct royal command, would wander in and out. A giant carved hatstand, which once had pride of place in the palace bedroom, stood in the office's central corridor – a hindrance to all, but an almost untouchable totem of regal favour. On my way back from a meeting with government officials, one of my colleagues took me to visit a hotel swimming pool.

'Our King was great man', he said, referring not to the current King George Tupou V but to his revered father, King George Tupou IV, as we bowed our heads in awe at an empty swimming pool about 20 metres in length. Why we were standing by the pool was unclear but I didn't wish to disturb the solemnity of the moment with questions. 'He used to swim here', my colleague eventually explained after a short silence. 'He promised the people of Tonga that we should all lose weight, starting with himself. Every day he would come here and swim and, in the end, he lost 5 pounds.' I agreed that the late king was indeed a model for his people and as we left I noticed a small red carpet on the other side of the room leading up a couple of steps to the edge of the now empty pool.

The local organisation I was working for, being in many senses a product of the establishment, was linked intricately with the peculiarities of Tongan monarchic patronage. While I had some sense of what this might be like from Mafua's tales, it only dawned on me at the airport that this was, in fact, reality. Unbeknownst to me, I arrived in Tonga on the same flight as a member of the royal family. As we touched down, a military brass band, its members dressed in red coats and brilliant white-plumed pith helmets, marched up and down the tarmac playing the national anthem before being left behind by the royal's jeep, which, bearing an enormous royal standard, took off down Tongatapu's one road, surrounded by motorcycle outriders.

The obscurity and idiosyncrasy of the Tongan political system reflected an extreme form of Polynesian hierarchy (also evident in the chiefly structures of Samoa and precolonial Hawaii) and of the country's unique position as the only Pacific nation – in a still deeply colonial region – to have escaped imperial subjugation. While Tonga remained independent, it fell within a British sphere of influence and this led to the absorption of the style and substance of British nineteenth-century politics. Tonga had the region's first written constitution, which prescribed a Westminster system but actually strengthened indigenous political structures by enshrining the legal, property ownership and political rights of the monarchy and the landed nobility, which comprised thirty politically significant families whose lords had the right to govern. In style, the Tongan political system also appeared odd, with an insistence on traditional clothes, elaborate nineteenth-century military uniforms bedecked in braid, coloured sashes and the pomp and circumstance of the British Raj miniaturised and transported to the small Pacific island. But this, too, was a piece of political theatre, designed to reinforce the concept of what anthropologist Marshall Sahlins has described as the 'domesticated stranger king'.

In Tonga, unlike much of the region, there are no migration myths. Instead, the earliest foundation stories talk of the inhabitants of the main island, Tongatapu, as 'small, black and descended from worms'. Others suggest that early rulers 'descended from the skies' following the union of a divine father with a Tongan mother. The fusion of these stories suggests an invading ruler who had cleverly combined elements of a divine origins myth with the suggestion that the monarchy was an integral part of indigenous society – hence their being descended from worms. This form of archaic kingship, as Sahlins has written, 'makes its appearance from outside the society. Initially a stranger and something of a terror, the king is absorbed and domesticated by the indigenous people, a process that passes by way of his symbolic death and rebirth as a local god.'

Seen in this context, the miniature Raj of the Pacific – ermine-clad nobles and Sandhurst-educated, monocle-sporting kings separated from each other and from the constitutionally enshrined 'commoner' class by wealth, power and even distinct dialects – appeared marginally less incongruous. The anomalous traditions had been co-opted by an indigenous hierarchy seeking to retain power and influence. The Tongans understood and adapted to the Pacific the lessons of Tsar Alexander II of Russia: reform from above before you are reformed from below.

On the final evening of my Tongan visit, I saw the royal cavalcade again – this time halted outside a small house whose entrance was guarded by brass cannons. I stopped to watch, and after a few minutes an enormous man wobbled at a stately pace along a red carpet from the house to the royal car, while his guards stood to attention and saluted. He got in, but the car door remained open, and the guards stood frozen at attention. Some minutes passed before a minute dog bounded out of the house, along the carpet and into the car. In a second the door slammed, the outriders ripped their motorbike throttles, and the cavalcade surged powerfully onto the road, forcing the passing traffic onto an embankment. Their majesties, large and small, progressed imperially home beneath the fluttering royal standard, leaving behind a roar, a tail of dust and the gentle lapping of the waves against the Pacific shore.

*

At 6.48 am on 1 October 2009 an underwater earthquake off the coast of Samoa caused a massive, fast-moving displacement of water. Fifteen minutes later, this slammed into the palm-fronded coastal villages of southern Upolu, the tourist heart of Samoa's main island. More than one hundred people were crushed or drowned, and more than 5000 were affected by waves that, owing to the towering cliffs overlooking the village of Lalomanu, reached up to 15 metres high. Footage soon emerged of the vast tsunami sweeping across the beachfronts of Samoa, smashing houses and lifting cars like children's toys in a bathtub. The image of one of the 'happy isles of Oceania' pounded by what was presented as a random act of unstoppable natural brutality resonated vividly, reminiscent of the images of the 2004 Asian tsunami, and hit a tourist nerve. The 'Samoa tsunami', as it became known, connected with the global nexus of beach culture, cheap resorts and holidays in the sun. In addition to the loss of life and destruction of property, the tsunami was presented as a 'coconut catastrophe' that sent shockwaves through tourist hubs from the Pacific to Thailand and the Costa del Sol.

The island of Niuatoputapu, aka 'tin can island', 300 kilometres from the earthquake's epicentre and belonging not to Samoa but to the Kingdom of Tonga, was not one of those fashionable beachside locations. Before it sank in Tonga's worst disaster, the aging and unseaworthy *Princess Ashika* had taken over two weeks of chunderous chugging across open seas to get there. Unable to get near the island because of the reef, the *Ashika* had lowered passengers and supplies into smaller motor boats which then made their way back to the island through a specially cut corridor in the reef. In this way, the island's staples of huge vats of expired Salisbury corned beef, tuna, packet noodles, damp cardboard cylinders of stale Pringles and assorted Arnott's digestive and chocolate biscuits were imported.

Despite this, the island managed to maintain a population of 800 people, clustered in small hamlets along the sea front – Hihifo,

Vaipoa and Falehau – and on the island of Tafahi. All were rubble by the time I arrived almost three weeks after the tsunami, sent to assess options for 'early recovery' programs. The imprint of left-over normality lingered on in the abandoned furniture, the cleared paths and the rubble-strewn outline of where houses once stood.

While the world's eyes were fixed on Samoa during the tsunami, higher waves of greater force flattened three of the four hamlets of Niuatoputapu. Many residents were caught in the waves, which reached up to 6 metres high, and nine people died – on an island of less than one thousand people, a catastrophic loss. Samoa received a tsunami warning fifteen minutes before impact, but there was no warning in Niuatoputapu. Residents felt a light tremor, but it was no different from previous tremors, except that it lasted almost ten minutes. A few minutes after that, the first of three increasingly large waves struck.

With a Tongan colleague, Iengi, I flew first to the island of Vava'u in an antique Douglas DC-3, described as a collection of parts flying in loose formation, and then transferred to a mosquito-like Islander for the journey to Niuatoputapu. As we loaded up on the tarmac there was a delay while the eight passengers already onboard had to be re-seated: to maintain the aircraft's balance, a colossal noble had to be placed by himself at the back of the plane. I was the loser in this readjustment and ended up crammed at the front between the pilot and the permanent secretary to the cabinet – a man named Busby. During the flight, almost incomprehensibly above the roar of the propeller, Busby described the World Bank's Niua reconstruction plan: 150 Californian bungalows made from imported brick and concrete that were to be built in neat rows and at vast expense on an inaccessible island without a port in the middle of the Pacific Ocean.

Of the four hamlets, Hihifo was the worst hit, and there was nothing left standing there except the shell of someone's lovingly constructed blue-tiled concrete bathroom, on which a gleaming white toilet bowl perched without a roof, walls or attached house, looking out over the sea. The rest was rubble: bricks, concrete and hideously twisted iron sheets lay strewn about the remains of the village. The pulverised wreck of a car sat on top of what had once been a roof, now lying on the ground.

Through the rubble and debris a road and some paths had been cleared by a New Zealand navy unit sent up from Tongatapu. The ship carrying them had been too big to land, and they had created a helicopter air-bridge to the island in order to deliver supplies and help in the clean-up.

Near the entrance to the village, a slightly battered community noticeboard had survived and, in a malapropism that had turned into an apocalyptic temptation of fate, read:

Community
Leader
Eradication
Around
Niuatoputapu

Laura Jeffery's book *Niuatoputapu: story of a tsunami* compiled stories of the immediate aftermath of the tsunami from those who had survived. Residents described how they had stayed alive, the lack of prior warning, the sudden panic of animals, and the realisation that bigger and bigger waves were successively on their way. Villagers had been going about their daily routines one minute and clung to the tops of trees or the roofs of their disintegrating houses the next. In a few cases, farmers had risen early to tend their taro patches on higher ground behind the villages. They were unaware of what had happened during the day, and when they returned after work that evening they found that their world had literally been washed away.

Mafi Hoa:

I was at home with my family preparing breakfast that morning when I heard people in the road shouting: 'the sea is coming' ... I got in my van and saw the track outside my house was wet and later I realised this had been caused by a first wave.

Further along the track a pig was running around as if it had gone mad, and then I saw a second wave, perhaps a couple of metres high, surging up ashore behind the bank, and then an even larger wave beyond that a few hundred metres away. This wave was higher than the coconut trees and I felt a surge of panic and began reversing up the road.

By this time, people had jumped into the back of my van, onto the roof too, and others were clinging to the sides, standing on the running board. I was keeping an eye on the larger wave all the time, which by now had lifted and was floating an entire house towards us.

Mica Patolo:

I woke up early that morning to go fishing. I felt the earthquake and was on my way home when I saw the sea surging up the reef and I ran into a bush and climbed a tree. There was a small wave at first and though I was safe from that one when the water dropped down I ran to a bigger tree. I was lucky I did because a bigger wave came soon afterwards. From the tree I could see pieces of my house floating by and I was so worried for my daughters that I began to cry. When the bigger wave had gone, I climbed down from the tree but our house was gone, there was nothing left at all, and it was much the same for the village, nothing but wreckage, and fish flapping on the ground. I met someone and was told that most people had fled to the bush, so

I went to look for my daughters there and I was so relieved when I finally found both of my daughters safe and well.

Ipeni Vakata:

I was at home when the earthquake started. I'd never seen a wave that big in the channel before but even so it wasn't so big as to frighten me. But it took my boat and I started to walk along the beach and then into the sea to retrieve it.

Then suddenly there was another wave coming, a bigger one, maybe 3 metres and I remember being rolled in the wave as it took me inland. I managed to stand in the water, but I could see another wave, a really tall one already following and I swam towards a tree and climbed it. Then I clung with all my strength as the wave hit me and I was lucky because the tree stayed rooted and I continued to hold on until eventually the sea receded.

Strangely, amid the wreckage caused by the tsunami, I felt almost at home. Far from being the shock they once were, disasters had become almost familiar scenes – the constant accompaniments, however grim and destructive, of human settlement and construction. And in this place so different from my own, the destruction – the entire reason for my visit – was also a point of connection.

While the villages had been destroyed, the agricultural land, at a higher altitude, fortunately remained untouched. Everyone had moved from the villages to live in shanties and tents in their gardens. What had gone, however, were the food stocks, and the water wells near the coast had been contaminated with saltwater. Beyond the digestive biscuits, stale chocolate and tinned beef in the one remaining general store, there was almost nothing to eat and very little to drink.

Iengi and I slept on the floor of a school that had escaped damage and ate one meal a day – boiled rice mixed with tinned beef – cooked over an open fire made of broken pieces of people's former homes. As I walked between the villages one afternoon, comparing elaborate reconstruction plans with more practical concerns of recovery (shelter and water), a small party of children followed me – the strange, pale foreigner – through the rubble. They clearly had taken pity on my wanderings and each brought delicious, refreshing gifts of food. And so I found myself standing in the sun on my own, the proud possessor of half a dozen watermelons – extravagant gifts for a total stranger from people in the midst of food and water shortages and whose island lives had been shattered only a few weeks before.

When we left Niuatoputapu, we stopped on the island of Vava'u for a connecting flight to Tongatapu. After the dry heat, destruction, solemnity and generosity of the Niuans, 'normality' in the tourist centre was bizarre, and Iengi and I felt equally out of place. 'These strange foreigners', Iengi muttered to me under his breath, as we watched a group of international yachting families dress up for Halloween. 'How was it over there?' asked a friendly yachtie dressed up as a pirate, and it took me a second to remember that I too was a foreigner.

*

'It's the Chinese', said the taxi driver, as we steered our way back from the airport into the centre of town. Tropical Cyclone Gita hit Tonga in 2018 and I found myself once more heading down the familiar airport road, looking for signs of damage as an in-coming aid coordinator. There didn't appear to be much and so I asked the driver how he was doing. 'Not good' came the response. No – the cyclone did not damage his house or that of anyone in his village.

He had plenty of food, everyone was okay and his job had not been affected. He was, however, exercised about the growing presence of Chinese-run businesses in the Tongan capital and, in the wake of the cyclone, had grave concerns about them.

'You won't believe it', he told me. 'They brought in lots of Juicy Fruit chewing gum but it's fake. They have a whole container of gum but it's not Juicy Fruit. The Chinese swap it with something else.'

'The only thing that didn't blow down was my office', complained the head of the local NGO I have arrived to assist and who seemed less agitated by the great Chinese gum conspiracy than the taxi driver. 'I've been trying to get rid of this termite-infested ruin for years, and it's still there.' He picked up a cigarette lighter from his desk and toyed with it for a second before flicking the flint and examining the flame with close interest. 'Although, it's not impossible, a fire could break out at any time', he said ominously.

This disaster response was very different from many others I had experienced. The damage was relatively light, and the cyclone, rather genially, had slowed down on impact. The recovery, for the most part, was fast. It was only rather late in the day that international assistance was called for and a crowd of United Nations agencies and a few NGOs flew in from Suva to make up the numbers. Discussion in the government had already moved beyond the emergency phase and debates about how much money could be obtained from the World Bank filled the lunch spots near the administration buildings in town. Much to everyone's delight, Tonga had just dropped into the UN's list of least developed countries, which qualified the government for a system of international grants that did not have to be repaid.

'Time to invest in shares in ANZ', opined a large official sporting a crested tie, a neatly clipped moustache and a tightly furled umbrella.

A younger colleague leaned over and added, 'The big issue with concessional loans is the Reserve Bank.'

Both concurred, after a short pause, that the Ministry of Finance was an Apex Ministry.

I left the cafe and made my way to a meeting with Salesi, an official with the Ministry of Infrastructure, which was housed in a ramshackle shed a long way from town and definitely nowhere near the apex.

When I arrived Salesi struggled down the corridor and looked hardly able to walk. 'Gout', he muttered. 'I need to buy a skateboard.' He sank painfully into his chair, which, like all government chairs in Tonga, was covered in a regal crimson and bore the king's monogram in gold. These monograms were also the last significant investment in each ministry, and revealed their respective place in the administrative hierarchy. Finance chairs, bearing gilded crowns and the monogram 'GVIT' (George Tupou VI – the reigning monarch), were at the centre of current bureaucratic desirability. The faded crimson of Infrastructure, however, bearing the insignia 'GIIIT', lagged behind the rest of the government by several reigns.

'Well, I'm advising the government with the World Bank, you know', said an aging American of wraith-like proportions as she emerged, eyes bulging with dissatisfaction, from behind a cubicle. Salesi, immobile with gout on his aging crimson throne, had no means of escape, and introduced me to Prunella.

'I'm designing the emergency response to Cyclone Ian', she informed me by way of introduction. 'You should follow what we've done.'

I asked why she was still designing the emergency phase of the response, since Cyclone Ian had occurred some years before.

'We got it wrong the first time round', Prunella replied pertly. 'We thought we would run out of money, and so we built very small houses, not really suitable for Tongans, who are quite big, so we had to start again. But we've got great documentation now', she said, beaming, as she returned to an immense multicoloured spreadsheet.

Salesi and I exchanged glances. 'Let's see if we can find a skateboard', he said.

*

While the emergency response to Cyclone Gita had been quick, thanks to the rapid mobilisation by the government and Tongan Red Cross, there were some who had missed out. Several months later, a family I visited had lost the roof and most of the walls of their house and were still sheltering under a tarpaulin. The house had once been a charming building, with high ceilings, a steep roof and leisurely verandas, but age and termites had ensured that it was blown apart as the powerful cyclonic winds came through. On what remained standing, there were pictures of the Chicago cityscape and an embroidery reading 'Home Sweet Home'. Built carefully over generations, the house now consisted of a single habitable room furnished with a soaking polyester mattress under the gaping tarpaulin.

'It leaks', said the owner as we stood in a large puddle of water on the bedroom floor, looking up at the open sky. The cyclone had been vindictive in its randomness. None of the other properties in the area had been damaged, yet this one house had been destroyed. 'We don't have any money to repair', he continued. 'I'm a builder. I know what to do. I have a hammer and some strong brothers, but we can't afford the materials.' Next door, a well-constructed and well-heeled Mormon church had been completely untouched by the storm. Knowing that the Mormons were one of the largest religious groups in Tonga and, like other religious institutions in the country, required significant financial donations from church members, I asked if they had helped. 'They won't help us. We're not Mormons', he said, glancing resentfully at their neatly clipped lawns and pristine white buildings.

As I left, a truck bearing the logo of the Sudeep Supermarket chain drove up to what remained of the house, and a bunch of happy workers with red Sudeep Supermarket hats jumped out and posed for a photo in front of the ruin. The manager strolled up to me. 'Great brand promotion', he said cheerfully, and they drove off.

*

That night, at the hotel, there was great excitement. Jacinda Ardern, the newly minted New Zealand prime minister, had decided to visit Tonga in the wake of the cyclone and had been seen moving around the nation's capital in a large bus all day, along with a trade, governmental and NGO entourage. In the bar and the reception area of the hotel, aid workers and officials lingered in the hope of pressing the flesh. A number of the aid workers, who had been busy out in the field all day, had made an effort and had dug out formal shirts for the occasion. They waited in high anticipation. Ardern had already changed the language of her government and was being held up as a leader for a new and more progressive generation than her predecessor. After a decade of conservative rule, hopes were high that she would revive more generous traditions of aid, trade and foreign policy. So, freshly shaved, showered and shirted, Ardern's extended court gathered, awaiting the prime-ministerial presence. But after a long day of shaking hands, smiling and making speeches, the premier was tired, and word soon got out that she had decided not to come down and mingle and had gone to bed instead. Slowly the atmosphere turned sour. Delegates who had until that point refrained from a second drink in order to remain cogent now flocked to the bar for a third and fourth, shirts untucked and buttons undone.

'You know, I miss Bill', said one aid worker, referring to Ardern's predecessor as prime minister. 'Good old Bill, he wasn't very charismatic, but you could always have a chat with Bill. Jacinda sets the right tone and says the right thing but ... Bill would have come down. He was solid.'

'We don't know why we're here', said a youth representative. He continued, 'I mean, I like travelling round in the bus and going to openings and hearing nice things, but what's the point?'

As the new prime minister slept, knives were being sharpened long into the night by her apparent friends, suddenly deprived of a moment in the limelight.

I left the reception and joined a colleague for dinner at a nearby sports bar. 'I've just spent a year writing my own book', said Houston King, an aid worker who had recently left the army to work as a logistics manager for a New Zealand charity operating in the Pacific. We sat with a beer and fish and chips underneath a vast television that was broadcasting a rugby match from Christchurch. Houston, although riveted, seemed to have no interest in the game and had decided to tell me his life story out of the corner of his mouth as he stared unblinkingly at the grunting scrimmages on the screen in front of us. 'You know, I wasn't happy in my last few years in the army, so I saw a psychologist to ask what's wrong with me. "You've grown out of it", she said. "It happens every now and again – we get someone who starts to think for themselves, and when that happens the army's no longer the place for them." So I resigned and took myself off to Koh Samui for five years and wrote this self-help book.'

His eyes still hadn't left the television, a new round of beers had been procured, and I was becoming anxious that I was about to hear at length the spiritual development of Houston King.

'The book's about finding yourself through the discipline of action', he summarised in a brisk military manner. 'For example, clothes. When I travel, I have three sets of clothes: good, medium and worn. They rotate: good to medium, medium to worn, and worn – out. That's it.'

There was a protracted silence while I waited for him to continue, trying to discover the greater significance of the story. Were the clothes an analogy for something that I didn't quite understand? I steeled myself for an uninvited onslaught of life advice. But that really was it. Houston hadn't wasted his words and had already shared the fruits of his period of self-reflection in Koh Samui. As this dawned on me, I was instantly grateful for having been spared. There was no yoga, no Buddha, no moment of spiritual awakening. If it didn't mean anything, the advice was, at least, mercifully brief.

'Anyway, it's a no-go. Fuck'n' Deepak Chopra's cornered the self-help market', Houston said bluntly as he necked another beer and continued to eye the game that was playing out on the television.

A diving instructor joined us, and while Houston watched the rugby, Stanley stared in the other direction, out of the window into the night. 'It's dark out there', he said eventually, his eyes searching the blackness. 'It's a terrible thing, the ocean: vast and powerful', he continued in a soft Yorkshire accent whose modulations seemed to match the slow pulse of the incoming tide. 'The other day, when I were diving out there, I looked and I looked into the deep of the Tonga Trench, over 10 kilometres down – deeper into the earth than Mount Everest is high – and I thought, I thought to myself, I thought, "No – this is no way to die". I always carry my breathing gear in front of me, so I can keep an eye on it. Just in case I'm down there at 50 metres. If you do everything right, by the book, it's perfectly safe', he continued unconvincingly. 'But down there, in the deep, you never really know.'

And with that, he ceased talking and continued to stare out into the night, weighing the prospect of an aquatic demise while Houston stared blankly at the rugby stalemate on the television screen above.

Part 2

EMPIRE OF THE SEA:
POST-COLONIAL ENCOUNTERS

5

THE UNITED STATES OF PALAU

'I'm Bond, James Bond', Palau's former vice-president said over his beer. He chuckled loudly. 'At least, that's what I used to tell the Americans whenever they came here. They didn't know how to take me at first, but they eventually got that it was a joke.' And to clarify: 'I don't really think I'm James Bond.' He then waved the waiter over, ordered a martini and looked at me with his eyebrows raised.

'You know what I'm going to say now?' he said, inviting me into his James Bond joke.

'Something about them being shaken, not stirred?' I responded, playing along.

'No!' He roared with laughter. 'I'll have two of them – two for me, none for you.' He doubled over, chuckling again at his own joke. 'Jeez', he continued, once he had recovered, 'we used to crack up at the UN'.

At a meeting of the United Nations General Assembly in New York, the former vice-president had found himself seated between the representatives of North Korea and Saudi Arabia. After a few awkward moments of silence wondering how he could entertain his stiff and uncommunicable neighbours, he leaned over and whispered, 'You'll never guess what. I'm Bond, James Bond.'

'So am I' came the instant reply from the North Korean delegate, and they collapsed giggling in the back row like two inattentive schoolboys.

'But the Saudi guy didn't get it. They're no fun', he observed.

Why Palau, a microstate of more than 20,000 people in the western Pacific, bothered sending anyone to the United Nations was beyond me. As a US dependency, the country always voted according to instructions from Washington. The demanding role attached to the vice-president when overseas had been to deliberate and say 'yes' when asked to do so by the US Department of Pacific Affairs. He had recently lost office in a closely contested election but was still on the campaign, hoping to get back in next time. His wife, Marjoram, was head of a local NGO. Every action was, directly or indirectly, related to the maintenance of family influence and the electoral cycle.

'Remember to vote for me next time', the former vice-president told the waiter. He turned back to the table and said, in a stage whisper, 'Those voters are bastards. You can't rely on them.'

A voice from the other end of the table pitched in. 'He probably can't vote anyway, Daddy. He's from the Philippines or somewhere, so don't waste your effort.'

We had been joined in the restaurant by the former vice president's daughter, who announced immediately that her being there to talk with us meant her parents were calling in a favour; this meant she wouldn't have to see them for the rest of the week. She was accompanied by her boyfriend, a champion free diver who dreamed of spear fishing and spent the evening practising breath control. After remaining motionless for minutes at a time, he would suddenly expand his enormous lungs, and the countdown to the next breath – some time away – would begin again. 'He's the silent type', muttered the former vice-president with approval.

*

The Republic of Palau, lying close to the Philippines, was an American Pacific territory until 1994, when it signed the deal known by the Orwellian name of the Compact of Free Association, which granted Palau nominal independence in something resembling a condition of sovereign dependency on the United States. Prior to this Palau was a German, a Japanese and, following World War Two, a US territory. Elements of its multiple colonial masters lingered on. Palauans with names like Siegfried Nakamura hung out in well-chilled American diners with Bud Lights, musing over the gridiron while being served by Filipina waitresses and kept afloat by US aid grants (including $250 million to accommodate former Guantanamo Bay inmates from China's Uyghur minority).

While the country had a small but lively downtown with shops and a restaurant catering to its growing demand as a tourist destination, the formal capital was on an adjacent island and suggested a very different set of influences and national aspirations. In the capital Ngerulmud, on the island of Babeldaob, is an enormous replica of Capitol Hill, which the government of Taiwan constructed in gratitude for diplomatic recognition by Washington, DC. Shimmering white buildings arise from the surrounding paddock, crowned with domes and connected by sweeping colonnaded walkways that link the legislature, the judiciary and the executive. The congress and senate meet there, while each of the sixteen state governors, answerable to their own state legislature, has offices in the executive building – all for a total national population of around 20,000. Amazingly, in this relatively wealthy island microcosm of the United States, the civil service ran on a patronage basis, just like on the 'mainland' as America was still often called by Palauans. The effective functions of government stopped every four years, as one rent-seeking group of politically connected administrators replaced the other, with each turn of the electoral cycle. The campaigns emphasised, in the slogan of one candidate, 'Honor, family, military'.

In 2012, Palau was hit by Typhoon Bopha. While the typhoon caused major devastation affecting 100,000 families in the Philippines, in Palau only a few hundred families were affected, so the country received less initial assistance and attention. In local terms, however, it was a major disaster, for which the local disaster management authorities led the response. Three months after the typhoon hit, having worked on the aid response in the Philippines, I went to Palau to scope out what further humanitarian assistance might be necessary.

On my first morning, I went out with some volunteers to see what the typhoon had done to parts of Palau and how the recovery effort had gone. It was hours before we came across the first damaged areas – not because these were far away but because the route chosen circuitously passed a number of shops and gardens where the finest produce of Palau could be obtained in order to fuel our visit. The volunteers stacked the boot with cans of Coke, Fanta and sickly pineapple juice, pastries, chips and several packets of chocolate biscuits. They then ordered and collected a whole roast chicken and several fish dishes. When we were finally under way, they ate large numbers of chocolates and munched on a bitter local berry mixed with a peculiar concoction of miso soup and Kool-Aid. At one point the car hit a small speed hump, and the driver turned to me and slurred, through a mouth plugged with betel nut and tobacco, that the speed humps were enough exercise for the day.

Eventually, we came to a coastal village that had been damaged in the typhoon. In total, nearly one hundred houses had been destroyed along the coast, and some agricultural lands had been damaged. However, the government, with significant US backing, had had the response in hand a few months after the typhoon hit. Most of the houses had been entirely reconstructed, and lingering humanitarian concerns consisted of arguments about what colour they should be painted. There were signs of life continuing as usual: some folk were out fishing and others were putting the final touches on newly rebuilt and restored houses. Chickens ran freely around a big yard at the entrance to the village and there was the bustling orderliness of a busy community. Several large, recently constructed houses attested to where the cyclone had hit, but the recovery seemed to have been quick and well funded and life seemed to have returned to normal. There was, in my view, little to see other than a small, pleasant village quickly getting on with things.

As we left, one of the volunteers turned to me with tears in her eyes and shook her head. 'It's so tragic', she said. 'They have no money and are so poor. We need to go and eat.'

The car took us to a park and my colleagues brought out the picnic they had spent so much of the morning collecting. With pride, one of them offered me a plate of a local delicacy: spam sushi. As I struggled to find a way out of eating neat little parcels of spam carefully wrapped in seaweed, a look of grave concern came over her face. 'Are you anti-spam?' she asked, worried that she might have caused offence.

'No, no', I replied hastily as, stomach churning, I selected the largest parcel as diplomatic evidence of my basic pro-spam position, chugging it down with the aid of a bottle of green Kool-Aid.

*

My visits to Palau always featured many hours visiting a local organisation whose offices were housed in a former Japanese World War Two air-raid bunker. A small, heavy metal door on enormous hinges plus 1.5-metre-thick walls made the inside dark, cold and mildewy, and the atmosphere was airless and oppressive. The ceiling was not quite high enough for an adult to stand straight, and the staff and volunteers walked around inside as if perpetually bowing to one another. Old mannequins used in first aid instruction lay scattered across the floor, and treading across the moist, stale carpet in the musty half-light felt like being in the den of a psychopathic mass murderer.

To escape these uncongenial environs, I would go down the road with my colleagues to Chief's Diner – a 1950s American restaurant with glossy fake-leather booths to sit in and a menu that included minute steak for breakfast. Couples on dates could be seen sipping soda together and periodically looking romantically into each other's eyes. When conversation dried up, they studied the enormous television screens broadcasting baseball games with the same moist-eyed reverence. So American was the Palau I was experiencing that I wondered if any serious indigenous culture still existed. I had heard that there was a Council of Chiefs that still held significant political sway in the country and one day I wondered out loud if these bearers of ancient tradition might provide an alternative worldview to the predominating Americana.

In response, a colleague tapped me on the arm and said, in hushed tones, that perhaps the biggest chief of them all, the chief of the most populous town, Koror, was currently dining at the bar. I looked across and saw a large, walrus-moustachioed man with a suitably chiefly mane of snow-white hair that reached his shoulders.

As we went up to pay the bill, I was deferentially introduced, and I said what an honour it was to meet him. Hoping to draw him out on his chiefly duties, I observed that it must take enormous experience and dedication to be a great chief. He looked up from his burger and chips, twitched the walrus moustache a little and ordered another Budweiser.

Assuming that my conversational ploy had failed, I paid the bill and was about to walk off when the chief grabbed my arm.

'Look', he said, waving a beefy hand at the television screen. I squinted at the baseball match in progress and wondered what I was supposed to be looking at. 'It's the Chiefs playing!' he roared. With great pride, he jabbed his index finger into his chest and, with a mouth full of beery chips, said, 'Like me!'

*

I was trying, one afternoon, to make a trip in an enormous four-wheel-drive pick-up truck belonging to Palau's disaster management authority. There was a big hole in the floor on the driver's side, and every now and then I looked down and was unnerved by the sight of the road whizzing by under my thong-clad feet. The truck had little steering and virtually no brakes, and I had been advised that if I needed to stop urgently the best course of action was to drive onto the curb or aim at the nearest hill. Eventually losing all control, I lurched onto the wrong side of the road and through a pedestrian crossing, finally ending up on a small embankment next to a boathouse.

'Hey, there's room on the boat if you want to join us.' A group of students at the boathouse had seen me 'parking' the truck and called across as I emerged, ashen faced, from the vehicle.

'Sure', I said, pretending that I had always intended to head in their direction, 'I'll come with you.' With an attempt at studied detachment to hide my embarrassment, I hauled a large rock over to the truck and stuck it behind the back wheel while secretly hoping that the wrecker's yard would have it crushed into a ball of metal by the time I got back.

Flushed, I turned to the students. 'By the way', I asked, with as much offhand casualness as I could muster, 'who are you and where are we going?'

They were Americans from the University of Guam and were with their teacher on a class excursion. As we sped out of the harbour on a small motorboat, an incredible seascape emerged: the Rock Islands. Over the millennia their limestone base had slowly corroded and formed a secluded labyrinth of clear turquoise waterways in the middle of the Palauan lagoon. On reaching the labyrinth, the boat slowed to a stop. Drawn by the mesmerising colour of the water, I dived into its cool, clear, salty depths. As I came up for air, I was startled to find what resembled a ghost ship, and my companions had turned a ghoulish white against the bright Pacific sky. The corroded limestone mud from the bottom of the waterway was said to be good for the skin, and the students had dived down, collected handfuls of it, then plastered themselves in it from head to foot.

Having swum over to an arched opening in one of the walls of the labyrinth, I trod water for a few minutes, letting the gentle undulations of the ocean lap against the underside of my chin while I looked out from the shallow tranquility of the labyrinth onto the darker expanse of the lagoon and the Pacific beyond.

'We're going!' someone shouted, but I lingered for a moment, immersed in the wind and swell and squawk of island birds. I paddled back to the boat as the engine started, and we made our way through the narrow passages and ravines sheltered from the wider sea, then out into the lagoon.

'Get in carefully', said the teacher, detecting my reluctance to enter the water. 'You don't want to squash them but you'll be fine.' I hesitated instinctively. Leaping into a lake filled with millions of jellyfish while clad in only a pair of swimming shorts seemed a recipe for disaster. Inching myself off a small wooden pier, I inhaled sharply and slid down into the cold, dark, brackish water, fearing a thousand agonising stings as hungry, vengeful jellyfish swarmed towards me. When I got my bearings and had suffered no immediate attack, I took in the outlandish sight. The centre of the Eil Malk island in Palau's South Lagoon had, over the millennia, eroded to form a hidden, forested inland lake that had filled in with frequent rainwater. Somehow, centuries ago, some jellyfish had managed to get in, perhaps blown in by an ancient cyclone beyond human memory. Finding themselves alone in the lake with no predators, and in the absence of any need for self-defence, the jellyfish had not only prospered but had evolved without a sting.

The simple act of moving from the lake's depths into the sunlight, refracted through the surface water, was enough for an approximated eight million of them to survive. I was instantly surrounded by tens of thousands of light-pink jellyfish that seemed to float in endless streams out of darker waters at the bottom of the lake, like an infinity of lava lamps endlessly morphing as they blobbed around an enclosed space. They proceeded slowly but efficiently with a sudden pulse-like contraction of their mushroom-shaped heads, propelling them towards the surface. I was transfixed. The water was so packed with jellyfish that I moved carefully to avoid accidentally slicing them apart with my flippers. Frequently, I would feel a soft and gentle blob against my skin, little harder than a breath of air, and I developed an instant affection for these wonderful, ridiculous and harmless creatures.

And yet, by 2016, after thousands of years of evolution, the great Jellyfish Lake of Palau would be under threat. Warmer water temperatures in the Pacific combined with an El Niño event had produced a serious drought. The lack of rain meant that the lake – dependent on the open skies to replenish its freshwater – became more saline. All of this, in addition to the impact of more than 600 tourists a day, led to a plummeting jellyfish population. Where once there had been thirty million of the extraordinary stingless creatures, evolved specifically to live in a small lake in the middle of Eil Malk island, only around 600,000 would remain when the lake was re-opened to tourism in 2019 after a two year closure. When I swam in the lake, there were so many of them that I unwittingly bumped into ten or twenty every minute and sent them spiralling back down towards the bottom of the lake.

At the height of the drought – a sign of the ecological fragility of this unique environment – they were thought to have disappeared.

I swam the length and breadth of the lake amazed, tickled and absorbed by the sight of the jellyfish that were then still in their incalculable multitudes. Finally, fearing that I'd spent so long exploring that the students might have left without me, I made my way back to the pier only to find that the students hadn't moved. Most of them were sitting down and those that were in the water had remained close by or still clinging on. One of the students, weighed down by an enormous underwater camera, appeared totally marooned on a nearby rock, unsure as to how to get his expensive photographic equipment safely back to land. The teacher noticed my surprise.

'They're always like this', she said. 'They're not used to moving around and any form of exercise exhausts them. We try to get them out and show them other parts of the Pacific away from Guam, but they just prefer to sit in groups and not go anywhere.'

On the way back to the boathouse, after several failed attempts, I managed to engage one of the students in conversation. They had been kind and generous in inviting me to go with them initially, and I wanted to learn more about them. One student, Ashley, who seemed slightly worldlier than the others, told me that her family had moved to Guam, an American Pacific territory, after her parents were made redundant in the mainland United States. The tuition rates at the University of Guam were considerably lower than elsewhere, and there were job prospects servicing the US military bases on the island. These were the kinds of predictable, decently paid jobs that have all but disappeared from the American Rust Belt but can still be found in – or servicing – the government and the military in the Pacific, and so her parents had found work.

Professing a deep fascination with everything Korean, from the country's history to her love of kimchi, Ashley announced that her dream was to become an English teacher there. Encouraged by her enthusiasm, I mentioned that I had once lived there for a period, including a disastrous few months teaching English to a succession of uncontrollable five year olds whom I could only entertain, much to the school authority's annoyance, by turning the classroom into a miniature soccer field. 'Everyone's wanting to teach in Korea now', she said brightly. The former military base set in the isolation of Guam, known during the Cold War as the Pacific's 'Coral Curtain', and US dependencies like Palau, had now become a gateway to Asia and a new future.

6

NEW CALEDONIA AND THE MEMORY OF REBELLION

Voices shouting from a triangular black speakerphone in the middle of the room were barely intelligible amid the oceanic swell of static also coming down the line. Around me, wiser heads nodded sagely; some notes were passed. 'Good as gold' came a New Zealand voice, suddenly clear, from somewhere out there, deep beyond the reef, although what this referred to I couldn't say. There was more static, a glorious crunching of vowels and electric contortions as if a microphone were being pushed hard into the sand of some remote island in the hope of hearing from the earth itself – a swirling, oppressive, ear-jarring cacophony that spoke of fierce winds, rising seas and imminent destruction. The telephonic static was more grimly articulate than the humans themselves.

Twenty of us had crowded around the speakerphone in a conference room in the Melbourne office of the international NGO where I had recently been employed. Strong winds – possibly cyclone strength – had been reported on an outer island in Tonga and my colleagues had sprung into action. A 'Pacific Taskforce' was convened and, despite being new to the organisation, I had been invited to participate. 'This is it', I thought, sensing that I was about to witness a mighty global institution leap to the assistance of one of its smallest members in a remote, sparsely populated outer island of the Pacific Ocean. How would the NGO respond? Who knew what was going on? Those in the room stared sternly into the middle distance or impassively contemplated a bleak oblivion of grey office partitions, keep cups and an ancient oil painting of a palliative care nurse reading quietly to an elderly, moustachioed gent who was clearly transitioning – as the NGO's new management would say – into the next world. Was this the sort of extraterrestrial slippage that awaited the Tongan island? Around the room eyes were set, lips pursed. There was silence and static.

'We are sending a Man of War.' It sounded as though a disembodied Inspector Clouseau had joined the call and was met with nodding, this time more vigorous. The French authorities in New Caledonia, relying on a century-old dictionary, had decided to send a naval vessel that happened to be on exercises nearby to assess the Tongan wreckage. The call ended quickly – someone had done something and the Taskforce could reassemble later to assess the findings from the French navy. Clutching their badges of office – mugs of weak tea, ID cards on luridly coloured lanyards, and small bundles of notebooks, pens and highlighters – the taskforce members returned to their cubicles to tend to an array of emails, forms, templates, and colour-coded spreadsheets that give shape to a day in the life of NGO headquarter staff.

At fifteen hundred hours, fortified by several coffee catch-ups and water-cooler conversations, the Taskforce reassembled. The numbers had now increased and the room was even greyer and more airless than ever as the members packed in to see what the French 'Man of War' had found. Once again, the speakerphone crackled from the middle of the room. 'Good as Gold' came the disembodied New Zealander again from somewhere out in the ether while an international dialling tone boinged a thirty-digit mobile number seeking contact with New Caledonia.

"ello, 'ello', intoned another muffled Inspector Clouseau. The assembled Pacific Taskforce collectively leant in to hear what had happened: taut lines of facial concentration circled the room, closing in on the black box at its centre. In the absence of information, a fervid collective imagination had taken hold and conjured up the worst possible mental images of destruction. Had the cyclone made landfall? Had anyone survived? What clinical statistics of houses damaged, crops torn apart and lives lost would serve as aid-speak's disembodied proxies to describe the destruction of an island life? As the static hissed, and time dragged between responses, the taskforce's collective imagination grew grimmer still. Mouths curved downwards in stony anticipation while visages assumed the official blankness of a passport photograph. It was clearly bad, they seemed to suggest, but was it really, really bad?

'Ze Man of War' resumed Inspector Clouseau, 'we 'ave lost it.'

Strong winds had failed to form a cyclone and had caused almost no damage at all. A tropical depression lifted after a few days of heavy rain and the Tongan island had returned to its sunlit rituals while the Man of War, now relocated, began its slow, imperial chug back to New Caledonia. Officers in starched white tropical uniforms and gold braid sauntered around the upper deck under a flying French tricolour as their ship headed to the quiet colonial town of Noumea – a quaint relic of another age that had lingered on in the era of the atom bomb and the rise of China. At NGO headquarters, following the circulation of a file note and an administrative trail of densely typed meeting minutes adorned with 'learnings' and 'actions', the once mighty Pacific Taskforce disbanded.

A few weeks later, in order to find out more about the mysterious disappearing Man of War, I found myself on a plane heading for Noumea. At the airport, a comical interrogation ensued. Owing to the recent outbreak of SARS virus, all the New Caledonian officials were now wearing enormous black gas masks. This did not deter them in their line of duty and I was subjected to an incomprehensible series of questions in French-accented English through a Darth Vader gas mask. Routine enquiries about how long I intended to stay and which hotel I had in mind became spine chilling when accompanied by the Dark Lord's mechanised emphysema and apocalyptic vocal timbre. The Voice of Death politely enquired whether I preferred tasteful beachside apartments or the convenience of an international business hotel downtown. There was some excellent snorkelling to be had up north, Monsieur Vader opined in a basso profundo death rattle, but the girls in Noumea were prettier. It seemed that the ghost of Peter Sellers had returned to play merry hell with French officialdom.

In previous Pacific travels, I had loved the frontier town feel of Honiara, the bougainvillea-clad hills of Port Moresby and Suva's neat gardens and lingering Anglophilia. If I had found much to enjoy and explore in these crumbling yet vibrant postcolonial cities, nothing prepared me for Noumea. This was European colonialism restored to its pre-lapsarian heyday; Suva, under British rule, would have looked like this almost half a century ago. Neat and trim and gleaming white, Noumea seemed to have dropped straight from the French Riviera to the South Pacific – the chic perfection of Nice and Saint Tropez had replaced the diesel fumes, betel nut, kava bars and rasta rebellion of the independent cities in the rest of the region. Neat lines of gleaming yachts bobbed languidly in the harbour while health-conscious Europeans jogged along the town's immaculate, palm-fronded foreshore wearing 1980s revival psychedelic lycra and gleaming white running shoes. Domestic French television channels beamed quiz-shows, reality TV and sporting contests from Paris into Noumea's bars and hotels, while daily flights ensured that no one missed out on the latest crisp editions of *Paris Match* or *Marie Claire*. Tanned and relaxed Europeans exuded the casual self-confidence of dominion while the local Kanaks – in a Gallic twist on American race relations – when not behind bars were seen behind the bar, mixing expensive cocktails with alcohol shipped from France and overseeing the perfect steak tartare. In fact, what struck me as I walked along the waterfront and through parts of Noumea's downtown was that the city was predominantly white, and even the waiters, shop assistants and tour operators – performing menial work often undertaken by locals in other contexts – were French.

If commerce was dominated by Europeans, the banknotes themselves seemed otherworldly. Although New Caledonia was part of France and therefore part of the European Union, here there were no neutral Euros with their unifying symbolism of circles and bridges holding out a mild hope of pan-continental solidarity in an increasingly fractious era. Instead, the monetary symbols of the nation state were defiantly in evidence. The magnificent French Pacific franc was more a document of empire than a denomination of currency. It fitted in no known wallet and was emblazoned with Pasifika. On one side, the French tricolour fluttered above a bare-breasted image of Liberty leading on the revolution, while the reverse featured an idealised Polynesian woman with chiselled features, chocolate skin and an exuberant crown of frangipani. It was as if Gaugin himself had designed the banknotes. Nineteenth-century imperial erotica with Pacific themes lived on in the territory's daily exchange of currency as an insistent reminder of who was boss.

In the era of Bitcoin and increasingly cashless societies, the French Polynesian Franc was a theatrical currency that looked as if it had previously served as a casino prop in the film *Casablanca*, and it was easy to imagine an underworld cast of collaborationists, resistance fighters, refugees and international jetsam gambling desperately under the cynical eye of Humphrey Bogart at Rick's Café Americain.

That evening, I was sitting with a colleague in the bar of a massive whitewashed tourist hotel near the beach that was completely empty. 'Just imagine', he drawled, Bogart-like, while languidly stirring a glass of Pernod. 'If this place was independent, it would be just like the rest of the Pacific.'

*

'You teach me English, I'll teach you muscle-building', offered Bruce, a giant former soldier in the French Marine Corps. We had found ourselves crammed into a small desk in a schoolroom several hours outside Noumea waiting, like overgrown children, for class to begin. In an effort to prepare Pacific Islanders for future disasters, a regional training program had been developed to run a simulation of a humanitarian crisis. This was attended by potential disaster responders from countries throughout the region and took place in an old scout camp several hours' drive from the capital. Bruce, at a loose end in early retirement in Noumea, had volunteered his military experience to the cause and we both waited eagerly on our first day to learn what to do in a crisis.

The day began early, in the Spartan tradition of scout camps around the world. Despite its tropical image, rural New Caledonia was surprisingly cold and, sharing a room with colleagues from Solomon Islands, Vanuatu, and Papua New Guinea, we huddled, shivering, in our cots, waiting for the sun to rise. A beaming Frenchman had marched in before dawn – 'It's not Siberia', he said jovially. Making my way in the tepid early light to the shower block, I became aware of the unusually cheery sounds of early morning ablutions. While the islanders maintained a low profile, the Europeans were in their element. Singing and gasping with pleasure as ice-cold water from the showers met the chill of first light.

'It's not Siberia, you know', repeated someone else in the adjacent cubicle, having noticed my reticence to dive enthusiastically into the shower's stinging jet of ice. The cheery echo of what seemed to have become the official mantra made me suspect that I had, in fact, ended up in the wrong country. To hell with Siberia, I thought, and plunged into the character-building spring waters of New Caledonia whose bracing chill was the one feature of the island that in any way resembled Scotland. Only a few hours in, and the training was already turning into some kind of humanitarian gulag – with early starts, body building and cold showers essential components of physical conditioning for emergency response.

Bruce and I spent three days companionably squeezed into our school desk as PowerPoint slide after PowerPoint slide lit up on the other side of the room. Supply chains were presented and discussed, the quality of tarpaulins (and whether or not they should contain reinforced eyeholes) was analysed, lengthy checklists were introduced, and exhilarating customs procedures were outlined. There were presentations on how to do assessments and how to make distributions of aid items. The importance of manifests and way bills in logistics processes was duly emphasised. 'And always remember to smile', said one instructor, adopting an unnerving grin of almost Californian insincerity in demonstration. 'Imagine what you would feel like if you were a refugee', she said, 'a smile always helps.' The presentations continued and, after initial intense concentration on the finer details of humanitarian logistics, a gradual mental numbness began to encroach. 'At least it's not Siberia', a colleague from Vanuatu whispered as we exchanged bleary-eyed glances deep into the afternoon of the fourth day. Bruce, while maintaining a perfectly correct military posture, was completely asleep.

By now the time had come to put everything we had learned into practice. Teams were assigned to direct a humanitarian response imaginatively set in an invented Pacific nation: the Republic of

Utopia. I found myself allied with an architect, a retired airline hostess and a former Commonwealth Games one hundred-metre sprinter – a combination of backgrounds, ages and occupations specifically designed to ensure maximum discord. Together, we would save Utopia from the menace of a swiftly moving Category 4 cyclone bent on destruction. The drone of the PowerPoint presentations had ended; we were turfed out of our dorm rooms and had set up camp to await the arrival of the cyclone and instructions as to where, using our new skills, we would manage the humanitarian response.

Things went badly from the beginning. After somehow managing to erect a tent together, the initial demands of the exercise proved almost impossible. An attempt to draw a rough map showing key settlements and major infrastructure on the small island of Utopia – roads, schools, hospitals, ports and landing strips – proved too difficult. The professional sprinter turned out to be an amateur artist and spent the next three days collecting flowers and hunting in the bush for materials to make paints. The architect, true to his profession, got instantly lost in a succession of ever more complex house designs to which the former flight attendant contributed with a hitherto unrealised passion for filing. Forgetting the urgency of humanitarian action, each successive design was lovingly labelled, categorised and put away for reference by posterity.

In their enthusiasm for procedure, the Utopian state authorities – our former instructors – had developed a large bureaucracy, no doubt in parallel with that of New Caledonia itself, and I spent the days traipsing from one end of the scout camp to the other, play-acting with pretend bureaucrats who presided over school desks stacked with forms and wielding ever larger and more important rubber stamps. Each visit to these menacing figures ended in rebuff – the forms were never filled out correctly, the stamps had not been issued in the right order, the cut-off for submissions had just ended and one bureaucrat was perpetually unavailable owing to a pre-existing golf appointment.

In desperation, our disaster response team resorted to the tactic of the marginalised and the dispossessed: crime. The flight attendant abandoned the files and used her institutional knowledge of airports to forge a series of documents that we hoped would pass as official documents for an array of equally fake government officials bent on administrative obstruction. Yet as we laboured to mislead the state authorities, the Vanuatuan sprinter's map of Utopia slowly progressed. Adding contours, colours, and topography made from layers of frangipani leaves and carefully mixed paints from local soils of deep browns and rustic reds, the map revealed a cartographic palimpsest that was a wonder to behold. If useless for the actual purpose of organising information to guide humanitarian decision-making, the map was, at least, a thing of beauty.

That night, as we continued to stumble our way through the exercise, a real cyclone warning was received in the scout camp, with initial strong winds and the possibility of landfall in a few days' time. The exercise suddenly took on a more serious aspect as we realised this was the very event we were now training for. Moments later, a torrential rain started, hammering down on the camp and making communication all but impossible. After a light start, periodic gusts of wind intensified until an almighty vent blew away the tent entirely, sending it cascading through a paddock and off into the night, taking all the architect's drawings, the flight attendant's files and most of our food supplies. Now drenched and covered in mud after an unsuccessful attempt to recover the tent, the disaster response team huddled next to an old outhouse, away from the rain and biting wind. Someone produced a small camp stove and we all shared the warm broth from a bowl of instant noodles while wondering what to do next.

Our initial attempt to manage, albeit in a simulation, an emergency in the Republic of Utopia had failed disastrously. Imagination and reality had intersected when, preparing to respond to an invented emergency, the tailwinds from a real cyclone blew away our camp. Wet, cold, filthy, tired, hungry and struggling to see through the sleet, we crawled around the side of the hut – a light was on in the other side of the scout camp and we made our way slowly towards it. Through the horizontal rain, the building gradually became clearer, and once inside we were met by the erstwhile bureaucrats of Utopia. The room was bright and warm, food was served by the real-life indigenous people of New Caledonia, and the tables rang with wine and good company. 'Interns not allowed' read a sign on the door. By now completely disillusioned, the disaster response team huddled together. 'This really is a gulag', said the sprinter and, as he looked into the warm room with its warm food and saw the animated, rosy-cheeked administrators, he became aware of a beautiful map hanging on the wall. The State of Utopia, evoked with deep-hued russet and sepia and frangipani, looked out over the State of New Caledonia and the interns grubbing around outside.

As the exercise ended, the journey back was sullen. The training had gone badly, and we participants were by now tired and homesick and generally fed up with each other. To make matters worse, the disaster response team had embarked on a piss-up by raiding the scout camp's liquor store. Being significantly more civilised than their puritanical counterparts elsewhere, the French scouting movement had left crates of wine in an easily accessible storeroom. As a result, the long drive to Noumea was frequently interrupted as members of our corps asked the driver to stop the bus in order to get out and throw up. Some of us didn't quite make it and puked forlornly out the window as the bus hurtled towards the capital. Once back in Noumea, we nursed our collective hangover in front of day-time TV beamed from Paris. Breathing heavily, with sallow eyes and green gills, the team tried to forget the last few days with regional French cooking programs, talk shows, and makeover programs. Would Henri, a drab computer programmer from Lille, invite Chantale, a graphic designer from a Parisian suburb, on a date following a haircut and a carefully selected new outfit? What really was the secret to making the perfect pig's offal sausage in Lyon? From deep in the Pacific Ocean, answers came by way of the occasional regurgitative groans from a nearby lavatory.

*

The ambivalence I had detected about France's position in the Pacific had long roots. Viewing New Caledonia as a francophone equivalent of British penal colonies and settlement in New Zealand and Australia, sections of the French administration refused the idea that New Caledonia was a colonial outpost. '*La Nouvelle Calédonie*', I was told, '*c'est la France.*' It had representation in the French and European parliaments. Throughout the 1980s, until the Matignon and Noumea Accords that had ceded greater political autonomy and the concept of '*équilibrage*', to reduce the profound inequity between European south and the Kanak (indigenous) north, this idea had been contested. The Kanak Socialist National Liberation Front had been brutally suppressed by French police, the caldoche (descendants of nineteenth-century French prisoners) who staunchly supported the French state, with whom the more politically liberal residents of metropolitan Noumea had been in conflict. Political reforms and greater re-distribution of the New Caledonia's profits from nickel mining, as well as the promise of a referendum on independence in 2018, had staved off further confrontation. These concessions were substantial and, in France's bloody late-colonial history, unprecedented. They were spearheaded by the Kanak independence leader Jean-Marie Tjibao, who was later assassinated by more militant independence activists who thought his negotiations with the French State were insufficiently radical. At the memorial Centre Jean Marie Tjibao in Noumea, visitors were invited to place their hands against an impression of his as a gesture of reconciliation. An injection of funds, government programs and retirees into New Caledonia ensured almost certain rejection of the impending independence referendum.

*

'As for me, I was tall, skinny, dishevelled, wild, brazen, sunburned, and often decorated with torn clothing held together with pins', wrote Louise Michel, in her memoir, about her childhood self. Michel was a French anarchist who came to prominence in 1871 on the barricades of the Paris Commune, for which she was sentenced to transportation to the convict settlement in New Caledonia. She had had an idyllic upbringing in a crumbling chateau, largely unsupervised by a grandfather who spent his time reading Voltaire. The chateau's grounds were 'dominated by two Tombs visited occasionally by partridges, a tortoise, a roebuck, some wild boars, a wolf, barn-owls, bats, several broods of orphaned hares that we had raised by spoon-feeding.'

Michel's initial sympathy was for animals and she railed against any ill-treatment of them. She recalled a pastime for farm labourers: 'they cut frogs in two, leaving the front part creeping along in the sun, eyes horribly popping out, front legs trembling as they try to flee under the ground. In the bright sunlight their soft, enormous eyes shine with reproach.' This sense of prevailing injustice soon transferred to her analysis of human society, both in relations between economic classes and between men and women. She had been given a lute to play, which she did with her cousin, a boy called Jules. 'In one stormy discussion on the merits of the sexes, Jules maintained that if I learned from the schoolbooks he had brought with him during the vacation and learned so that I was more or less on his level, it was only because I was an anomaly. So I took my lute', she wrote later 'and threw it at him'. She piercingly ridiculed the sexism of education and upbringing of her era. Girls were taught 'a pile of nonsense supported by childlike logic' while boys were made to 'swallow little balls of science until they choke. For both of us it is a ridiculous education.'

Her experience of a bad harvest was transforming. Just as animals had been brutally exploited by humans and girls had been subjugated by men in the educational system, a bad harvest led to the immiseration of the poor. Witnessing rural starvation firsthand, she was appalled by the callousness of the authorities, whose view was that 'the poor people should submit to that which they cannot prevent'. From that point, for Louise Michel, 'everything intermingled in a single song, a single dream, a single love: the Revolution'.

'Barbarian that I am, I love cannon, the smell of powder, machine gun bullets in the air', she observed, before contrasting the way her female comrades had fought and the lesser martial instincts of the men. 'Our male friends are more susceptible to faintheartedness than we women are. She may feel ripped open to her very womb, but she remains unmoved. Without hate, without anger, without pity for herself or others, whether her heart bleeds or not, she can say, "It must be done." Such were the women of the Commune. During Bloody Week, women erected and defended the barricade at the Place Blanche – and held it till they died.' When the Paris Commune was eventually defeated, Michel was arrested and was fortunate not to be shot. 'I threw a bottle at the gendarme', she recalled of the moment. 'A nearby officer rebuked me, and I told that my only regret was that I had thrown the bottle at a tool of government rather than the head of it.'

The court report at the time described Louise Michel as '36 years old, petite, brunette, and with a very developed forehead which recedes abruptly. Her nose, mouth and chin are very prominent, and her features reveal an extreme severity. She dresses entirely in black.' Her trial was brief and her statement from the dock was even briefer: 'I don't want to defend myself nor do I want to be defended. I belong completely to the Social Revolution', she announced to the gallery as she was sentenced to transportation to New Caledonia.

In the internment camp there were no resources or provisions and the convicts had to make their own tools. They lived in conditions Michel describes as 'Stone Age' and she considered trying to make a raft and escape to Sydney. She was allowed to mix with the Kanak population and quickly came to the conclusion that 'The Kanaks were seeking the same liberty we had sought in the Commune' and provided advice and moral support to the insurrection of 1878 against French rule, at one stage tearing the red scarf she had worn in Paris in two and handing it to leaders of the insurrection whose anti-colonial political organisation became known as *les foulads rouges* – the red scarfs. Two of her friends in the revolt against French rule had come to say goodbye before taking up the fight:

> They slipped into the ocean. The sea was bad, and they may never have arrived across the bay, or perhaps they were killed in the fighting. I never saw either of them again, and I don't know which of the two deaths took them, but they were brave with the bravery that black and white both have ...
>
> The Kanak Insurrection of 1878 failed. The strength and longing of human hearts was shown once again, but the whites shot down the rebels as we were mowed down in front of Bastion 37 and on the plains of Satory. When they sent the head of Atai [a revolutionary leader] to Paris, I wondered who the real headhunters were ... Versailles government could give the natives lessons in cannibalism.

By 2018, however, the first of three promised votes on New Caledonian independence had failed. I was, by then, travelling in Bougainville, a region of Papua New Guinea that was also preparing for its own independence referendum and locals were following the events in New Caledonia closely. In Bougainville, there was bewilderment and then understanding. 'Why had "our Melanesian brothers" not voted for their own country?' wondered the Bougainvilleans, facing their own independence vote after a long, bloody and hard-fought struggle. But then there was discussion. France's attitude to its Pacific territories had begun to change and while disputes remained about the equal access of Kanaks, European and Caledoche (settler) New Caledonians to the resources of the State, 'France', it was acknowledged, was 'not PNG'.

After the bloodshed of the 1970s and 1980s, reconciliation had been paramount in French–Kanak relations and was symbolised by the construction of the extraordinary Centre Jean Marie Tjibaou, designed by architect Renzo Piano. No such monument or sentiment existed in Bougainville. 'They have education, access to the European Union, they have a large degree of autonomy, and they have a future with France', reasoned the Bougainvilleans, listing the things they would have liked from their own national government. 'No wonder they voted to remain.'

7

MARSHALL ISLANDS: BOMBS, BASES AND THE ENCROACHING SEA

'There was a lot of talk in the office about annihilation', shouted Gretel above the din of a televised basketball game while waiting at the airport in Honolulu for a flight to Majuro in the Marshall Islands. The Warriors had just opened up a fourteen-point lead over the Kings as she recounted her experiences of the accidental air raid alert that had led Hawaiians to believe they were under nuclear attack from Pyongyang. Some Hawaiians had taken this news in the Waikiki spirit, and a video of a man sending his last message to the world had gone viral. 'If you are watching this it means I'm dead', he began solemnly and then, as the camera panned to the cloudless skies of another sunny afternoon in Hawaii, he continued: 'So, since we have about twenty-five minutes remaining until impact, it's a beautiful day and I'm going to play a round of golf.' Had Gretel been similarly phlegmatic about impending nuclear incineration, an echo of a modern-day Francis Drake indulging in one last game of bowls before facing the Spanish Armada?

'I texted my family to tell them I loved them and then hid in the bathroom with a cup of coffee', she replied more prosaically.

'If you've ever sky-dived, that was the feeling. There aren't any evacuation centres in Hawaii or anywhere you could go, so we just sat there with that terrible feeling of falling. You felt it in your stomach. It didn't happen, it didn't change anything. When they sounded the all clear and I went outside, there were these big orange displays above the traffic lights downtown saying, "THERE IS NO THREAT". We all felt giddy for days later.'

The basketball game continued to blare from the speakers in the airport lounge as the Kings staged a comeback. Through the noise, a travelling businessman from New Zealand had overheard our conversation and decided to have his two cents' worth.

'It's a strange world, even in New Zealand, the government's changed', he interjected. 'They don't care about economic growth and no one wants to work hard any more. And that's why they changed from the Nationals to Labor', he maintained – as if Pyongyang had unduly influenced politics in Auckland and the ascent of New Zealand's new prime minister, Jacinda Ardern, was somehow a victory for North Korean supremo Kim Jong-un.

During the flight to Majuro, I stared out the window and wondered what those moments must have been like and how people going about their everyday business would have responded to the realisation of an impending nuclear attack. In offices, would the annihilation chat occur by the proverbial water cooler or in a departmental meeting? Would there would be a last address by HR on 'end state entitlements' (incrementally available depending on final salary grade) or perhaps a few minutes to clear out some last emails? But my reverie was interrupted by the real-life intercom system.

'Those terminating on Majuro will deplane now.' A chill went down my spine – there seemed to be too much recent talk of termination.

The flight from Honolulu to the Marshalls was filled by locals returning home to their families and by men with close-cropped hair and disproportionately large arms. They were soldiers and contractors on their way to the US military base in Kwajalein, the largest of the Marshallese atoll chains. These had been rented from the country since independence in 1979, in a deal that is known as the Compact of Free Association. The plane was early and there was little discussion at the baggage carousel at that hour of the morning. The men all put on matching sets of Bose headphones or stared into the middle distance, silent and absorbed in their separate auditory worlds, noiselessly cocooned in the same technological world that steered missile delivery systems, launched in California, through the stratosphere to land in the 'catcher's mitt' of the Kwajalein lagoon. Every now and again, words would be exchanged and I was able to make out a number of distinctly Australian voices mingling with the Americans, relaxed and easy in each other's company, sharing the latest apps on their iPhones – soldiers bound for the same place and a common duty.

George W. Bush once famously asserted that he saw Australia's role in the Pacific as 'sheriff'. Here, then, was the sheriff in action: the quiet, unremarkable, out-of-sight and unobtrusive integration of Australian forces into an American command structure on a remote atoll in the Marshall Islands. As the US defence establishment accidentally sets off a missile attack warning in Hawaii and a man in the White House lies in bed watching reality television and boasts that his button is the biggest of them all, I wondered what could possibly go wrong? On a television screen in the airport in Majuro, the basketball game was on repeat. The Kings and the Warriors were now tied and were facing a tense final quarter.

*

Over the first few days of my visit, I roamed the streets, walking as far and as fast as possible in the heat, trying to get a sense of place and to find my bearings. Majuro on the ground looked much as it does from the air: a long, thin sliver of atoll in the middle of the ocean, with a single road running its length. An endless succession of cars reached traffic jam proportions at peak hour and when school finished, ploughing a slow and careful route up and back, to avoid potholes, pigs, speed humps and children.

I walked excitedly, wanting to explore the road, the shops and the few side alleys of the atoll. But this sense of adventure slowly turned sour. The total absence of shade and the churning dust kicked up by the passing traffic made exploration by foot hard work. And my curiosity came up against the limits of geography, isolation, poverty and the largely untold disaster of Pacific urbanisation. The street, and the shops along it, had little appeal, being dominated by a succession of retail outlets called 'EZ Price' with the questionable mottos 'Buy more save more' and 'You name it we got it'. The stores were covered with advertisements for newly arrived thermal underwear. Perhaps winters in Majuro were harsher than I imagined.

Like the cars, most of the shops had blacked-out windows to repel the sun, and this gave the town a shut-down feel. In an effort to encourage customers who might find the darkened windows off-putting, the shopkeepers had put up multiple orange fluoro signs that read 'Yes, we are open'. In the middle of the Pacific Ocean, thousands of kilometres from the continental United States, this seemed only to reinforce a sense of commercial desolation. In a chain called 'Payless' I picked up a product that contained a mysterious green-coloured ingredient and looked very much like cheap sunscreen. I inspected the label more closely, to see what it was. 'Warning', it read. 'Using this product will expose you to chemicals known in the State of California to cause cancer.' In Majuro, even terminal illness comes with a discount.

As I looked more closely, the predominant features of the Majuro landscape were cars, clothes and containers. Rusting carcasses of old cars were piled up on the side of the road to make way for new ones. Second-hand clothing stores displayed their dusty wares: singlets, shorts and old jeans. The New Hope Shop, a dark and airless concrete box, was selling an array of mildewy second-hand clothes. Despite the brief optimism of its name, a few minutes inside revealed that even the future would be faded and used. Shipping containers, either in the dock, abandoned or somehow incorporated into people's houses along the waterfront, pocked the landscape.

After some time walking up and down, I stopped in a small second-hand shop to escape sun, heat and dust of the road. It was owned by an Indian businessman from Jaipur and, while pretending to look at faded khaki shorts and old t-shirts, I chatted with him about that city's Rajput palaces and kite festivals. 'How do you find living in Majuro after growing up in in Jaipur?' I then asked, but the question was unfair and the comparison could only be a doleful one. He looked across the room where a picture of his long-dead parents was nailed to the wall behind a collection of discount deodorants. There was a pause before he said, with a combination of resignation and finality, 'I've been here twelve years' – a statement of fact that came across in an exhalation of hope and the gradual extinguishing of migrant ambition. I left the shop carrying an overpriced and undersized pair of camouflage sandals bought more out of sympathy than necessity.

The Majuro atoll was only a few hundred metres wide, yet the sea was invisible – as if the streets, shops and houses had turned in on themselves and away from the ocean. In other Pacific countries, the geographical confines of small islands were enlarged by the presence of the elements. Vast skies and great oceans disappeared into the horizon, leaving a sense of wonder and enormity. But here the road, the cars, the concrete and the dust were now the natural environment. An article in the *Marshall Islands Journal*, the local newspaper, confirmed my worst suspicions. This wasn't just a case of poor planning and urban poverty; it was also a conscious choice. The article was about renovations at a local school and the *Journal* had printed 'before' and 'after' shots. Gone were the beach and the palm trees and a meandering dirt track up to the school gates. These had been replaced by a large car park with neatly demarked parking spaces, a big road of gleaming tarmac and a new high concrete fence. 'Better and brighter' read the headline.

And so, I took the alleys that presented themselves in the gaps between the houses to make for the sea, looking to wash away the dirt and dilapidation with an early afternoon swim. I picked up several large stones to throw at the inevitable stray dogs and wound my camera strap around my wrist to use as a high-tech ball and chain if they got too close. Suitably forearmed, I walked down one last alley, drawn by the sounds of the waves. But at the end of the road, instead of a Pacific island beach with swaying palms and the lapping of a lagoon, I faced a rubbish tip. Lining the shore were piles of plastic bottles, packaging, old car tyres and tangled metal objects, too badly rusted and wrecked to imagine what they must once have been. A small pig next to me grunted amicably and for a moment we stood together looking over the piles of debris.

On the mudflat in front that led to the ocean, a succession of concrete pylons stood solemn and tomb-like, etched against the sky and the sea. They resembled a version of the Easter Island *moai* rendered in squat slabs of concrete, an impassive testament to the god of economic progress. Close by, a dog's carcass, floating on the incoming tide, thudded dully against a concrete sea wall. I walked back past the houses, over the main road and across the street, hoping that the ocean side a few hundred metres away would be better. But this was just the same, although with a greater prevalence of rusting car parts and ruined hulks of old fishing boats. Beyond this, moored in the distance, was the sleek outline of the Google yacht – a vast aquatic pleasure dome, bristling with antennae and helicopters for use of executives, that was secure in a faraway jurisdiction, out of sight and out of mind.

My camera strap got entangled in its casing, and I missed the shot. But the image remained with me, emblematic – to me, at least – of the paradox of Majuro. Through the rusting grille of an open house window, a small child was playing with a bright-red toy car as her mother squatted nearby doing the washing in a large blue plastic tub. The moment seemed mundane and fun, yet they were encaged by the seawalls and the detritus of urban life.

No wonder the houses faced the street, not the water, and that the focus of life was the one narrow road up and down the atoll, and not the sea. Once, the ocean had brought life and news and connection by boat to the outside world. Only sixty years ago, before readily accessible plane travel, the oceans were the highways of the world, as they had been for millennia. But now they were a dump. My meandering had brought me closer to a pack of large dogs a few houses away. They had just noticed my presence and were beginning to assemble. I hailed a passing cab and sank into the air-conditioned comfort of the back seat, relieved to have evaded the fangs of the gathering strays. In place of the government channel, which broadcast development statistics and updates on departmental initiatives, the driver was tuned to newly minted Radio 504 Zumba and the cabin resounded with the professional bonhomie of its hosts, who outdid each other with stories of how much they could eat.

'You murdered that plate last night, man' came the banter between songs. 'Respect, man – that's what I'm sayin'. Keep it real, man.'

And in the freezing cabin in a traffic jam, the pop lyrics poured out of Radio 504 Zumba until a government health warning of viral pink eye brought a momentary reprieve.

I wanted to speak with young people about their hopes for the future, and so I asked the taxi driver to drop me at the College of the Marshall Islands (CMI), a community college that prepared young Marshallese to complete undergraduate degrees at colleges in the United States. How did they, I wondered, 'keep it real'. This was a comparatively privileged group. They were college students with pathways to some form of professional employment in the US government or the Marshall Islands government. I had also made arrangements to meet with the local organisation Waan Aelōñ in Majel (WAM), which took unemployed youth and taught them the ancient arts of canoe building and navigation. There was a stark contrast. Tradition for the poor, who had become marginalised and displaced in the urban sprawl of Majuro, versus aspiration and emigration for the rich. Three CMI students were hanging around the students' union when I visited. Thurston, Schuyler, Walter and I sat down to a Hawaiian pizza with pepperoni and a large bucket of iced Coke. Wearing baseball caps and polo shirts, they were the model of CMI students: attentive, funny, quizzical and open. Thurston's t-shirt commemorated the USS *Missouri*, a floating memorial to the Japanese attack on Pearl Harbour and a modern-day American pilgrimage site.

The students had come back to the Marshalls to attend college after living in Hawaii. They wanted to reconnect with Marshalls culture, since this was where they were from. I asked if they all came from Majuro and in reply they listed all the islands from which their relatives and antecedents had come. While broadly homogenous, each island had its own culture, specificity, traditions and local inflections that deserved recognition and acknowledgement. The recitation reminded me of a form of ancestor worship, a listing of the generations where atolls took on a personality and stood for cultural inheritance and continuity. 'We still know some of the old stories and songs and the different islands our ancestors came from are important to us', Schuyler observed, suggesting, perhaps, that he was not totally convinced by his new tertiary-educated, urban identity.

There were other, more mundane, reasons for their enrolment. The college provided a shortcut to university in Hawaii and the

US mainland, as they termed it, and meant they could complete a degree in two years, not three. Continued education at the University of Hawaii, Eastern Oregon State and the Jesuit-run Chaminade University of Honolulu beckoned for the ambitious and the academically able.

Did they intend to come back? Certainly, they *intended* to, replied Thurston, and those who had received Marshall Islands government scholarships had to serve an indentured period of two years working for the administration or in local schools. 'But really only the rich return', he observed. They were the ones with education and connections and who could benefit from the opportunities and avenues to the further generation of wealth by having senior positions and careers in an independent state of 53,000 people. Ministerial appointments, influential and profitable jobs in trade and fisheries regulation (or the ignoring of regulations), ambassadorships, sinecures at the United Nations, and travel to more salubrious destinations – conferences in New York and Geneva – all beckoned. So, too, did the gravy train of development: resilience, climate change adaptation, governance reform and yet more overseas meetings and conferences could make for an interesting, high-profile and profitable career. It was not uncommon to see a mixture of Marshallese names among those of Peace Corps volunteers who had stayed on and monopolised business, politics, NGOs and cultural production.

And where does everyone else end up, I asked?

'Springdale, Arkansas', replied Walter immediately, in a manner that suggested he was staring down the barrel of this option. Springdale, he explained, was the location of a chicken processing plant. The owners had once relied on cheap labour provided by underpaid, undocumented immigrants. However, tiring of legal problems associated with this, they hit upon a solution: employ Marshallese. For the operators of the chicken plant, Marshallese were the ideal workers. They were poor, had few options, and crucially they had the right to live, work and study in the United States. They would work twelve-hour shifts six days a week, degutting chickens for virtually no money, and this was legal. Years later, nearly twenty per cent of the citizens of Marshall Islands had voted on the future with their feet. Not for them were the urban intensity of Majuro and Ebeye – the country's two main urban centres. Degutting chickens in Springdale, Arkansas, was, for many, the path to the future.

As I left the College of the Marshall Islands, I picked up a copy of a student literary magazine, *Ettonaak*. In it, a contributor called Tuna Turner had written a poem entitled 'Now'. It described the aspirations and perspectives of a contemporary generation whose members, unlike their parents and grandparents, had grown up in an urbanised present and did not pine for an idealised life in the outer islands.

I sit and listen
F-bombs dropped and n-words thrown
We are a group ...

Drake, Rihanna, J. Cole, Lil Wayne –
They speak to us
We know their struggles
We too were grown in the ghetto
The streets of Jenrok
The slums of Delap ...[1]

We are modern, we are hip, we are now

Was this a more enquiring generation – worldly, troubled, rebellious and questioning – than an earlier generation of Marshallese

---

1 Densely populated areas of urban Majuro.

who had trustingly left their atoll homes to the American promise to 'end war and create conditions of peace for all mankind' that presaged the arrival of the hydrogen bomb? But it turned out that Tuna Turner was Fijian, not Marshallese, and had grown up in a different, independent and more questioning cultural environment.

My thoughts returned to some of the young Marshallese I had met: Thurston with his neat 'USS Missouri, Pearl Harbour' polo shirt, Walter dreaming about degutting chickens in Arkansas, and an eight-year-old girl who told me her president was Donald Trump. To them, Hawaii was the 'big island', while the continental United States was (as it was for Palauans) simply 'the mainland'. What did this imply about how Marshall Islanders viewed themselves colloquially, I wondered? Were the Marshalls, therefore, the 'little island' to Hawaii, an atoll dependency of the mainland, a small orbital rock caught in an American gravitational pull?

In search of a more questioning outlook, I met with Kelly Lorennij, a Jane Austen–reading reporter at the *Marshall Islands Journal*. I was curious to know whether this bookishness was an affectation or whether Austen really did translate from eighteenth-century England to twenty-first–century Majuro. Unfairly, I suspected that Kelly had watched a version of *Pride and Prejudice* on television and was in thrall to a teenage crush on Mr Darcy.

'Austen is much misunderstood', Kelly explained within minutes of meeting me and between strums of a ukulele, 'everyone thinks of *Pride and Prejudice*, but I'm interested in her unfinished novels. They are about small, insular societies, full of hierarchy and social convention, and so are very familiar to the modern Pacific. And they're funny. The novels translate over time and between customs well, but for many Marshallese youth, especially in urban areas, there is a real problem about which culture they are part of and some are not part of any – they can't speak either English or Marshallese fluently.'

This was a sentiment echoed by one of the most prominent advocates for the Marshall Islands; the poet and climate change activist Kathy Jetñil-Kijiner. She had shot to fame at the United Nations General Assembly by reciting a poem 'Dear Matafele Peinam' to her daughter and had defiantly called for 'canoes blocking coal ships' to prevent the worst ravages of climate change on small island states for future generations:

I want to tell you about that lagoon
that lucid, sleepy lagoon
lounging against the sunrise

Men say that one day
that lagoon will devour you

they say it will gnaw at the shoreline
chew at the roots of your breadfruit trees
gulp down rows of your seawalls
and crunch your island's shattered bones

At this point in the United Nations meeting, she carried the well-mannered infant Matafele Peinam herself onto the podium. If only for a few minutes, her arrival instantly changed the tone and outlook of the otherwise unsentimental governmental representatives who had gathered for a United Nations conference in New York. Grey-suited diplomats used to operating in the adults-only world of international diplomacy suddenly went weak at the knees at the sight of the innocent Marshallese infant – a content and healthy child whose only problem was that her future was in their hands.

It was a striking performance but also one that echoed in some ways the less storied lives of youth in Majuro. As Kelly Lorennij had pointed out to me earlier, in harking back to tradition Jetñil-Kijiner was also alive to traditions lost. Language was one of these endangered traditions. In 'On the couch with Būbū Neien', Jetñil-Kijiner laments that, having grown up in Hawaii and attended American schools, she has been deracinated and can't communicate effectively with her grandmother:

I can't speak fluent Marshallese.
English syllables accent
the walls of my voice, pronounce me
Ashamed
so I bury my native tongue
beneath a borrowed one.

It was an irony, then, that, as the most powerful voice in the international language of English for the survival of the local and the indigenous, she struggles in her own language.

Back in Majuro – away from the high-powered world of the United Nations in New York, high youth unemployment, lack of self-esteem, and a newly hybrid urban culture somewhere between Marshallese tradition and an American cultural domination – young people were taking things into their own hands. They were either migrating, dropping out and staying at home, living unobtrusively with their extended families or, increasingly, committing suicide.

Another option for the young and not particularly well connected was to join the US military. I met with Edmund Etao, a journalist from the island of Ebeye within the Kwajalein lagoon that serviced the American military base on Kwajalein Atoll itself. Growing up in what was frequently termed the 'slum of the Pacific', Edmund had shown promise at school and had won a scholarship to attend an academically successful but otherwise hierarchical and disciplinarian Catholic boarding school in Chuuk – a state in the Republic of

Micronesia that neighboured the Marshall Islands. As his final term at the school approached, recruiters from the American military had appeared and had met with some of the smart and athletic students at the school.

'It was like holding up a long menu', Edmund told me, using the actual menu of the restaurant where we met as an example. 'They went through all the long list of possible jobs you could do in the military – from being a cook to doing the accounts to managing logistics – and many of these sounded boring. Then, having gone through all of these, they turned the page and suggested I might be more in interested 12 Bravo and that many people from my school had also chosen 12 Bravo and enjoyed it.' Edmund slowly ran his index finger down the long list of items on the menu, eventually hovering over a picture of a banana fritter with multiple scoops of brightly coloured ice-cream. It looked big and bold and highly appetising. 'This is how they presented 12 Bravo', he said. 'It looked so good, I signed on immediately.'

In 'choosing' 12 Bravo, Edmund had chosen a frontline combat unit. He completed two years of training in Texas, then was dispatched to Iraq with a bomb disposal squad and straight into the carnage of frontline combat. His training turned out to be outmoded and years behind the lethal developments in the local explosive devices and traps that he had been sent to defuse. His unit had initially been light and mobile, something Edmund preferred in the densely populated and built-up areas of downtown Baghdad. However, they had been transferred to a larger, armoured tank which lumbered slowly through the city, providing an open invitation to attackers and suicide bombers. Once, a man had driven a car bomb at speed into the tank, blowing up a crowded market place in the process. The appalling consequences were witnessed by the young Marshallese soldiers inside the tank. 'Only five of my unit died', said Edmund in a matter-of-fact tone. 'Everyone had PTSD but I think I was lucky.

I grew up in a big Marshallese family and this is something that the other soldiers didn't always have. If they didn't have that level of support growing up, then the PTSD was really bad.'

This reminded me of an interview with an American army psychologist who had acknowledged that humans on the whole don't especially like killing each other and that only special conditions enable it. In addition to urging the troops to 'embrace the word *death*', he had argued that the army couldn't on its own create the psychological conditions necessary to want to kill in battle. Instead, it needed to recruit soldiers from the poor and desperate, from broken homes and troubled pasts. 'In these cases, the work of making a combat soldier who is able and willing to kill is already half-done for us', he opined.

Edmund had survived but that had come at a cost. Among his PTSD symptoms were alcoholism, lingering fear of confined spaces and built-up cities, stationary traffic that meant you could be easily targeted, and deep levels of boredom after the constant adrenaline of the frontline. Among the worst things Edmund had to do in Iraq were home invasions to apprehend suspected militants or bomb makers. This was done in the dead of night and was often based on inaccurate intelligence. It was deeply shocking to the families as highly armed and adrenalised marines broke down their doors at 3 am. 'In the Marshalls, we're family people', Edmund told me. 'We take care of each other and it's the same in Iraq. When we broke down the doors, I recognised them – these big families, all the children running around, the relationships. To me it was wrong. But some of the other soldiers seemed to get off on it.'

During a leave from the army, Edmund had returned to his home island of Ebeye in the Kwajalein lagoon. This involved a transit through the Kwajalein military base itself before taking the twenty-minute ferry ride to Ebeye. Usually authorisation is needed to visit Kwajalein as a secure military establishment, but Edmund was entitled to enter because he was a serving member of the armed forces. Once inside, he discovered the quasi-apartheid of a military base in the remote Pacific.

Most of them were contractors. I can tell, even out of uniform, who is a soldier and who isn't – it's clear from their posture, their level of physical fitness, their hair and their clothes and I counted seven soldiers. I went to the bar and ordered a drink but was told I wasn't allowed to be there and needed to go to the Marshallese section. I showed them my ID and when they realised that I was serving in a combat zone they suddenly became very respectful and apologised, but it was part of a deeper culture, especially for military contractors.

Most of them were not members of the military and they were mainly white. Everything is provided for them because they are in – or with – the military. It's all subsidised. The schools are good and get extra resources from the US and have US teachers. There is a swimming pool, a movie theatre, ATMs, a golf course, a Burger King and even a bowling alley. You pay to use the alley but they give you the shoes for free. Later I met with the commanding officer who said I was welcome, but when he found out that I was from the neighbouring island of Ebeye he said, 'Please don't bring any of your Marshallese friends over.' There is all of this opulence – people get around in golf buggies – and yet a few minutes away 11,000 people live on top of one another on an island that is about a third of a kilometre.

I showed him a sign I had seen from the base on Kwajalein – the English version had read 'authorised personal only' but the Marshallese translation, it was explained to me, had been more expansive. 'No Marshallese allowed on these premises. Anybody caught will face imprisonment.'

Edmund nodded. 'That's right', he said laconically.

By this stage we were joined by Edmund's friend Francis. A product of the same high school as Edmund, he had joined not the army but the police. 'It's Kwajalein independence day. Let's celebrate liberation from the Japanese', he said cheerily before ordering a round of shots. We clinked glasses, toasted independence, and drank quickly. Seconds later, we exploded into a fits of rasping coughs from the appalling diesel fuel that we had just consumed. My stomach lurched and my throat burned.

'What the hell was that?' Edmund demanded, recovering slightly.

'A Bravo Shot', replied the policeman, pale but triumphant, 'named after the biggest of the Bikini Atoll nuclear tests.'

'That will fuck you up', grunted the barman.

After a brief pause and some heavy breathing, the grotesque concoction kickstarted further reminiscences from Edmund and the policeman about their schooldays discipline, the virtues of hard work, and the educational tradition of the Jesuits. 'They break you down but they build you up', said Francis before ordering another round. 'Made me what I am today.'

Eventually, the men exhausted their tales of high-school masochism and it was time to leave. But somewhere along the way, the drinks had dislodged fragments of Latin that their Jesuit teachers had instilled in them by way of education.

'*Ut omnes unum sint*', slurred Edmund in parting.

Francis staggered off with a wave and a vomitous '*ad maiorem Dei gloriam*' as he looked for a cab on Majuro's one and only road.

*

'Welcome and thank you for coming to MY FIRST BIRTHDAY MOUSTACHE PARTY' read the sign with a picture of a chirpy looking toddler called Jeremiah Lajutok Hemmy Nathan who was pictured wearing a three-piece suit and a fake moustache. I had spent a half hour crammed in the back of a pick-up truck with a number of disgruntled relatives of the young Jeremiah Lajutok Hemmy Nathan en route to his party. They were half-asleep children and some concerned mothers as the truck sped and swerved down the one road, buffeted by a growing wind, towards the edge of the island. Next to me, squashed up against an electric keyboard, was a rotund young man sporting a Chicago Bulls cap. After a while staring in different directions, I tried a gentle conversation starter.

'Do you play the keyboard?' I asked.

'No', came the response after a protracted silence.

'Are you in a band?' I persisted, still under the impression that possession of a keyboard suggested a musical interest.

'No', again came the response after some time.

I looked up at his cap, which miraculously stayed on his head despite the rush of air over the speeding vehicle. For a moment I considered asking if he was a Bulls supporter but I desisted, sensing the inevitable response.

We finally arrived at the first birthday moustache party and found ourselves in a queue to get in to a packed hall. Chicago Bulls and I stood glumly together as children careened around and music blasted from inside. Everyone else seemed to be having fun but we had got stuck, waiting – and, what was worse, with each other.

I again plucked up courage for another question. 'Are you also studying at the College?' I asked.

He brightened and ventured 'LA'. I knew just enough to interpret this not as Los Angeles but as Liberal Arts.

He looked pained and, after struggling through another period of awkward silence as I stared at my feet, he uttered 'English'.

I was rescued from this social limbo by an eight year old. Thurston, my host, was busy organising the food, music and dancing and swung by with his young niece. 'Keep an eye on him, Lula' was all he said, gesturing towards me, and she looked distinctly unimpressed. A few minutes later he re-emerged with an even smaller child and plonked it in Lula's arms, at which she looked even more put out.

I asked what the matter was and if she was enjoying herself. 'It's okay' came the reply 'but much bigger than my first birthday'. She was annoyed at having been outdone and, to make matters worse, she had also been given the task of babysitting me.

It was a formal yet joyous occasion. Lines and lines of tables, ordered by social status, faced dancers who performed a hybrid of stylised Polynesian movements combined with Western 'twisting', as it was called. As was done on Tuvalu, especially energetic dancers would charge around with bottles of cologne, spraying guests and dancers; here, they would also hurl pre-packaged gifts into the audience or at anyone who looked like they were not enjoying themselves or nodding off. The band, including Chicago Bulls clutching his keyboard, sat above the dancers on an empty stage. They didn't play any instruments and only occasionally sang. Most of the time they sat staring back at the audience and making minute adjustments to the stereo equipment. Lula and I observed it all from the back of the hall.

Somehow, the constant beat, the convulsions of the dancers, the cool evening breeze and warmth of the guests turned what I feared on arrival might be a protracted evening into one of increasing entertainment. I sat and watched, but this was all everyone else was doing. The lack of milling and conversation actually seemed an advantage. There were no forced conversations, no awkward gambits about jobs or schools, or the weather. There were no anxious moments when either there was no one to talk with or a risk of being cornered by the mad uncle or the resident bore. Perhaps this was a product of an island society in which everyone is known. There was no great need for small talk or introductions, but the feeling was one of great warmth and welcome, of fun and celebration, inwardly expressed. Suddenly, unprompted, Lula and I burst out laughing.

Food arrived and, having scanned the plate, I started eating a delicious pile of fresh tuna marinated in coconut milk. Lula stopped me in my tracks with a disgusted look. 'Eating tuna! You're strange', she observed, 'I like eating thumbs', and she started gnawing at her hands. After a few unsuccessful seconds of this, the allure of the prehensile digit wore off and she turned to a succulent bit of lobster. But this was also unsatisfactory and Lula, on discovering that one of the orange-coloured feelers was, in fact, an eye, started enthusiastically gnawing again. 'Eyes are nice', she said between slurps.

In Marshallese society, the first birthday party or *kemem* was clearly important – more so, in fact, than marriage. In part, this was due to the cultural conventions of a society with a high infant mortality rate. If the child made it to one year old, then it was more likely to survive. The occasion was also the marker, in the Marshall Islands, of an accession to full personhood and was often the point at which the child would be named. It was better therefore to delay celebrations and emotional investment as much as possible until it was certain that the child would live. But there was another more interesting possibility. Micronesian islands tended to be matrilineal: the predominant relationship that would ultimately pass on land and political authority was between mother and child, especially the daughter. Micronesian culture had changed, especially with the arrival of cash, Christianity and increasingly rapid urbanisation in which detached, nuclear families were beginning to assert themselves, and which in both religion and legislation favoured men.

In the contemporary hybrid, men occupied the public and political space and dominated in decision-making forums like parliaments and traditional councils. However, the pre-Christian and pre-contact matrilineal tradition of inheritance and cultural connection still survived. In the Marshall Islands, the atoll where your mother was born remained home, just as claims to land and title came through the mother's family. This was reinforced by the fading but still current tradition of burying the umbilical cord of a new born baby in the mother's home atoll as a not particularly metaphorical connection to the child's maternal homeland. In this way, the celebration of the survival of a child until one year of age was central – the infant for whom the moustache party was held would be an heir to the mother's culture, land titles, and tradition.

Having arrived back at the hotel well after midnight, I walked down to the edge of the lagoon and looked out in the darkness, swathed in the cool, salty breeze, as I contemplated the distant hulks of fishing boats sheltering from the ocean.

*

In the hotel the next day, the curtains had been drawn against another brilliant day in Majuro. A group of Americans and Marshallese gathered expectantly for the Superbowl involving the New England Patriots verses the Philadelphia Eagles. The Eagles, as the commentators put it, were the underdogs. There were two televisions turned up to maximum volume and there was an air of tense excitement in the bar whose crowd of yachties, regulars, hangers-on and the generally homesick gathered to worship the ritual of American football.

While I was watching the Superbowl, Hugh Laurie's impersonation of Bruce Springsteen came to mind. Laurie, wearing a bandana and plaid lumber jack shirt, sings an interminable song whose only words are 'America, America, America, America' until Stephen Fry arrives on stage and hits him over the head with a brick. But this was real. Each of the players appeared on screen, announcing their names and the university sports program that had given them a scholarship in Steroid Studies. 'Rick Hauer, Virginia Tech', 'John Jones, Alabama' 'Leroy Smith, RU' they grunted as they appeared on air before the growing excitement of the crowd. A first singer poured out his heart with the moving words 'America, America, from sea to shining sea. America, America, from sea to shining sea'. This was swiftly followed by a singer calling herself Pink, with a rendition of 'America the Brave' followed by the US national anthem. One was beginning to get the point and, looking around, I discovered there was a distinct absence of bricks.

But it did not end here. The flags of the five main divisions of the armed forces were unfurled as a group of veterans gathered in the middle of the field and one was selected to toss the coin. These were no ordinary veterans of the sort I'd seen in Pearl Habour sporting baseball caps with an image of a medal and the word *veteran* written clearly on the front to invite the obligatory 'thank you for your service' from a Filipino ticket attendant. These veterans were recipients of the Medal of Honour, bestowed for displaying the highest degree of valour in action against 'the enemy' (which enemy was left undefined). Herschel 'Loony' Wilson (now known by his Superbowl title as 'Flipper Wilson'), a hero of Iwo Jima, tossed the coin. The crowd and the lines of pompom girls went wild with Midwestern glamour as the teams in their crash helmets and tight trousers ran out and started punching the air to psych themselves up. 'Beautiful baby' murmured some of the salty viewers who were now packing the bar and gulping down quantities of iced tea and Bud Light Platinum.

Nearby, two Australian patrol boat operators were having an ethical discussion under the din of the Superbowl. 'There are a lot of differences between us', said one, talking about his local girlfriend. 'She's really poor and everything but in the end she gets what she wants and I get what I want.'

'Yeah' grunted his drinking partner before turning to the woman behind the bar and ordering two more beers. Encouraged by his mate, he adds a slurry 'You're not single are you?' to his request for more Budweiser.

I decided to leave. Outside, as I walked along the main street, children played a fun game. A group of nine year olds stood on the side of the road and the objective of the game was to persuade a smaller, confused and highly excited child of perhaps five years to dash across in front of the passing traffic. On Majuro, there was clearly not enough to do.

8

EBEYE: A TALE OF TWO ATOLLS

On the bus to the airport, I sat next to an older man smoking a cigarette. He appeared friendly and we started to talk, reminiscing about mutual acquaintances in Pohnpei, the capital island of the Republic of Micronesia, which I had visited a few years before. I asked what brought him to Majuro.

'Explosives', he answered laconically. 'Usually we blow up the reef and grind the coral for aggregate.' As we parted, he held out his hand and said, 'Come visit me in Pohnpei, you'll find me at my nightclub', before taking an extra long, deep drag on his cigarette.

The flight arrived at Kwajalein and passengers were taken by ferry to Ebeye. While Kwajalein itself was an American military base with restricted access, I was escorted in a golf buggy from the airport to the ferry terminal. It reminded me of a trip I'd made to visit the Miraflores Lock in the Panama Canal, also once a highly restricted military zone where the Americans had lived lives of subsidised bliss. This was a land where employment was not only full but well paid and where welfare, housing and entertainment were provided. All but a few Panamanians were excluded; the few were those needed to service the Americans. It was the same in Kwajalein, in a contemporary incarnation. Here, it was not as vicious perhaps, and was softened by money, but the world of Jim Crowe still existed – a Pacific apartheid out of sight and out of mind.

As I waited in Kwajalein for the ferry to Ebeye, I saw a group of soldiers disembarking in the opposite direction towards a sign that read 'Kwajalein US Army Garrison – a community of excellence'.

'Where are you from?' asked one, addressing a fellow soldier.

'Panama', said the other. 'I grew up in the Canal Zone – do you know it?' The Panamian presented his ID card to the guard.

'Appreciate your service', said the guard mechanically.

At the ferry terminal, some Mormons, a few United Nations employees and some ordinary passengers returning from Majuro sat for two hours in something called the 'American Diner', a cafe draped in American flags and offering American food. A menu whose other side was decorated with an image of a fluttering stars-and-stripes flag, listed appetising culinary options: American ⅓ lb Cheeseburger; Big Chicago ⅔ lb Cheeseburger; All American ¼ lb Dog; Chilli & Cheese Dog.

With three hours before the ferry was due, I looked around at the diner, the Mormons and the depressed-looking locals who had also been herded into this human holding pen. My companion at the diner was a goateed American from Nebraska who was working at a United Nations agency with close funding links to the US government.

'There will be no jobs in the future and soon robots will learn to think and take over all essential human functions. Eventually we will consider the humans – the flesh-and-blood species – as some kind of curious anachronism to the technologically improved version', he said, leaning back against a Coke dispenser.

Next to us, the Mormons talked about God and their Mission to Ebeye. A waitress tapped me on the shoulder and asked if I had ordered a Chilli & Cheese Dog.

It all suddenly seemed a terribly long way from home.

*

'Let's play chess', said Jeban Riklon, a retired senator in the Marshall Islands parliament. 'There's a tournament for Kwajalein Day.' Under a gazebo in the local chief's house, on the island of Ebeye in the Kwajalein lagoon, a group gathered around a chess board. There was silence and deep concentration from players and the onlookers who murmured with approval as far-sighted moves are made. The games were attacking and were played at speed as pieces were dispatched with vigorous and definitive clunks on the board. I lost my first six games quickly. There was no time to think. Each successive move only met with a lethal response, putting what I had thought were well considered positions into jeopardy. The older players dominated the earlier rounds, but the evening became more exciting as the young guns turned up and a knockout prize of three hundred dollars was announced. The chief, an old man in a wheelchair who had had a stroke and lost the use of one arm, deployed his good arm lethally on the chess board. But even he was eventually defeated in the later stages of the tournament, and the competition heated up with little deference for age or position. I lingered on, long past midnight and long after I had been knocked out of the competition, enjoying the night and the competitive absorption of the games. It was little wonder the Marshallese were so good at chess. Once the world's finest navigators who sailed the Pacific Ocean in small outrigger canoes, they had mastered the patterns of the waves and the sea. To them the chess board was child's play.

I had been told many things about Ebeye but one phrase turned up constantly: the slum of the Pacific. Eleven thousand people living on a third of a square kilometre of coral atoll in the Kwajalein lagoon. It is also next to the US military base on the Kwajalein atoll itself, resembling the slum settlements that adjoin places of immense resources and investment worldwide. The base was also known as the Ronald Reagan Ballistic Missile Defense Test Site and was the technological centre point of Reagan's Star Wars program. Here, a lethal game of catch was played between Kwajalein and the Vandenberg military base in California as each launched missiles at the other and tried to intercept them with the debris falling into the lagoon.

'Remote Pacific location is ideal for permissive safety and environmental constraints' said an early report on the attractions of Kwajalein, the largest lagoon in the world, for the purposes of missile testing. While the base crawled with scientists, engineers, analysts, contractors, technocrats and a few soldiers, Ebeye was where the cleaners, constructions workers, nannies, and low-skilled, casual labour came from and where they lived, a twenty-minute ferry ride away. On Kwajalein Atoll, there were neat roads organised in a grid and large, evenly spaced white bungalows for families living on the base. The bachelors' quarters were pleasant apartments with ocean views and everyone cycled or got about by golf buggy. The roads were perfectly maintained and clearly signposted and the atoll had its own yacht club and golf course. The school on Kwajalein received extra funding from the US government and was one of the best in the US; much to the amazement of a teacher from Ebeye who visited, the school had interactive whiteboards and ran a dizzying array of after-school programs, from sailing to theatre studies. Next to this highly subsidised opulence, Ebeye looked very poor indeed. From a brief glimpse of Kwajalein, I could see why the label 'slum of the Pacific' had stuck.

Although I had been warned of the horrors of the Ebeye 'slum', I was pleasantly surprised. There was one ring-road around the island and a winding maze of smaller pathways in the centre that wove between built-up houses. There were neat streets, well-kept houses, and a couple of commercial stores near the ferry terminal. Friendly people were everywhere and, as it was cooler in the evenings, they stayed out late playing sport and socialising. After a few days, I'd never felt so safe or at ease in a community I did not know and whose language

I did not speak. The term *slum* that everyone had used seemed to be overdoing it somewhat. I had never seen so many children in one place before – thousands of charging, running, cavorting, playing children filled the streets and the footpaths. They played everything from clapping games to American football, baseball, volleyball and a game that involved hurling flat volleyballs at each other as hard as possible. Some of the smaller children gathered under a water tank, absorbed for hours in complicated games of marbles. Those less interested in fierce sporting contests quietly sang and strummed their ukuleles. For boys, the major sport was basketball and the streets were filled with homemade rings cobbled together with pieces of wood and bent plastic for the basket. The streets were a constant hum of movement and energy as the games progressed and groups got together and dispersed. This continued – with a brief lull during school hours – for most of the day until eleven in the evening when the local police took it upon themselves to give Ebeye's parents a hand and drove around the ring-road, sirens blaring, in order to enforce a children's curfew.

But below the cheerful exterior, resentment was beginning to simmer. While professing how much they liked the island and how it was their home, many of the people I spoke with broke into soft, unobtrusive tears as I questioned them about Ebeye and their hopes and fears for the future. 'There are no mountains and no McDonald's but here is my heart', said one person, who asked not to be identified because it is such a small place. And yet, after years away studying for higher degrees in international relations and economics, he had deep concerns for the island's future. The local public school was one of the worst in the country and was under-resourced and unable to cope with so many children. There were about two thousand children in school, but an equal number who do not go to school at all. Religious schools, like the Seventh Day Adventists and the Mormons, had sprung up, opportunistically, and offered marginally better options in a bid for souls. But even these options were expensive and catered only to ten per cent of the population.

Diabetes was at almost epidemic levels, and domestic violence and teenage pregnancies were on the rise – 'children giving birth to children' as a local teacher described the latter. This also effectively ended the young mothers' educational chances as most were kicked out of school when it became obvious they were pregnant. 'They can come back later', said another local teacher justifying this exclusion, although when I asked her if any actually did return she offered a perfunctory 'no'.

Unemployment was high and while relatively well-paid menial jobs could be obtained on the base, these were mainly in construction and were unreliable as long-term, regular work prospects.

'People are getting fed up', said one person I met, who also requested anonymity. 'We are hungrier, poorer and life is harder. The Iokwe spirit (the Marshallese cultural tradition of welcome and solidarity) won't be enough and we'll kill each other one day, I think', he told me.

A major cause of growing frustration, especially from the educated and ambitious young people of Ebeye, lay with the traditional landowners. While the government represented the state and the people, it did not own any land. The rent for the Ronald Reagan Ballistic Missile Test Site on Kwajalein Atoll – around nineteen million US dollars a year – went to the traditional leaders and incrementally came down to the community. The leaders were tempted to take larger and larger portions of the pie. Few of these leaders chose to remain on Ebeye and were reported to reside instead in ever-greater splendour in the United States, despite the growing poverty of the local population and the signal inadequacy of the civil institutions that were supposed to provide for them: the school and the hospital. Even the food provision was deeply questionable.

Lacking obvious eating options other than a dirty fried chicken joint known as 'Triple J' (perhaps a play on jaundice, giardia and gastroenteritis, I thought to myself), I followed the example of another traveller and stocked up on food from the local supermarket next to the ferry terminal to get through the week. But the offerings were grim. After a depressing half hour walking with diminishing enthusiasm along the aisles, I could find nothing that I particularly wanted to eat. There were expensive imported fruits, most of which were battered and bruised from transportation and left to rot on the shelves. Even more expensive were the serried rows of potato chips. There were whole aisles of instant noodles and eventually I found a freezer that contained some only recently expired processed cheese. Nothing seemed to have any nutritional value at all beyond an immediate hit of salt or sugar or both. I was starving, so after deliberating over my purchases, I headed back to the hotel and consumed a makeshift dinner made less unpalatable by a couple of San Miguel Pilsens from the Philippines.

That night I suffered a migraine, couldn't sleep and developed a fever. Standing helped slightly but this proved to be an impossible position in which to sleep and anything involving light was agony. Eventually, I crawled off the bed and unplugged an alarm clock whose lime green digital display had been causing untold agony in my brain for hours. By four in the morning I felt nauseous and spent the remaining hours before dawn throwing up before I finally drifted off to sleep.

By nine, I was awake again and feeling remarkably sprightly. The sun beamed down and I headed off enthusiastically to Triple J's for a mug of brown-coloured water that passed for coffee and a stale egg sandwich. It was bright, the breeze from the lagoon was cool and suddenly I felt fantastic.

*

'You know, they've found plutonium in the lagoon', said Abacca Anjain-Maddison, a former Marshall Islands senator from the atoll of Rongelap. Her family had been evacuated because of radioactive fallout from the 1954 'Bravo Shot' blown across vast distances by strong winds from Bikini Atoll where the test took place. At over a thousand times the strength of the Hiroshima bomb, 'Bravo Shot' was the largest hydrogen bomb ever detonated by the United States. Abacca now lived on Ebeye, home to many of the nuclear evacuees from different islands and their descendants. 'Of course, they won't tell us any more about it or help us understand how dangerous it is', she said. 'We found the information in declassified US documents. As far as the US is concerned, Rongelap Atoll and the Kwajalein lagoon are safe.' She doubted this and, despite significant US pressure to return to their home, Rongelapese displaced to Ebeye and other parts of the Marshall Islands were refusing to go. 'We believe it's unsafe', Abacca told me. 'If you can't eat the coconuts or the fish how safe can it be for human habitation?' She had recently returned from Sweden where the network she represented, the International Coalition Against Nuclear Weapons (ICAN) had just been awarded the Nobel Peace Prize. 'The US always thinks it can tell us what to do, we are always getting American advisors and experts. But we have to teach Americans their history. The tests didn't just happen here – they are not the Bikini tests or the Enewetak tests – they are American tests and are part of US nuclear and Cold War history. We have to show them that we are human too', she told me.

There was a lack of information about the consequences of nuclear pollution and about what the bits of destroyed rockets from the Star Wars program and its successors meant for the environmental health of the lagoon. 'We can't even afford this anymore', lamented the director of Ebeye's Environmental Protection Authority, gesturing at the grimy hotel room where his office was located. He showed me a presentation he gave regularly at schools.

It was about lead poisoning in fish and the diagrams suggested that this was caused by the rubbish waste site at the end of the atoll. 'Don't eat the fish', he told me sternly, while drawing my attention to a diagram of some green and unhappy-looking fish next to some equally green and unhappy-looking humans. In a bizarre transfer of environmental responsibility, some of the diagrams suggested that the lead poisoning was caused by a waste site at one end of the atoll and therefore by Ebeye's poor garbage management. They didn't mention the potentially lethal plutonium, strontium and caesium, the missile casings and other military-grade waste known to be in the lagoon, its glistening waters becoming less idyllic by the minute.

I asked about sewage. This is often a major problem in other low-lying atoll states where untreated waste flows into the shallows.

'Either people use the beach or, if they use a toilet, the sewerage is flushed untreated into the lagoon. Either way, don't eat the fish' he said.

Retired senator Jeban Riklon was born on Rongelap after his mother had returned there having divorced her husband on Ebeye in 1952. It turned out to be a disastrous move. Jeban was a nuclear survivor and as a young boy he had been covered in radioactive ash. 'We had heard of snow', he recalled, 'and this is what we thought the white ash was, so I went out and played in it, along with all my friends.' He became nauseous, his hair fell out, and there were lesions all over his young body. 'Every time there is a missile test now', he told me, 'children get sick.'

I heard this frequently from worried parents who live with the fear of testing, the effects of cancers and the memory of the 'jellyfish babies' born with no bones to mothers who had been contaminated with nuclear radiation while pregnant. 'The children often get flu-like symptoms – headaches, nausea, fever – when the testing occurs. We know when this is because the US closes the base at Kwajalein and doesn't let anyone in. They won't give us any information about what is going on and refuse to share medical information about the possible consequences of living in a rocket range. Whenever there is a test, chickens die by themselves. People want to know "Why do chickens keep dying?"'

'It reminds me of the US in the 1950s', said Alson Kelen, master navigator, who grew up on Kwajalein where his family were exiled prior to the 'Bravo Shot' nuclear test on Bikini Atoll. He is a former mayor of the Bikini Atoll community now living on the islands of Kili and Ejit, permanently displaced from their expansive island chain and confined to two small atolls thousands of kilometres away. Coming from a long line of canoe builders, Alson's father was a military carpenter and he grew up on Kwajalein. 'There's a lot of discrimination – you're not allowed to be treated at the hospital there', he recalled. Islanders now require authorisation to go to Kwajalein. 'I understand that military sites might be off limits', said Alson, 'but we can't even go to the supermarket or the laundry without permission.' Even then, there were strict limits on the amount that could be purchased from the market and it could not be taken off the island Kwajalein itself.

I tried to get a sense of what this discrimination actually looked like in its daily experience. Almost all the Marshallese on Ebeye I spoke with raised this as a major concern. 'They say we're monkeys, that we're stupid and lazy, and they say this to our faces', said one Marshall Islands government employee, who asked not to be named.

Marcella Sakaio, principal of the College of the Marshall Islands extension campus on Ebeye, told me about the importance of school communities, how really effective educational institutions involve the students, teachers and parents. Her son attended the well-provisioned school on Kwajalein, but Marcella herself was excluded from the island. 'I was not allowed on the base after business hours and so I could never attend sports or theatre or any extracurricular activities. Once, my son won a scholarship to go to a science lab in Arizona. When the other parents realised that a Marshallese and not an American had won, they complained, and in the end two scholarships were awarded. It was the only year that this happened.' Her son eventually joined the army himself and progressed rapidly in the military through hard work and volunteering for multiple deployments. 'His senior officers are always surprised about the number of missions he has completed', she told me. Though she was deeply worried for his safety, she told me he had earned enough to pay for his siblings' education.

He once arranged for Marcella to visit him in the United States, and they stayed on an army base in Texas. 'It was totally different to Kwajalein', she said. 'Kwajalein made me paranoid. There were places we could and couldn't go; you have to have permission and they check you all the time. At the base in America I was scared to go anywhere, but my son laughed and said it was totally different here. "It's not Kwaj", he told me.'

As I was leaving the college campus I caught sight of a copy of Paulo Freire's book *Pedagogy of the Oppressed* in a classroom. In it, Freire, a Christian socialist who pioneered literacy programs for Brazil's poor, argued that the true value of education is in the development of a critical consciousness through which the poor, the oppressed and the colonised come to question – and ultimately to change – the economic and political processes that underpin their subjugation. Had I witnessed a kernel of politicisation – 'conscientization', as Freire called it – in Ebeye? Later, I emailed Marcella to ask.

'I don't know', she replied immediately. Then, referring to the Freire's book, she added, 'I think someone must have left it here, I haven't read it either.'

Leaving Ebeye on the ferry to Kwajalein and a flight back to Majuro, Vernon, an older American man, craggy and tousled, and wearing a Marshall Islands t-shirt, sat opposite me. Conversation started pleasantly: What brings you here? How do you like it? He was married to a woman from Ebeye, and, after two years as a contractor on the base, was going to work in Dallas–Fort Worth, Texas, where she was to join him. 'I sing four-part harmony', he said, 'so for the next three to five years I'm going to work and sing.'

But then, out of the blue, he started talking about Donald Trump. 'You won't read about it, but he's doing great', said Vernon. 'What he's saying is America will look after our own interests, and you other countries can look after your interests. Australians, Marshallese can all speak for themselves; we're not going to do it. Just look at the UN and NATO: we give them a shock by not supporting them any longer, and everyone else starts paying up for once. The only country, other than the US, to meet its obligations is Sweden.'

I asked what he thought about the reports of Russian influence in the elections that had brought Tump to power.

'It's all the Democrats', he shot back. He said Trump was doing a great job rolling back the influence of former president Barack Obama, but that Obama was the one using the Federal Bureau of Investigation to spy on Trump. 'You should check out the website "People Killed by the Clintons" if you want to see how corrupt they really are. Trump's done nothing like that and is trying to make life better for us – putting Americans first. The stock market is up twenty per cent, and there are more jobs than ever before. You know, the blacks and minorities and the people who represent them really don't complain, because they all have jobs now, thanks to Trump – these jobs didn't exist under the Democrats. And he's doing something about the illegal Mexicans – we've got more of them in California than the entire population of Australia. We just can't cope. So who do you help, the cute-looking Mexican child in poverty or the veteran who has served his country? My heart goes out to them, it really does, but my priority is with Americans, just as Australia's priority is with Australians. You try getting into Australia if you're an illegal.'

Did Vernon consider himself to be a Republican? 'I'm neutral', he declared improbably, then clarified, 'I'm a libertarian.' As if to emphasise his lack of classical ideological convictions, he started talking about how badly the Marshallese on the base had been treated. 'The new company wanted to cut their pay right back. Guys who had been making fifteen dollars an hour now make six or seven. That's why I resigned – I choose my jobs as much as possible on the basis of moral integrity, not how much money you can make. I worked delivering Domino's pizzas a while ago; there were people doing that for a living. They had families. How do you make that work? Trump's doing something about it, but the Democrats aren't.'

Was he concerned by the polarisation of American politics?

'Yes', he said. 'It's the Democrats.'

They're the ones who take their children to rallies with signs that say 'Fuck Trump'. Look at all the presidents who have been assassinated – all Republicans killed by Democrats. They want to let everybody in, they abolished slavery, they profit from deals with Iran. The Republicans are only interested in money; they're as bad as the religious right: they say they have the correct answer to everything. You know, I've got friends who are Mormons, and I say to them, 'Imagine what Jesus Christ would say if he came across a homosexual couple.' He'd say what he always says and offer them God's love. You know, I've read the Bible, Torah, Koran; I've studied Buddhism. They don't say anything about these things. I'm glad to be moving to Texas. I'll be among people who think the same way I do.

He walked off as we arrived at the checkpoint at Kwajalein, and I sat down in the holding pen, disoriented by our recent conversation. Above me a sign read, 'TODAY'S FPCON IS: ALPHA'.

Entering the departure lounge at the airport on Kwajalein was like walking out of the Pacific into another country. Some white contractors were joking about finding new jobs now that there was a new company running the base. One was going to Saudi Arabia, a few to Texas; others were returning to new jobs in Kwajalein. I saw Vernon chatting with a group of identically clad, middle-aged, overweight men in loose polo shirts, baggy shorts and baseball caps: a collection of right-wing Michael Moores. To avoid eye contact and having to talk with him again, I moved quickly over to a series of exhibits from Kwajalein laid out in a glass case and pretended to study them intensely. There was a rusting helmet from World War Two, some dog tags and an ancient machine-gun barrel. Most of the cabinet, however, was taken up by a collection of vintage Coke bottles

Above it, a television blared a broadcast from the army channel, Defense Media Activity. There were interviews with proud sergeants standing in front of their Humvees and ads for financial management services. The channel is multicultural – an African–American financial advisor talked with a Pacific Islands colonel, followed by a Hispanic general offering words of wisdom about duty, service and the importance of financial planning. This is the modern American military: the poor young people from the imperial periphery forging a life and career. Around me were the Trump-voting contractors: better paid, white and pining for a largely vanished world of American apartheid that now exists only on remote, mainly civilian bases like those on Kwajalein and the now-defunct Panama Canal Zone. The winter Olympics were on, and a casual viewer could have been forgiven for thinking that there was only one country competing as a succession of American medal winners, flushed from their victories in the snow, filled the humid waiting room on Kwajalein Atoll.

As the flight was finally called, I walked out onto the tarmac and turned back. 'Kwajalein US Army Garrison – a community of excellence' said the sign on the base gates.

9

MAJURO AND THE LEGACY OF NUCLEAR TESTING

While the atomic bombs on Bikini Atoll were the most infamous of American nuclear tests in the Pacific, tests on Runit Island in the Enewetak atoll group had left some of the most haunting physical remnants of the era. Here, 73,000 cubic metres of nuclear waste had been dumped into a vast crater and covered with a concrete sarcophagus known as the Runit Dome. I wanted to talk with people from Enewetak and, if possible, visit the testing site. Like other remote island groups in the Marshalls, Enewetak was represented in the capital by a 'town hall'. This was situated on the third level of Majuro's tallest building, with a total of five storeys, and next to bracing wafts from a set of urinals.

'All you journalists are the same', said the administrator.

I was surprised: it was unusual in my experience of the Pacific to meet with such forthright views immediately expressed. 'What do you want to go there for and what do you give back? You ask your questions, make money and go away again. Anyway, if you really want to go there you can. There's a boat that can drop you there, but nobody knows when it will return, or you can charter a plane.

The choice is yours. If you really must visit the radioactive dome you can, but you do so at your own risk.'

I mumbled in protest: I wasn't making money and only wished to record people's experiences respectfully, if they wanted to talk. If Enewetak representatives didn't want to talk with me then 'no' was a perfectly good answer.

The administrator looked at me for a moment, then asked where I was from. 'Ah, Australia', he sighed. 'Do you know the job site www.seek.com?' It turned out that he was from the Philippines, as was the entire administrative unit of the town hall. 'I was supposed to go to London', he said, 'but the job fell through and I came here instead.' He had been an accountant and administration manager for the last thirteen years. 'Sometimes I look for jobs in Australia', he said wistfully. It seemed like a minor capitulation. His initial annoyance at my appearance had evaporated.

Given that I now knew he was not from the contaminated atoll, I felt more inclined to push my case. 'Would you mind if I spoke to some of the people from Enewetak?' I asked.

The administrator sighed and gestured towards the mayor's office. 'Good luck if you can find him', he said. 'The mayor usually spends most of the day at brunch.'

Failing to locate him, I headed to the Rongelap town hall, which was open and bustling and not staffed by overprotective administrators.

'Yes, I remember the tests well', said Isao Sakaio, a resident in his seventies, who had come to the town hall to claim his monthly pension. He told me stories that I had heard from several sources. The second sun; the children playing in what they thought was snow, which transpired to be nuclear fallout; the peeling skin, lesions and hair that came out in clumps. 'It tasted like cement', Isao observed, pursing his lips as if to conjure up the taste.

Given his direct personal experience of the nuclear testing, I asked what he thought about the ongoing close relationship between the Marshall Islands and the United States.

'They're so clever, the Americans', he replied. 'They can make these bombs and planes; they're so much more advanced than we are. We don't have anything like that and are really quite backward.' As this nuclear survivor spoke reverentially about the superiority of American technology, I wondered whether, in a terrible accident during his escape from the contaminated island, he had swallowed a 1950s nuclear propaganda film whole.

Continuing my search for information, I left the town hall and went back out onto the street. I followed a sign pointing to the Nuclear Claims Tribunal, which I found innocuously located in a building on the main shopping strip, between the post office and the bank. But despite a prominent sign outside, the office itself was hard to find inside. After running up and down dusty stairwells, I eventually saw a chipped printed notice at the bottom of a window next to Room 209. The door was open and the office inside looked like something from the mid-1990s. Ancient Apple Macintosh computers were piled up in the corners and a microfilm reader sat in the centre of the room. Empty desks and swivel chairs had an expectant look that suggested their occupants had ducked out for a quick lunch in 1995 and never returned. The sole remaining person, a surprised-looking employee sitting behind a desk, said to me, 'I'm just making a few calls, but help yourself to the files.' She returned to studying her phone.

The Nuclear Claims Tribunal was established under the Compact of Free Association between the United States and the Marshall Islands in 1986 and at the time of my visit in 2018 had awarded over $2 billion in medical compensation and for property damage to people who could no longer return to their ancestral homelands. However, less than $4 million had actually been disbursed, and the day-to-day functioning of the tribunal effectively ceased in

2011 for lack of funding. Twenty-three million dollars of the $96 million awarded by the tribunal was still owing on total health-related compensation payments, meaning that nearly a quarter of all health-related payments made by the US government to people suffering from the effects of radiation exposure was unpaid. In 2004 the US National Cancer Institute estimated that roughly half of the extra cancers likely to occur as a result of nuclear fallout were still to develop.

Lined against the walls of the tribunal office were boxes and boxes of case files named for the main atolls subjected to the nuclear tests and those subsequently uninhabitable because of nuclear fallout. Amid the dust and jumble of files, I didn't know where to begin. But, despite my curiosity and the open invitation of the tribunal's remaining employee, I decided not to look in the files marked 'Rongelap' and 'Enewetak', knowing that these contained the private medical histories of people who had experienced extraordinary suffering. Instead, I turned to some rusty ringbinders and fell headlong into the past. The fading facsimiles and aging reports inside, covered in dust and dead cockroaches, told a story of willful and permanent destruction. In total, sixty-seven nuclear tests were carried out by the US military in the Marshalls. Reading through a bland-looking table appended to one of the faxes, I found that some of the Marshall Islands' northern atolls have been declared off-limits for human habitation for the next 24,000 years.

In the 1990s, I discovered, a geo-engineering firm from New Zealand, called Darroch, conducted an assessment of the islands in the Bikini chain as well as Bikini Atoll itself. I found comprehensive lists and descriptions of each of the islands, which are mainly coral atolls, low and flat, with some vegetation but not much. Few were deemed able to 'support permanent habitation' and, after a few pages, I found that a chilling phrase kept recurring: 'Atoll no longer present, vaporised'. On Bikini Atoll, the most famous of the nuclear test sites, the report made some optimistic observations. Despite the presence of caesium-137 and strontium-90, radioactive substances that are absorbed by plants and animals and constitute a high level of contamination, thus making an affected area unfit for human habitation, the report claimed that 'with its unique history, extensive beaches, and excellent scuba diving, and the attraction of the Bravo crater (one mile wide and 400 feet deep), [it] could certainly be one of the Marshall Islands' leading tourist attractions'.

The tone of many of the declassified documents contained in the files was that of a chummy, pipe-smoking Ivy League common room. The *Proceedings of the Second Interdisciplinary Conference on Selected Effects of a General War* directly addressed the likely consequences of a nuclear conflict. Starting the conference in a jocular tone, Dr Dunham, a facilitator, reflected on his role: 'I gather that my function is that of an initiator in the sense that one talks about initiators in atomic weapons; the problem is whether I can produce enough neutrons to produce a chain reaction with this, our critical assembly here.' Laughter among the attendees. 'A fascinating question' that the distinguished scientific gentlemen should consider, Dunham continued, was how pilots would react when they discovered 'that they had received a lethal dose of radiation' while flying.

However, it was a description by Dr Merril Eisenbud of the US Atomic Energy Commission of the research possibilities afforded by testing in the Marshall Islands that revealed most about the United States' intentions for the nuclear tests, beyond just how large an explosion could be made. Declassified documents have shown that the fallout was more extensive and less accidental than officially claimed. The reason given by US authorities for the contamination of other atolls that were not directly part of the Castle Bravo test in Bikini was an unexpected and sudden gust of wind at high altitude. The wind direction, however, was known to authorities well in advance. At the same time, the US Department of Energy's sinister Project 4.1 was altered from being 'an inquiry into the effects of radiation in mice' to its effects on humans when the scientific opportunities from 'inadvertent' radioactive fallout became clear. With the Bikini test, these opportunities were soon to become available. At the time, Eisenbud said, 'It will be very interesting to go back and get good environmental data: how many per square mile, what isotopes are involved and a sample of food changes in many humans through their urines, so as to get a measure of the human uptake when people live in a contaminated environment. Now, data of this type has never been available. While it is true that these people do not live, I would say, the way Westerners do, civilized people, it is nevertheless also true that these people are more like us than mice.'

By 1954 but prior to the Castle Bravo test on Bikini Atoll, Marshall Islanders had become deeply concerned about the extent and effects of the nuclear testing on their islands. In total, sixty-seven large nuclear devices were detonated on small atolls in the Marshall Islands between 1946 and 1958 at a rate equivalent to one and a half Hiroshima bombs per day for twelve years. Finding the American administration unresponsive to their concerns, the Marshallese petitioned the United Nations Trusteeship Council, which had granted the United States mandate rights over the Marshall Islands. The council had nominal oversight of governance in territories the United Nations had entrusted to the victorious powers after World War Two. 'No stone will be left unturned to safeguard the present and future wellbeing of the Islanders', diplomats had pledged at the time. In their appeal, the Marshallese wrote, 'The Marshallese people are not only fearful of the danger to their persons from these deadly weapons in case of another miscalculation, but they are also concerned for the increasing number of people removed from their land ... Land means a great deal to the Marshallese. It means more than just a place where you can plant your food crops and build your houses or a place where you can bury your dead. It is the very life of the people. Take away their land and their spirits go also.' This was, predictably, ignored. 'There are only 90,000 of them', Henry Kissinger, the US Secretary of State, remarked on hearing about Marshallese objections to nuclear bombardment. 'Who gives a damn?'

*

On 1 March 1954, when Bikini Atoll in the Marshall Islands was evacuated to make way for the 'Bravo Shot' nuclear test, the Bikinians were told the test was 'to end war and for the good of mankind'. After a final visit and church service at the island's graveyard, the Bikinians left their ancient atoll home, thinking they would soon be back and singing, as a friendly gesture to the Americans, 'you are my sunshine, my only sunshine, you make me happy when skies are grey'. They were outnumbered on the horizon by 242 naval ships, 156 aircraft, 42,000 military personnel and 25,000 radiation recording devices.

'There were two suns that day', a survivor from the atoll of Rongelap, a hundred kilometres from Bikini, told me. 'We thought the world was ending.'

Alson Kelen is a traditional navigator, former mayor of Bikini Atoll, and founder of WAM. 'Canoe building and navigation in the Marshall Islands originated in Bikini', he said. 'The trees were planted on the windward side of the atoll to ensure they grew curved for the boats' hulls. The trees grew slowly and so grandparents planted for their grandchildren. The boats were light and fast – able to speed on the winds for nearly a thousand kilometres between the dispersed atolls in days.'

'Marshallese navigate with their stomachs', he continued. 'We practise "wave navigation", feeling the swell of the ocean and recognising its direction. During the day, I close my eyes to sense the movement of the ocean. The atolls, the trees, the canoe-building, the ancient navigation: to us everything is connected. It stopped on 1 March 1954.' Like the Russian, British, French, and Chinese nuclear tests, the US tests targeted remote, indigenous lands and people who were regarded as 'savages'.

Because the nuclear waste left on Enewetak Atoll wasn't sealed, the radioactive matter leached through the porous coral and was gradually washed into the ocean as sea levels rose. Consequently, the Marshall Islands are 'where the atomic age meets the climate change era', observed Alson Kelen.

There was pressure for the Bikini community to return. In a meeting at the American Embassy, Kelen was told to return but not to 'eat fish or coconuts or dig the soil and we were told to keep our children inside. I asked the officials if they realised we are adults'.

'We will never go back to Bikini', he said. 'It lives on as an idea, a culture we preserve through teaching navigation and canoe-making. This is not just about preserving tradition – it is about finding a sustainable future.'

I asked Alson about relations with the United States.

'We can't undo the past' he replied. 'I know that I am never going back to Bikini and we have such close connections now with America – I was educated there, many Marshallese live or have family there'.

He picked up a textbook used to teach English to young people in the canoe program. It was a massive hardback tome on American history, unironically called *A Free People*. In a gesture of magnanimity, Alson held up the book and said, 'I would be happy if there was a section in here on nuclear testing, but in America nobody knows anything about it.'

A week later, when I had left the Marshall Islands and was back in Australia, I met with Tilman Ruff, a physician and academic at the

University of Melbourne, who founded the International Campaign to Abolish Nuclear Weapons which won the Nobel Peace Prize in 2017. I wanted to put to him some of the questions about nuclear testing that had been put to me in the Marshall Islands. I started by asking him about Abacca Anjain-Maddison's concerns about the presence of plutonium in the Kwajalein lagoon.

'Plutonium is manmade', he said. 'It's something we've put out there and it doesn't exist in nature. There's plutonium all over Central Australia now that didn't exist before the tests at Maralinga in the 1950s and 1960s.' He gestured towards the street in front of us, the pedestrians and the passing traffic. 'It's a heavy element', he continued, 'and despite having a half-life of 24,000 years [it] doesn't spread widely into the surrounding environment. The best thing for plutonium is that it sinks to the bottom of a lagoon somewhere and gets stuck in mud.' It seemed a low-tech solution to a high-tech problem, but I was relieved that this most noxious of chemicals doesn't just leach endless toxicity into the atmosphere and the oceans. 'The real problems are strontium-90 and caesium-137', Tilman continued. 'These get taken up by the plants and animals and enter the environment. They can be inhaled or ingested and are cancer causing.'

I asked him about the intergenerational effects of radiation exposure. Now that the generation initially exposed to radiation is dying off, what is in store for their children and grandchildren?

'We don't know for sure, but once genetic damage has been done, it's in the system. It's quite likely that cancers will recur in subsequent generations.'

I was also concerned about the stories I'd heard about Marshallese children getting sick because of their association with the ongoing missile testing in the Kwajalein lagoon. I asked Professor Tilman if there might be a link.

'It's impossible to say, but the symptoms – fever, sweating, diarrhoea – are also those of ciguatera, a bacterium that lives on dying or damaged reefs, possibly further damaged by missile debris', Tilman observed.

What did he think about the pressure on people to return to islands where there had been testing or fallout? Could they safely return, as Alson Kelen and the community from Bikini Atoll had been asked to do?

'It might be possible, especially for older people', Tilman said, 'or for periodic cultural or religious reasons. But it would be inadvisable to live there.' He paused for a second before adding firmly, 'I wouldn't do it.'

As we were leaving, I asked him how the International Campaign to Abolish Nuclear Weapons was progressing in its call for a treaty. There are treaties against landmines, rightly considered among the most inhumane of military technologies, but not against the weapons that could bring about the end of life on earth.

'We're gaining momentum', he said, 'but there's a strange dichotomy. Many states are completely behind the treaty, but there are a few, the major nuclear powers, that vehemently oppose it. But I think there's a growing ethical consensus which the big powers are finding it increasingly difficult to ignore.' With that, he headed back to his office and, later, to India to meet with physicians against nuclear weapons and continue the slow process of building ethical momentum through reason, argument and the simple premise that planetary destruction is undesirable and avoidable.

As American and Chinese security officers scuffled, during a presidential visit to Beijing, over the 'nuclear football' (the black leather briefcase containing the US president's nuclear launch codes), as Donald Trump and Kim Jong-un debated whose 'button' was bigger, as Australia embedded itself ever deeper into the US security network in Asia and the Pacific, and as anti-Chinese rhetoric heightened, the prospects of nuclear confrontation became eminently more real. During the Cold War, the logic of two nuclear-armed superpowers assured of mutual destruction may have kept the peace in Europe and North America, at least. But the proliferation of such weapons has unfrozen the Cold War, and once again they pose an existential threat to us all. For Marshall Islanders, as for indigenous communities in Russia, China, the United States, Australia and the other Pacific Islands where these devices have been detonated – to say nothing of the inhabitants of Hiroshima and Nagasaki – the nuclear past will live on for millennia.

Part 3

THE ONCE AND FUTURE OCEAN

10

LEAVING THE COOKS: DECLINE OF AN OUTER ISLAND

A bombed-out utility vehicle met me at the airstrip on the island of Mangaia in the Cook Islands. The airstrip was little more than a patch of neatly mowed grass next to the coast, and we were driven for a few minutes into a township that consisted of a main road, some government offices and a general store.

'You're going to meet the most important person on the island', the driver said before dropping us off at the store and accelerating away.

This turned out to be Babe, a young man with luscious shoulder-length locks, well-manicured nails and a tight-fitting fuchsia tank top. Babe ran the store and a guesthouse and was slightly out of breath. 'I'm so sorry', he apologised. 'I was mid-set.' He pointed to the tennis court opposite, where a seriously competitive tennis match was under way. Babe essentially managed the local economy while starring as the island's tennis impresario. He was Mangaia's number-one ranked player, unbeaten on an island where competition, if minimal, was fierce.

Through contacts in the Cook Islands, Babe already knew

we were coming and had brought in provisions. Two crates of beer and a carton of cigarettes were neatly packed and awaited collection.

'What about food?' I asked.

He smirked, nodding towards two shelves heavily stocked with spam, rice, Oreos and Fanta Orange. 'There are open courts at two this afternoon and Zumba class at 5 pm sharp', he announced as he trotted back to his tennis match.

This wasn't the start I had been hoping for.

'WELL HOW'S ABOUT THAT!' roared someone, loud and close, as I grimly contemplated four days of spam and Zumba. It wasn't apparent where this noise came from and, starting, I looked around but saw no one. 'OVER HERE! ARE YOU DEAF?' came the booming voice once again, and I realised that it came from a diminutive New Zealander with steely permed hair and the solid appearance of someone for whom the daily spam-fest had become a way of life. Glenys turned out to be one of the teachers at the local school. A lifetime of ordering massed ranks of children around had left her with the impression that she was constantly addressing a crowd whose attention might wander at any minute.

'I was just saying that —' I started.

But with foghorn generosity, she exploded, 'I'LL SHOW THE NEWBIES AROUND!' and hauled me outside to a waiting car.

Her tour was one of friendly monosyllabism and confirmed the reality of the sights before us in a remarkable unity of word and object. Glenys shouted her world into being, conjuring up her connection with the social history, identities and religious mythology of Mangaia through single words or short phrases that were bellowed at random intervals. 'SHOP!' she screeched as we drove past Babe's store, quickly followed by 'MAIN ROAD!' A few minutes later there was 'BIG ROCK', 'SHIPWRECK', 'PORT', 'MY HOUSE' and, in a rare moment of verbal effusiveness, 'SCHOOL WITH A MILLION-DOLLAR VIEW!'

I sat in the back of the car in awe of her volume and air of command. She was right: the school was remarkable. Perched high on a cliff top, sweeping lawns surrounded by bougainvillea and swaying coconut palms led out to a view of sun-crested waves breaking over the reef. The open-sided classrooms formed a semicircle, and immaculately uniformed students in pressed smocks and shirts were playing rounders in the afternoon sun.

Attempting to humour Glenys, I jokingly asked if I could enrol in the school as well.

'THAT'S STUPID!' she roared and, without a second's hesitation, returned to the tour. 'CLASSROOM', 'SPORTS CUPBOARD' ... On it went, and, like a reprimanded child, I slunk to the back of the group.

Lining us up outside a small class room thatched with gently rustling palm fronds, she announced, 'THIS IS WHERE WE DO OUR STUFF.' She quickly produced a whistle and blew three succinct blasts. Immediately, the rounders stopped and the children came running towards us. 'IN CROCODILE!' Glenys boomed, as thirty apprehensive eight year olds came into sight and stood in line, two by two.

Glenys, it turned out, was also the head of the local NGO I had come to visit. Prior to arriving in Mangaia I had been under the impression that its NGO led the Pacific in disaster management. I had envisioned grisly volunteers earnestly discussing logistics and relief supplies. The discussions, I had imagined, would be about tarpaulins and evacuation centres and how best to stock pre-positioned tools and kitchen sets and how long these supplies would last in storage. Within NGOs there was usually an order to proceedings that often ended with long community discussions, starting off with the practicalities of disaster response. This would move on to life in general as visitors tried to satisfy their curiosity about island life and well-informed islanders took the opportunity to compare news and observations from the outside world.

'TODAY', shrieked Glenys, glad to have an audience, 'WE'RE DELIVERING ORANGES.'

So the schoolchildren were co-opted volunteers and at another blast from the whistle, they picked up baskets of fruit that had been prepared earlier and stored in the classroom. I followed them as, at a further blast, they marched out of the school grounds in crocodile into the nearby village.

The village was orderly. Well-spaced wooden dwellings with neat tin roofs nestled into a small hill, surrounded by coconut and pandanus and abounding in flowers. Except for a strange silence, it seemed a model of small island community in the Pacific.

I followed some of the students, who had by now broken their marching formation and had divided up the houses between them. They knocked respectfully at the doors and called out to ask if anyone was home before stepping inside with slight trepidation. They were kind and gentle with their elders, staying for a few minutes, as they had been requested to do. But clearly this was not the natural world of a group of energetic, happy, optimistic children.

Inside, all of the houses were the same: dark and cool, as neat and attractive as the village was to walk through, and occupied by elderly people in varying degrees of incapacity. In most, pots and pans were washed and put away in the kitchen; pressed and folded clothes and bedding sat in well-arranged and freshly laundered piles on a chair in an adjoining corner; and family pictures, along with newspaper cuttings, lined the walls.

In the first house, no one seemed to be home – until one of the students found the resident, an elderly woman, curled up on a foam mattress on the floor. She could barely speak or move and seemed not to be able to see. The students kneeled close to her and announced that they had come with oranges. There was a silence as the old woman looked up at us but did not really seem to register that we were there.

I was unsure what to do and the children, so full of life while outside, were uncomfortable. But Glenys did not hesitate. She knelt down, holding the old lady's hands in her own, introduced herself and talked in soft, gentle tones so that, even if oral communication was impossible, she might sense that Glenys meant well. It was difficult to leave, and I wondered what the old lady would do with the basket of oranges left on the kitchen table.

Outside, Glenys and I stood in silence for a moment. 'We keep an eye on them and try to visit every day', she said quietly. 'Sometimes we have reading classes here, and the children read their favourite books out loud and tell stories.' As we waited for the house visits to finish, she looked around, suddenly tired. It was a strange sight: only minutes before she had been a busy, commanding presence, ordering and organising, on top of every activity and conversation. 'When I first moved here in the 1960s on a teaching placement fresh from New Zealand, the place was full of people and laughter, but the young families have all left. The remaining children are boarders now. But we're still here, we still look after the place.' And then she beamed suddenly – the moment's moroseness had passed. 'AND THE SCHOOL'S THE BLOODY BEST IN THE COOK ISLANDS!'

She raised the whistle to her lips and she blew sharply to rally the young volunteers. 'CROCODILE!' she cried.

Relieved to find that the Glenys had returned to her natural ebullience, I fell in line behind the marching students.

*

The symbol of Mangaia was the adze, both an agricultural tool and an instrument of war, carved with a mirror-image K, the stylistic representation of two brothers in battle who, outnumbered by the enemy, tied themselves together, back to back, with pandanus rope and fought on against the odds with their stone adzes. The motif of struggle against the inevitable led to the use of the adze as a path to peace through sacrifice. When the Mangaia tribes fought, the side that thought it was about to lose would call a truce. Legend had it that a youth would be selected for ceremonial sacrifice; he would be dismembered with the adze and his remains distributed evenly to the island's villages as a sign that the dispute had been settled: a brutal sacrifice for the greater good.

By the 2000s, however, the social compact symbolised by the adze had broken down. In the house that I visited, the woman lived alone, surrounded by wall-to-wall pictures of family and friends once from the island but now leading their lives elsewhere. Frozen moments of fun, excitement and merriment stared down in joyous but deafening silence on the one member of the family left behind. Over time, the combined processes of development, climate change and new economic opportunities were gradually starving the life of the island. There were still children in the school, but they had been sent back as boarders and their time on the island would only be temporary. Elderly people tended to their taro patches, but the intervening generation had all but vanished, present only in the interactions captured in the photos on the walls. Those left behind had been figuratively adzed for the sake of Mangaia's now-departed youth.

At its height, the island had more than 2000 residents, but these had now dwindled to a few hundred, mainly elderly people. In the 1960s and 1970s, several New Zealand teachers made their way to Mangaia and started working in the local school. Helped by their talent and enthusiasm, it quickly became one of the best in the country and educated successive generations of capable students. But those students promptly left for the main island of Rarotonga or for New Zealand, as better job opportunities opened up and the hard life of cultivating taro and yam patches became harder still, with saltwater intrusion into the soil from rising sea levels. The pull of urban centres, development in the form of education, and regular flights between Mangaia and the capital, in addition to the slowly rising sea, now meant that those who remained were either too old or too sick to leave.

*

Back at the store, Babe had chilled the crates of beer and was seated in the sun, revelling in the day's sales and another unstoppable tennis performance. I headed down to the shipwreck that Glenys had pointed out earlier – a ruined coal supply from the early 1900s whose rusting ribs remained, stuck fast against the rocks. In September 1904 *The New Zealand Herald* described the wreck of the 'fine new four-masted steel ship *Saragossa*, of Glasgow, 2285 tons, 20 days out from Newcastle, New South Wales, bound to San Francisco with a cargo of 3200 tons of coal'. Caught in a gale too close to the reef at three in the morning, the crew made a valiant attempt to turn the vessel away from the looming rocks. 'All hands', wrote the *Herald*'s own correspondent in Mangaia, 'were immediately called to 'bout ship. She answered her helm well, and came round on the port tack, but before she had time to gather way, she took the ground aft. Her head then fell off and the seas drove her bodily near to the edge of the reef, where she stuck hard and fast, listing seawards and bumping heavily, which soon caused the fore, main, and mizzen topmasts with all their hamper to go over the side, the jigger mast alone remaining firm.'

The crew were stuck on the ship a long way out. They fired a rocket to alert people on the island to their peril. 'Vaevaeongo – a Mangaian native and medallist of the Royal Humane Society, a hero for saving a life on a former occasion – managed to get hold of it and bring it to land.' Attached to the rocket was a 'stout rope', and with this, the extraordinary Vaevaeongo was able to pull the sailors safely to land. 'It took fully five hours to get the people ashore from the wreck ... as the heavy seas caused the ship to roll considerably and the hauling line occasionally got foul of the reef. As the rescued men reached the lowest dip of the rope while being hauled shorewards, they were frequently submerged in the crests of the seas driving in.' While the remains of the ship were later auctioned by its commanding officer, Captain Duncan, for £10 and 11 shillings, there is no mention in the *Herald*'s account of whether Vaevaeongo received another medal from the Royal Humane Society.

It was a calm evening, and despite the inauspicious remains of the *Saragossa* I dived into sea to swim away the sense of sadness from the village that had once been so full of life but was now, except for the school, largely silent. A small piece of coral sliced a fine inch-long cut in my foot. Lost in the sound of the sea and gentle play of the late afternoon waves, I didn't give it a second thought.

*

Back in Melbourne, I woke up feeling unwell. Sweat poured off my body and my temperature ran wild. I stumbled out of bed to get a glass of water, and a piercing pain shot through my leg. Looking down, I saw that my foot was scarlet and had ballooned unrecognisably. I could barely walk. I crawled downstairs, got on my bike and rolled myself downhill to a doctor.

'Septicaemia', he said gravely. 'How on earth did you do that?'

My blood was poisoned. The minute coral cut had suddenly flared up, more than a week later. This was an illness that, untreated, could be fatal in the remoter Pacific Islands without access to antibiotics. Even with a powerful dose of prescription drugs, I was in bed for a week.

'Injured during a first-hand investigation of the effects of climate change', I wrote to my colleagues in an all-too-transparent effort to lend credibility to an injury that had been sustained during an afternoon swim while I should have been at work. Passing the time feverishly while waiting for the antibiotics to take effect, I read the news.

A 24-year-old Iranian asylum seeker called Hamid Khazaei, who had been detained in the Australia-funded asylum-seeker detention centre on Papua New Guinea's Manus Island, had just died after being flown to Brisbane for medical treatment. He had a cut on his leg that had resulted in septicaemia. This remained untreated by the Australian authorities, who ignored the self-evident symptoms of severe illness until it was far, far too late. For want of a few readily available tablets, Hamid Kharzei had lost his life.

I thought again about Mangaia – a world without youth – and about the valiant rescue efforts of Vaevaeongo that had saved the crew of the *Saragossa*. I thought about the deliberate bureaucratic inertia of the government administrators who had ignored Hamid Khazaei's pleas for assistance.

In Mangaia, Glenys was still teaching, visiting, busily trying to fill the growing silence in her society. Individuals struggled but the state was supreme. Canberra couldn't even sign a medical script, and its functionaries were anonymous and protected. Unlike the brave and conscientious Vaevaeongo or the indomitable Glenys, they would sleep soundly through the distress flares of the night.

11

PORT MORESBY REVISITED

'We're quite junior, so we always get the shitty places', said the Italian mining engineer as we shared a lift from the hotel in Papua New Guinea's capital, Port Moresby, to a weekend snorkelling spot. He and his colleague, an older British expatriate, had finally forced themselves back into the car after several minutes of retching and deep breathing. The cause of this display was the driver, who, coming from a settlement on the outskirts of Port Moresby with neither water nor electricity, exuded a mild and not unpleasant fragrance of wood smoke. This evoked long evenings by a campfire rather than the testing whiff of unwashed humanity. To cope, the Italian had tried holding his breath, then, when this had failed, held his head out of the window before deciding that the heat, humidity and dust were too much for him. He then filled his lungs again before plunging back into the wood smoke aroma of the car, repeating this process through the ninety-minute journey to the beach. His colleague merely clenched his jaw, said nothing and fixed his eyes on the road, his inner contortions given away only by the occasional quivering of a nostril. 'This is one of the most uncivilised places I've been to', continued the Italian. 'The money's good, though', he said, 'and when we get better jobs after this it'll be someone else's turn to come to the crap places.' We drove on in silence, the Italian like a strange snout-less dog, with his head out the window. His British colleague said nothing but opened his wallet and gently stroked its soft leather, absentmindedly running a finger over an array of credit cards. These were funded by the world's largest liquid natural gas project, which piped vast quantities of fuel from the New Guinea highlands to a processing plant outside Port Moresby.

'And of course, once I'd retired', said Sir Moi Avei, a former deputy prime minister, as he settled into post-prandial mode later that evening, 'Gough and I would spend our time together in Paris, where we were both on the board of UNESCO.' I had been invited to help run a disaster preparedness workshop in a village called Boera near Port Moresby and had been billeted with Sir Moi's family in a wooden house that was built over the ocean on stilts. He had a keen interest in the liquid natural gas project and his general good humour was aided by a succession of mud crabs. He began reminiscing about his days entertaining Gough Whitlam in France, where they'd both held honorary position with the United Nation's cultural and scientific organisation. In that house on stilts, I slept blissfully in the cool night breeze and listened to the lapping of the waves under the house. In the mornings I awoke to sunrise over the ocean and the smell of freshly ground Goroka coffee, from the New Guinean highlands. After a short walk through the village, followed by hordes of enthusiastic children, I would arrive at the workshop venue.

The first morning was spectacular. The dusty track by the beach was adorned with a red carpet that led up to a rickety platform from where the governor-general of Papua New Guinea gave a speech to open the workshop. There was a morality play in which dancers and actors wearing billboards labelled 'HIV/AIDS', 'OBESITY', 'FLOODING', 'CYCLONES', 'WAR' and 'CONFLICT' were vanquished by other dancers and actors in billboards representing 'DEVELOPMENT', 'GENDER EQUALITY', 'EDUCATION' and 'DISASTER PREPAREDNESS'. The final word was left to the director of a liquid natural gas project. 'All Papua New Guineans will be better off', he said and declared that a planned pipeline that would run through the village would end poverty, bring wealth and provide a lasting basis for peace and prosperity. 'Let us rejoice', he said, and with that, each of us was presented with a set of curled pig's tusks to wear around our necks. The human billboards cheered, the crowd clapped, the children hooted, the red carpet was rolled up, the dignitaries left.

A week later, the residents of the idyllic seaside village of Boera were on fire. The village lay in the path of the liquid natural gas pipeline, and the presence of all those dignitaries and the highly visible activities of the NGO for which I worked were parts of a public reassurance campaign about the beneficence of mining and the bright futures for all of the various villages that agreed to give up their land. Yet the politics of natural resource management in Papua New Guinea were violent and fractious. Critics of the liquid natural gas project claimed that it would deprive the indigenous people of access to fishing, hunting, water and gardening rights. A neighbouring village, sensing a greater share of the profits, objected to proposed village boundaries and increased their claim to the projected allocation of compensation payments for land needed to build the pipeline. In the ensuing riot, local volunteers who only a week earlier had play-acted disaster response while laughing with their friends were back again and doing it for real.

*

'We can take you to see all the new roads and infrastructure construction in Port Moresby', offered Joseph and Samuel in unison, two brothers in their seventies who had, respectively, held prominent roles in the Papua New Guinean judiciary and civil service during their careers. I baulked slightly at this offer, fascinating as road construction doubtless would be. 'But first', said Joseph, sensing my hesitation, 'let's talk about the past.' I warmed to the two rotund, jolly brothers immediately. They had navigated successful lives and careers through rural upbringings when trips to the nation's capital took a week by canoe, through independence, the tumult of Papua New Guinean politics and government, and into active retirements working on development projects and mediation and supporting innumerable relatives with resources, advice, connections and family business ventures. They were fortunate in that they had finished school at a time when the country's first university, the venerable University of Papua New Guinea, was established and were among its early student cohort. They were fluent in English, educated and worldly, given opportunities that had not been available to others in their family who had stayed at home to continue farming or had found manual work in the mines.

But if Joseph and Samuel were justly proud of their own achievements, they were more sceptical of those of their country since independence. 'We were students in the same year as Sir Michael Somare but we never joined his Corned Beef Club', said Samuel. The club became legendary and was where student radicals at the university would gather to discuss politics and independence while eating succulent slices of corned beef.

'I remember sunset that sad day', continued Joseph, with a tear in his eye, taking up from where Samuel had left off and referring to independence day, 16 September 1975. 'The governor-general was there, Gough Whitlam was there, Michael Somare was there. We stood on a hill overlooking the event, and, as the sun sank and the Australian flag was lowered for the last time and the bugles ceased to play, there was a sigh. People were in tears. It felt like we had lost a relative, and we were not prepared for this.'

I was surprised. Not since Kipling had anyone ever lamented the dying bugles of empire in this way. On the wall above the brothers in the hotel where we met was a photograph of Prince Charles, who also attended the independence day ceremonies. When it was taken, he had been about to leave Port Moresby and was standing on the tarmac at the airport, Jackson Field, with a group of Australian administrators in full 1970s splendour: safari suits, long hair and sideburns. Charles stood awkwardly at the centre of the photo in a braided white uniform with gold epaulettes and serried rows of medals, with one hand holding a plumed pith helmet and the other clutching a sword. Like Charles, it seemed that the brothers Joseph and Samuel were not entirely of their times, grown up under the colonial administration and never quite having adjusted to the new order.

'You could say we are a lost generation', said Samuel, 'but there were many who didn't want to see the Australians go.'

I asked if the old regime hadn't been essentially unbearable, with its kiaps, the all-powerful administrators and patrol officers of the colonial state.

'You know, Tom', said Joseph, 'it was segregation at its best, and there was law and order. We used to joke that "kiap" stood for "keep the indigenous always primitive". They were strict but we knew where we stood. In fact, as a youngster I wanted to be a patrol officer. They had smart khaki uniforms and big, shiny shoes – the boots of authority', he said, with a momentary gleam of envy and delight. He then recounted a story about how the kiaps would scare local workers and keep them labouring hard by placing a pair of spectacles on a table before leaving a worksite. The kiaps claimed that the glasses kept watch while they were away. When they returned, they would stage mock consultations with the glasses, which, possessed of magical powers of observation, would report who had been working hard and who had been slacking off while the Australian overlords had been absent.

'Anyway', Stephen interjected, mercifully moving on from his homily to authority and the masochistic rituals of colonial administrators, 'we are Papuan and supported Papuan rights. We never wanted to be in one country with the highlanders; they fight and dominate everything. We Papuans are too gentle, too civilised.'

*

The next day, I headed to Hanuabada, an ancient village on the harbour in the centre of Port Moresby in a battered blue school bus lent to me by the brothers. The village was where the first members of the London Missionary Society arrived in Port Moresby in the 1870s. A missionary from the Cook Islands was the first to land, set up a church and start preaching to the locals and was remembered each year with a week of feasting and celebrations.

Deciding that I was some kind of missionary, one of the Hanuabada residents introduced me to a studious man in a tin shed who purported to be writing a history of the missionary society. As we approached, he made a great point of writing something serious and protracted in his notebook. My guide whispered in my ear about not disturbing the deacon at work, and I sat for some minutes watching this single-minded ecclesiastical penmanship in action.

'How can I help?' he said at last, looking up from his dirty exercise book.

I explained that I was interested in visiting and learning more about Hanuabada and, seeking to establish a bond, ventured that I too might be writing about the experience.

He looked horrified. 'There's a process, you understand', he told me sternly. 'We've made some significant finds, but I must clear these with the editorial committee before I can talk about them.'

'Is this where the London Missionary Society arrived in Papua New Guinea?' I asked.

'That is beyond my current purview', replied the deacon, 'although I should be happy to discuss this further once the editorial committee has endorsed and validated our findings, as I initially indicated.'

I pressed on. After all, what could possibly be controversial about the ancient history of a few missionaries?

'Well', he eventually conceded, looking around cautiously, as if aware that he was being injudicious in leaking information to me. 'Some of the dates may be slightly different, and we may have misspelt some of the names. And now, I really must ask you to save further questions until after the committee has met.' And with that, he returned ostentatiously to making important marks in his notebook.

Hanuabada is a Motu village and its language, Motuan, still carries strong Polynesian echoes. Despite the genetic diversity of its population, who are clearly from all parts of Papua New Guinea and perhaps the wider Pacific, they share a common language derived from early Tongan and Samoan trade and settlements and are a linguistic and cultural minority in the heart of Port Moresby.

'As you can see, I'm Melanesian', said Edea Sisia Nou referring to his dark skin, 'but culturally we Motuans are similar to Polynesians.'

I had come across Edea, now in his seventies, sitting under a tarpaulin on the main street or Hanuabada. The village of his youth had been utterly different from the community I visited, perilously perched on stilts above the water and hemmed in by the urban growth of Port Moresby. 'There were few people here then', he told me, 'and we didn't really wear clothes much. Covering up started to become common in the 1960s. There were big fish that came right up to the shore.' Glancing up at a hill leading to one of the city's main ring-roads, he continued, 'Behind us was the bush, and our gardens used to be there as well. There were birds everywhere. There are no birds now.'

Instead of birdsong, I could hear the rush of passing traffic; in place of large fish meandering up the shore, there was a large floating dump filled with plastic bags, instant noodle sachets and soft drink bottles. The gardens and the bush had been gradually paved over and the population had increased. This left little option other than to build out into the ocean. Long plank walkways stretched out to sea. Houses had been built on either side of the walkways, connecting to it via short planks that were propped up on stilts in the mud. Despite the apparent precariousness, these stilt suburbs caught the breeze and were fresh and clean. Facing the harbour and the horizon, the stilted wooden village seemed a world away from the road construction and plate-glass modernity of Port Moresby's encroaching central business district.

But Edea Sisia Nou had lost more than the village of his childhood. 'There was a fire eight months ago', he recalled. 'It was a hundred metres away, but a spark caught in the rubbish and it travelled all the way to my house, which burned down. I have been waiting for assistance for the last eight months.' He had been given a pile of wood beams a couple of months earlier, but they had been insufficient for a new house, which in any case he couldn't build by himself. But he was philosophical.

You know, I have saved something from the past. When I visited the Cook Islands for the centenary of the London Missionary Society arrival here, everyone from the Pacific had their own dance. But we Motuans didn't have any and I felt sad that we had nothing to offer of ourselves. The missionaries banned dancing, along with our music, because they said it was heathen. Then I remembered an old man – an Adventist – who knew our dance. I persuaded him, against his religion, to teach me. I told him that, even though his religion forbade it, if he died without passing his knowledge on, a part of our culture would die forever.

So, I learned the dance from him and taught it to all the children. Now each November we perform for a week. It is a beautiful dance, it is our dance, and we call it 'The bandicoot'.

As I made my way to the end of the village, I met two men smoking cigarettes. Their house was over the water but close to the land and was strewn with rubbish. One of the men, wearing a cap bearing the logo of the Manchester United, was an engineer with a local telecommunications company. 'I don't live here any more', he said. 'I rent a flat in town and just come back for funerals. I want to control the environment where my children grow up, and for our family to get anywhere, we need to look after ourselves and get away from all this. Custom is important, but most of the time I want to work in an office, like engineers all over the world.'

His brother was a construction worker in the mines. 'I've just got back from a holiday in the Philippines', he told me, grinning lecherously while taking a deep drag of his cigarette. I suspected he had picked up an interest in sex tourism from his fly-in, fly-out mining colleagues in the New Guinean highlands.

Edea Sisia Nou's childhood and the charms of 'The bandicoot' seemed perilously close to extinction, as the missionaries, the miners, the ring-road and the expanding office blocks of the country's capital slowly overwhelmed the village in the sea.

*

A few days later, seeking guidance on how best to get a grasp on Port Moresby, I met with some Australian researchers at the yacht club. Having spent the day wandering around the local streets near my hotel and visiting the market, I suddenly found myself in Cairns. The yacht club's building was Australian, as was its clientele. From the balcony I looked out over a rusty sunset as dozens of bright-white yachts cast lengthening shadows from their neat moorings in the harbour.

'So you're not writing a guidebook?' said my contact, with an air of surprise and disappointment. 'Everyone I've asked here can tell you something about expat life. Like Joe, here; he's taken up golf in a big way and practises every weekend. Wendy does sailing, and Andy, who works in HR, sings in the choir. I guess if you want to know what Australians would be interested in, there's the war cemetery and a nice waterfall outside the city.' They ordered a round of soda water and peered at me expectantly.

In my alarm, I didn't have the time or imagination to make something up, so I defaulted to the truth and told them I was interested in visiting the settlements at the edge of town.

'Expats wouldn't go there', someone said bluntly.

The settlements, said to be the violent heart of Port Moresby, had given the city one of the worst reputations in the world. Pejoratively known as 'slums' or 'shanty towns', they had clustered on the outskirts of the city and provided inexpensive places to live for many who worked in the city in low-paid or semi-skilled jobs. The settlements were also centres of migration, particularly of young men from rural Papua New Guinea who had come to the city in search of jobs but had found only unemployment. The combination of poverty, lack of opportunity, and boredom made some of the settlements dangerous places for outsiders. On previous visits to the city I had been confined to a high-security hotel and not allowed to walk anywhere. If I wanted to go out in the evenings, I had to order a security escort from a company founded by ex-British marines called 'The Corps' whose staff, while not carrying firearms, were fearsome. They arrived in the back of a pick-up truck in full riot gear, carrying spiked clubs and accompanied by a German shepherd in a metal cage. This was a readiness for battle that added a frisson of uncertainty to the evening's dining options.

The longer I stayed in Port Moresby's expatriate enclaves, the less secure I felt. In the coastal villages and bustling markets everyone seemed to be more or less getting on with life, bar the odd pickpocket. On the hills overlooking the town's elegant harbour, however, the diplomatic residences and the houses of politicians and the wealthy business elite were shrouded in layers of razor wire, fencing, floodlights and surveillance equipment. Even in war zones, I hadn't seen so much fortification, and the zealous security provisions, so different from the reality of everyone else's life, produced a paradoxical sense of insecurity. 'In a city with such great inequality, the fences are a provocation', Samuel had observed when I first met him.

After my false start with the yacht club expatriates, a colleague put me in contact with Charles, a graduate student at the University of Papua New Guinea, who had lived in the settlements and offered to show me around. I met up with him one morning and we headed to Burns Peak, a community on a hill in the heart of Port Moresby, so I could meet some of what Charles called 'the boys'.

Inside the settlement, we passed through the market area, where small groups sat gambling, engrossed in card games that seemed to last all day. The gambling area was strewn with cards that had been hurled in victory, defeat or the prospect of modest gains. Fat red sausages sizzled on barbeques made from 44-gallon drums, and an enterprising resident had set up two dartboards for hire. Squatting around the fringes of the market were some of Port Moresby's ubiquitous betel nut sellers, purveying the stimulant that, when mixed with red limestone paste, made the teeth and gums red and produced great quantities of crimson saliva – the latter frequently projected across the streets and alleys of the capital.

We walked on, up a short hill that took us to a piece of level ground and a small wooden house with a New Guinean flag tucked into a rear window. Charles pointed to an old office chair leaning off the side of the hill, wedged between two trees. 'That's where I wrote part of my thesis on the Papua New Guinea Reserve Bank monetary policy', he said casually. 'It was shady and cool, and we had no electricity, so I had to study outside.'

Charles had put the word out that I wanted to meet people in Burns Peak, and about fifteen young men turned up to talk. For a while we sat around awkwardly, not really knowing what to say or why any of us were there. They sat on the stony ground, while I, as a guest, was given an upturned metal bucket on which to perch while asking questions. Someone supplied some betel nut, and another person ran down to the market to buy soft drinks; this seemed to oil the social wheels. But the men spoke very softly, almost inaudibly, and I found myself bent double as I asked about their lives and livelihoods, trying to hear what was being said.

'We have no work and there is nothing to do', one told me. Another added, 'We see our friends sometimes here in the settlement, sometimes in other places, but we don't go anywhere or do anything.'

Had any of them finished school? No one had got beyond grade eight.

'We didn't have enough money to continue', one said. Even schools in the public system charged a few hundred dollars, and this was unaffordable.

None of the men had a job, and I wondered if they had ever worked. There had recently been major construction in Port Moresby in preparation for an Asia-Pacific Economic Cooperation summit, at which leaders from Asia-Pacific nations would gather for a few days for talks on regional economic collaboration. It had occurred to me that, since the young men lived in the centre of the city, close to where the summit was to be held, there might have been employment opportunities on the construction sites. But it turned out that none of the young men had ever been employed.

'So we just stay around here', one of them said.

Several had been involved in an 'urban youth resilience program' run by some NGO. 'It was useless', they agreed. 'We spent a week learning about "life skills", they told us to be nice to each other, and there was a day on gender, a day on how to manage a bank account. But there was nothing about jobs and we've never been in a bank.'

The conversation continued in this vein, and I wondered how they managed to survive with no jobs and no money. Did anyone in their extended families have a job? A few hands went up, but not many.

'We steal', they said. 'Here, there is no garden, so we can't grow anything. We can't go fishing like the people on the coast. And so we steal whatever we can find, but especially mobile phones – Samsung, iPhones. You can get five hundred dollars for a new Samsung Galaxy, more if it is unlocked. Mostly, we just threaten people, and if they give their money or their phones we go away. Sometimes they resist, so we stick them a bit with the knife. Then we go and buy alcohol and maybe some marijuana and have a party, maybe find some girls.'

And when this glorious cycle was over, the funds had run out and the hangovers had worn off, it repeated. 'The only way we can eat is by stealing, so we can buy a sausage from the market', they said, referring to the unappetising red sausages I had seen being grilled earlier. 'That is dinner and breakfast as well. If we can't afford to eat and we get hungry we chew betel nut. It takes away the hunger.'

A young man near me whispered, 'Sometimes if we have nothing, we catch birds or dogs.' He continued, 'The dogs are good. If we have money we make an offer to an owner, or if we don't we just take one. We cook them slowly in an *umu* [underground oven] and add some special leaves and chilli. It's like kangaroo.'

Another young man, hearing this, said, 'Other people grow yams and taro, so stealing is our gardening.'

I enquired if they would call themselves a gang.

'Yes', they said instantly. 'We're the 007 gang.' And I noticed then that many of the them had '007' tattooed on one hand, in the flesh between the thumb and forefinger. 'There are many gangs around here', I was told. 'There is "13 Casino", "5 8" and "MXM", which stands for "mixed mates". We are all from different parts of Papua New Guinea, and so the names show which settlements we are allied with. But 007 is the strongest.'

'Of course it is', I said and immediately regretted my facetiousness, as the gang was a source of unity and pride for them and not to be made fun of.

'Sometimes we work together and sometimes we get angry and fight. We don't trade anything – like drugs – we just steal. Sometimes we fight each other when we're drunk, but we make up the next day and we look after each other.'

There was a young man with them who had been hit by a car as a six year old. He had been lucky to survive and had needed a tracheotomy. He was now about fourteen and breathed through a stent, but the accident and medical intervention had damaged his voice box, so he couldn't speak. 'We look after our brother', said the bigger, older members. 'We can understand what he says and translate for him, because he has no voice. If anyone teases him, we beat them up.'

I asked if there was violence between the different gangs and if they had different territories.

'Yes, we are in Burns Peak; the other gangs can't come here. Sometimes we fight with fists and knives, sometimes we get the gun.'

It turned out that 'the gun' was homemade. I did not see it, but from the description of pipes tied onto a wooden stock, it sounded more dangerous to the person firing than to anyone else.

'There are good crimes and bad crimes', said one, to much laughter. 'The good crimes are when you steal for other people.'

'The police chase us', chipped in another. 'They come into the settlement to beat us up and we all have scars from this. They come in and they try to hit us around the head.'

On inspection, I saw that a number of the young men had cuts to their faces and forearms from where they had tried to ward off blows, although none of the scarring was recent.

'Sometimes we are caught and go to prison, but we escape', said one of the older and perhaps wilier gang members.

I queried how they managed this, generating much laughter.

'We bring in some food or a bunch of flowers and hide a saw in it.'

The prisons are poorly maintained, the guards have low salaries and are uninterested, and so it is relatively easy to get out. Nonetheless, if the classic escape plot is almost comical, it also carries significant risk in real life.

'If the escape hole is not wide enough you can get stuck.'

One of the older 007 members added, 'And then the police come and really beat you up.' He meant it. This would clearly be more than just a few blows to the head.

Had they ever considered leaving, or going back to the villages that their parents came from?

'No, we are from here now. We can't live in the village; we don't know anything about village life. Burns Peak is our village and we have to stay here.'

As the conversation came to an end, I asked what they were up to for the rest of the day.

'Normal service resumes', smiled one young man.

Another, in a plastic top hat worn at a jaunty angle, said, 'We will go and tend our garden.'

They were the friendliest gang of thieves I had ever met. I was completely safe, although as I pulled out my iPhone to take a parting picture of the group, I felt all eyes darting alertly to the object in my hand. No one moved, the smiles remained, but they were aware, and I was glad it wasn't a Friday night, when alcohol flowed and fights started.

As Charles and I walked back down the hill, a tall, skinny man in a knitted Rasta beanie and a multi-coloured coat approached us. He was friendly and seemed to inhabit his own fantastical mental universe. 'See you later', he said. 'I'm just off to Las Vegas, the land of dreams.' He pointed to the sausage stands and betel nut sellers and small groups of people eking out a few cents over cards.

Later, we entered a crowded market place and Charles overheard another gang talking. 'Put im eye long white man', they said – keep an eye on the white man. Charles glared at them and they scampered off. Nearby, a plain-clothes policeman with aviator glasses and a big, flexible hosepipe administered occasional whacks to passers-by.

*

Back at the University of Papua New Guinea, I spoke to some of Charles's graduate class. 'Port Moresby has become much safer', said an Economics student. 'It used to be terrible in the 80s and 90s, but now you can walk everywhere, especially during the day, and the settlements aren't too bad.'

I wondered what had changed.

He thought for a second, then answered, 'Mobile phones. If there's any trouble, people can now call the police.'

I also suspected that the redesign of Port Moresby had something to do with it. In the run-up to the 2018 Asia-Pacific Economic Cooperation summit, the city had gone through a major beautification program funded by Chinese government loans. The old container port had been moved out of the centre of town to make way for a long, elegant stretch of waterside promenade. A modern plate-glass building set on an artificial rock platform in the harbour quoted the ancient building tradition of Papua New Guinean long houses while using the latest materials. Roads, even the adequate ones, had been dug up and re-tarmacked so the summit's delegates could enjoy the smoothest air-conditioned rides to their cool meeting venues. 'Port Moresby', read a road sign depicting a gleaming conference building, 'safe, clean, smart'. Elsewhere, drivers on the new roads had been exhorted to follow new standards of behaviour: 'Buckle up or bagarup'. It had been an expensive and in many ways effective campaign to change the image of the city.

It had also had its controversies. These included the purchase of fifty Maseratis in which to convey the distinguished summit guests and a ban on betel nut selling, a major industry for people in the settlements, who made a few dollars on the side for food and basic items from selling the appetite-suppressing nut. But the red stains of spit that covered the footpaths were deemed too much for the sensitive delegates, so the trade in the city, estimated to be worth perhaps $1 million a week (significant, given how small Port Moresby is and how poor its poorest residents are), was banned entirely or confined to the outskirts. The ban was often unenforceable, but it resulted in unaffordable fines, loss of income and blows from the cane-wielding plain-clothes police.

For Papua New Guinea's 'big men' managing the capital development projects, backslapping, bribes and golden handshakes were the order of the day. As one of the 007 gang told me, 'We're not the only problem in Port Moresby, but everyone else can bribe their way out of it if they get caught.' During my first visit to Port Moresby in 2008, the country's newspapers had contained reports in which a minister complained that he had been diddled by a logging company. With righteous indignation, he said that there had been an agreement with the company to 'relax' environmental regulations in exchange for brown envelopes of cash. The regulations had been duly relaxed by the minister, but he had not received his inducements. Subsequently, he went to the press with this outrage. Occupying the front pages, meanwhile, was an investigation into a decision by the chief of the capital development authority to spend hundreds of thousands of dollars on a city yoga program.

A major component of the redesign program had been a series of new ring-roads, strategically planned to go through the old settlements, which found themselves sitting on prime real estate. Mining companies, government agencies and the Hilton Hotels Corporation eyed off property development opportunities, and the settlements were in the way, although for the time being Burns Peak remained. Their splendid harbour views would command a high price, and there was much more money to be made and pocketed. Gleaming highways replaced the labyrinthine mazes of tin shacks and footpaths clinging to the hills of Port Moresby. Afterwards, no one knew where the people from the old settlements had gone, whether they were relocated or compensated, or what had happened to them. But it was clear that, like the birds of Hanuabada, they were no longer there.

12

SOLOMON ISLANDS:
GOOD BOY, CAN COUNT

'I'll call the manager immediately', said the Qantas check-in attendant with a tone of great alarm.

'No, no', I protested. 'I don't want to speak with anyone; there's no problem.'

But it was too late: management had been summoned and a more senior representative with an even more solicitous manner arrived to attend to my case and to allay my concerns. But I had no concerns.

I was travelling to the Solomon Islands on a last-minute urgent request, and the last remaining ticket on a same-day flight was in business class. Arriving at the airport, however, I had encountered a small group of Solomons volunteers from the NGO I was going out to support. They would not be travelling business class, and the contrast of preferential boarding, better meals, a glass of champagne and general pampering by obsequious airline staff while the volunteers were herded into cattle class filled me with dread. Surely this would only reinforce the worst preconceptions they might have of international assistance? I had already paid for the flight, but the 'optics' were so bad I couldn't go ahead, so I asked the airline for a downgrade.

The senior airline official, trained in the art of dispute resolution and agreeable compromise, was deterred but not defeated, and we engaged in a form of reverse haggling.

No, I didn't want priority boarding.

No, I didn't want my bags tagged so they came out first.

No, I didn't want any of the petty inducements that were so trivial in ordinary life but at thirty thousand feet became expensive perks in the airline's caste system.

'I'll have to clear this with Sydney', said the manager, perturbed by my throwing away of privileges that were the status symbol of the globally aspirant. Downward mobility was not something the airline industry, with its lounges, points systems and duty-free options, had yet encountered.

I had been summoned at short notice to Honiara to head off a pending sex scandal. Alarming reports had suddenly got back to headquarters that an international staff member had been living the high life and – if true – exploiting the trust, power and responsibilities incumbent on his position. I was dreading it. But I had no choice. The alleged behaviour was serious, and potentially improper although mercifully not criminal, and it had fallen to me investigate what substance there was to them.

I squeezed into my economy seat and, staring blankly into the headrest of the seat in front of me, considered the grim days ahead.

'You should join us', came a friendly voice, cutting through the gloom. It was one of the volunteers, plastic glass of champagne in hand. 'We've been upgraded', he said cheerily, as he breezed past on the way to some extra leg room and a bigger television screen.

When we got to Honiara, I found that my bags had been lost.

*

I spent the next few days in Honiara's expatriate enclaves trying to investigate the allegations of sexual misconduct. It was like a Salem witch trial. 'Did you see Goody Good or Goody Osburn with the devil?' I seemed to hear myself asking over and over again. But no one had seen anything. Locals remained tight lipped and said nothing or, if saying nothing was impossible to avoid, spoke at the same frequency as the nearest electronic object – air conditioner, ceiling fan, gurgling fridge – so as to be effectively inaudible. Scores of expatriates living, working and volunteering in Honiara came up to me sharing confidences and whispering stories – as I sat, trying to find neutral places to conduct interviews, in hotel lounges and air-conditioned cafes – and urging each other on with salacious details and lurid accounts. But it was all rumour polished into fact through successive retelling.

Fortunately, I was joined by a more seasoned investigator who asked harder hitting and more probing questions. 'I've lived in country towns', she said after several interviews. 'It's the same old rumour mill, but here it's taken on a life of its own.' And she started quoting, not from human resources manuals or studies of mass psychosis but from EM Forster's *A Passage to India*: 'Except for the Marabar caves – and they are twenty miles off – the city of Chandrapore presents nothing extraordinary.' The expatriates gossiping with each other in the Lime Lounge or over chilled Coronas by the pool were the modern equivalents of the 'Turtons and Burtons' of Chandrapore living in neo-colonial seclusion along a ridge overlooking the city. *A Passage to India*, which could be mistaken for Lonely Planet's *Solomon Islands*, observed, 'As for the civil station itself, it provokes no emotion. It charms not; neither does it repel. It is sensibly planned with a redbrick club on its brow ... and the bungalows are disposed along roads that intersect at right angles ... it shares nothing with the city except the overarching sky.'

Getting a lift to my hotel one evening with another expat, the wife of a diplomat posted to Honiara on mission, I noticed her deep-brown tan and air of profound relaxation. Suddenly irritable after a day of listening to interviewees, I remarked that she'd clearly been making the most of her time by the pool.

'It's not a tan at all – I'm Lebanese', came the terse response.

I wished I hadn't said anything.

As the investigation finally concluded, and as resignations were tendered and accepted with little mutual regret, it was a relief to escape the extended airport lounge of Honiara's hotels and offices and to walk down the street, liberated from the need to ask awkward questions of total strangers, and instead to inhale deep and joyous plumes of diesel and dust.

*

The town of Honiara still bore the hallmarks of the US army base and logistical centre that it had been until 1943, when the battle for Guadalcanal ended. The airport's name at the time, Henderson Field, recalled the US marine engineer officer who oversaw its construction. Even now, vast semicircular hangars of corrugated tin dotted the urban landscape, transformed from supply depots to mechanics' workshops and port offices. Newly constructed squat concrete buildings still evoked the sense of a supply hub, albeit on a less martial scale. Warehouses, building supplies and 'bulk stores' dominated the town. Alongside them were hundreds of small family-run stores selling clothing, plastic items and household supplies and managed almost entirely by newer Chinese migrants who sat on elevated stalls and observed the passing traffic, keeping an eye out for light-fingered customers and on the probity of their local employees. Unlike other Pacific town centres, where clothing shops had names to entice customers with local and international brands or exotic aspirations, the Honiara shops just announced, 'New bale': second-hand t-shirts and shorts packed in bulk and bought by the kilogram.

On the footpaths and in intimate clusters of busy stalls by the sides of the roads, island women ran betel nut stalls. All the stalls were identical and sold plump oval betel nuts, lime paste and cigarettes. The stalls were highly social and formed a kind of uncompetitive capitalism, since there was no differentiation in price, supply or quality, and the stalls were all grouped together.

I asked one stall holder how to choose a good betel nut.

'Go for a green one', she advised sagely.

But they were all green: every betel nut in every stall looked the same. So I took a plump one, bit the flesh open and popped the small brown nut into my mouth. The effects were instantaneous. My cheeks exploded with saliva, and I took a couple of quick steps away from the stall to expectorate dense streams into the nearby bushes. And then there was the rush. My head reeled as if I'd just inhaled a pint of espresso. I wobbled for a few minutes, spitting, chewing the bitter fruit and breathing deeply, before taking an erratic, light-headed course to the market, buzzing all the way.

Squatting on the pavement, newspaper sellers displayed copies of the *Solomon Star* and *Solomon Sun*, their headlines exhilarating: 'Legal corruption', shouted the *Star*. 'MPs siphon funds from hardworking citizens and tax-payers', 'Homes burnt in retaliation', 'Political party crisis: nation plunged into partyless state', cried the *Sun*. But the inner pages were less sensational. The *Star* carried a story about improvements in taro-planting techniques alongside a picture of men digging a hole. A writer in the *Sun* argued for fisheries reform under the headline 'Tuna managers in Pacific should reform transshipment controls'. It was a weird combination: grand political scandal accompanied by worthy updates. Openings, graduations, and photos of workshop participants celebrating their 'successful attendance' filled the inner pages.

By the market, bus operators touted for business. 'Need im wan fella' and 'Two fella, two fella' were the cries along the street as they sought passengers for their last remaining seats. Looking up at the entrance to the market, I was relieved to see that I had just missed a visit from Pastor Guy Cohen, an evangelical preacher and 'messianic leader' offering 'a word from Israel for our times and end times'.

As my luggage had still not arrived and I was desperate for a change of clothes, I spent the morning browsing through musty bundles of tattered Rip Curl t-shirts, ancient board shorts, frayed industrial work wear and oversize sports singlets. Discarded branding from companies selling power tools and mining equipment were also prominent among the capital's sartorial options. Economy was everything and I trawled through Fang's Discounts, Cheaprice and Bulk Shop (one of several) for something to wear. After an hour my 'to be considered' pile consisted of sloganised t-shirts. Would I look better in 'NEVER TOO OLD TO TRY SOMETHING NEW', 'NOURISH YOUR WHOLE DOG', or 'DOWNUNDER 1993' I wondered. Trade was quick, demand was high, and the best items disappeared fast.

Most of the shops were advertising for employees with wonky handwritten signs taped onto the reflective glass of their front doors. 'Vacancy', read one sign, for 'good boy, can count.' It was tempting to apply. In searching for my own clothes, I started to examine what others were wearing and found Honiara to be one of most stylish and diverse capitals in the Pacific. Streetwise, defiant and individualistic, it derived from a remarkable combination of influences. These ranged from the demure covering introduced by Christian missionaries to the hairstyles of global soccer stars and the militia look of Rambo films. For men, there were camouflage shorts, cool t-shirts, vast man-buns, hipster beards and vertical afros. For women, there was more demure attire evolved from the muumuu introduced by missionaries to hide what they perceived as 'pagan nakedness' but which was being slowly undermined by ever cooler t-shirts. In the end, I selected a slightly too-big t-shirt with a discreetly faded smurf on the back and a pair of straw-coloured cords torn off at the knee and held up with a piece of twine.

*

While the street names on the map sounded exotic – Mendana Avenue and Lenggakiki Road intersected with Hibiscus Avenue – the reality was not. Stubbing my toe on a protruding piece of metal, I looked down to find that it was a memorial plaque to the duke and duchess of Cambridge, who inaugurated Commonwealth Street in 2012 – a dusty, pockmarked side-street leading down to the port and garlanded with flame trees. But the sense that Honiara was less of a town and more of a supply depot never really left. Next to the flame trees were vast petrol silos and a container dock which crowded the town centre. NGOs and United Nations agencies had erected vast hoardings and signs that exhorted islanders to reach the long-expired Millennium Development Goals, wash their hands or eliminate illness. 'Side by side, a Movement for equality', announced another billboard before suggesting an array of social media options, in a country with limited internet access and mobile phone use, that would somehow alleviate domestic violence. The hotels and conference centres were adorned with coded messages to the development community. The 'PFIP/CBSI Workshop' was on the left, while 'UNDP's CBPFI consultation' was down the hall and jet-lagged development officials scurried between the two on their micro-visits from Canberra, Washington or Suva.

I walked on, past the government offices, and came to the statistics bureau which had decided to erect a giant flat-screen television facing the street. I stood before it, riveted by a succession of factoids being beamed out for public edification many of which turned out to be incorrect. The crude birth rate was apparently 37.7 per 1000, while the average household size was 5.4 people (based on the 2009 census), and the core inflation rate was 1.4 per cent. Life expectancy was sixty-six years for men and seventy-three years for women. Although 40 per cent of both men and women had completed some sort of secondary schooling, only 3 per cent of women and 9 per cent of men had attained post-secondary education. Captivating as this was, I moved on as a succession of new graphics emerged promising to outline contributions to gross domestic product in 2016 'by economic activity unit'. But, in the absence of cinemas, this evening's entertainment might have been as good as it was going to get.

After I had meandered for several hours, dusk was approaching and I had been strongly advised not to walk around after dark. I was not yet ready to return to the hotel, so I lingered on and eventually installed myself in the Little Tsing Tao restaurant. Small groups of Chinese men sat around smoking, drinking and staring into their phones. The food was delicious, and I attempted to make jolly repartee with the chef on this subject, but the language barrier was too great. I patted my stomach and gave a thumbs-up, but he just stared, perhaps not unreasonably alarmed at this Westerner in a smurf t-shirt whose shorts were kept up with twine. I didn't know how to mime that this was a temporary measure and that my bags would, hopefully, arrive on the next flight. A waitress with one eye sensed the goodwill, though, and as I left, called out a flat 'Thank yu Tumas'.

Out on the street it was pitch black and still. Most of the shops had closed, and in the distance strange green and red hues emitted from a few sporadically placed ATMs. I was confident but wary. I was doing what the guidebooks and security briefings told me not to do. I kept my eyes peeled and was focussed and alert. In the absence of streetlights I tried to keep to the path best illuminated by the moon. Groups of men and women were safe; single men I watched indirectly out of the corner of my eye; groups of men were identified early and avoided.

To my right, without warning, a large man with almost perpendicular dreadlocks brushed past me. 'Goodnight', he said softly.

Further on I came across a group of women with the Sisyphean task of sweeping the dusty road with short straw brushes. They were bent double, and with each vigorous flailing of a broom a cloud of dust was sent skywards, only to rearrange itself back on the road moments later. 'Goodnight', they called in cheery unison.

As I neared the hotel, I saw a group of teenagers sitting beneath the canopy of a flame tree chewing betel nut and projecting squirts of deep-red saliva onto the pavement. 'Sleep well', they shouted out as I passed.

By the time I was back in my room I had wished goodnight in person to what seemed like the entire city.

*

'You know, it was supposed to be Nicole Kidman but I got her chin wrong', said Sir Tommy Chan ruefully. 'The other is Angelina Jolie.'

Sir Tommy was the proprietor of the august Honiara Hotel, a large and rambling hotel that was once the pride of Honiara, and whose gentle decline over the years was one of the city's great attractions. Unofficially, he was known as the political kingmaker of the Solomon Islands, leading a minor parliamentary party whose votes were necessary for larger parties to form coalition government. 'But I never wanted to go into politics personally', he said, like all politicians, but then came an unexpected moment of frankness. 'Once you get in, people expect a lot of you and you just have to feed the bastards.' He had faced constant demands from his constituents for rice, noodles and roast pig. Tommy was no longer in parliament and claimed that he was taking a back seat. It was almost possible to believe him, but for the glint in his eye as he spoke, and I couldn't help noticing that lunches at his restaurant still ended up as headlines in the following day's papers. 'Sir Tommy, in coalition talks, calls for PM to resign', the *Solomon Star* had recently shouted from its front page. It was clear he had lost none of his love for politicking.

His real passion now was sculpture and he led me on a tour of dolphins, parrots and brightly coloured clown fish that he had made from fibreglass. The hotel car park featured a 6-foot-high guitar-playing parrot with a bottle of beer and a top hat that marked the entrance to a crumbling building that was once the 'Flamingo Club'. High above the Honiara Hotel reception, a vast crystal chandelier recorded the dust of ages past. But the pieces of which Tommy was most proud were the concrete mermaids, whose generous curves he produced with the aid of a series of woks from the hotel kitchen. 'I think this one's sexier', he said, indicating a mermaid whose vast concrete head and staring eyes were partly covered by streaks of sickly green and black polyester hair, thinned and faded from the sun. Beneath the mermaids, scum was floating across the lanes of the murky green pond.

Lurking in the hotel's three restaurants and in the cafe next to the entrance, I had tried to get an interview with Tommy over several days. Four flights of stairs next to a broken and rusty funicular led up to the room and I got fit going up and down, legs burning, to see if I could catch a glimpse of the enigmatic proprietor somewhere in his domain. But it appeared that he was watching me, and finally my patience was rewarded.

Tommy led me into a cool conference room for a discussion. He had placed piles of old photo albums on the table in front of us, clearly intent upon settling in for a protracted bout of reminiscence. 'I've often been told that I should write my autobiography', he began. My gloom mounted as he pushed the old albums and some dusty manila envelopes towards me. I started to flip through the albums: photos of the Honiara Hotel, founded in 1968 by Tommy's father, a migrant from Hong Kong, who had worked as a ship's engineer during British rule; old black-and-white snaps of colonial days, suddenly brightening into 1980s Kodak colour prints, which revealed common themes; Tommy resplendent in sideburns and a moustache, clutching the tail of a massive fish; Tommy doing a party trick involving water skiing while drinking from a frosty tin of XXXX lager. And then there were pictures of him at Buckingham Palace, where he had been numerous times in recognition of his services to charity, for which he was eventually knighted. 'I used to be just a businessman', he said, 'but someone once asked me if I had a heart. Of course, I have a heart.' Lapsing into Pijin, he added, 'Mi no heart, mi collapse, mi die, finis.' And then there were the photos of girls, dances, fashion parades, parties by the pool attended by the beautiful young socialites of the day, names now largely forgotten but whose moments of youth were captured in the Honiara Hotel's fading archives. It was a kind of late-flourishing jazz age that finally died out in about 1990, as the independent Solomon Islands ceased to require an imported governing class and as the remaining Europeans fled in the face of civil war. My eye was caught by a number of pictures of a paradisal white-sand resort. 'Burned down during the tensions', Tommy said, without elaborating.

But there was no time for sentimentality. Every few minutes a hotel employee entered the room with a bundle of documents for signature. Tommy's narrative of elections fought, political struggles won and views on the need for a reintroduction of corporal punishment were peppered with mutterings about the cost of mangoes for the kitchen and the lateness of his invitation to the Central Bank Christmas party, despite being chair of the board. A businessman had been hassling him about long-term room rental. 'Offer him a room, but no breakfast, no wifi and no massage', he barked down a phone. 'I don't like the look of him', he said, turning back to me. 'I study people's faces, and his eyebrows are too narrow. Untrustworthy.'

Suddenly I was being examined, Tommy's sharp eyes studying my physiognomy with alarming professionalism. He checked my ears and spent a long time looking at my nose in profile. 'Hm', he said, not particularly encouragingly. 'I need to see your palms to get a fuller picture.' He seized my left hand and jabbed a bony finger into the fleshy bits of my palm. 'Life, yes; heart, yes', he said, as if reading from a checklist. And then his eyes lit up. 'Property owner, I see' and then there was another, protracted 'Hmmm'.

'What's the verdict?' I asked apprehensively.

'Well', he replied, 'your head is good, nice and domed at the top, but narrows slightly in the middle. You were in the top five per cent of your school, but you were lazy or there were too many girls. Your nose is good – a bit weak in the middle, but nothing to be worried about. If the end gets any bigger, be concerned, but at your age it shouldn't matter. The eyes are far enough apart, and the teeth are good. You could have been a leader, but your ears are too small. My ears', he continued, with an air of satisfaction at having superior leadership qualities in this regard, 'are quite well shaped and are at the same level as my eyebrows.' He recommended that a way around my small ear difficulty might be to give more to charity. 'On the whole, never trust anyone whose jaw you can see from behind', he advised, before indicating that I need not worry personally on this front.

I asked whether he had had a chance to study the British royal family in this way on his various encounters with them, but he wouldn't be drawn.

'You know, they keep giving me all these damn medals. I've got so many of them now: St John's Ambulance Medal, OBE, Jubilee Medal, KBE. You name it, I've got it, and I don't know what to do with them all. I never even wanted the knighthood. I grew up during the colonial period, and the only people who ever had knighthoods were retirees or men about to die. That's not me – I've still got work to do!'

And with that, he announced that he wanted to show me something. We left the conference room and walked through the long, deserted bar with its empty lounges and vast chandeliers and past a great banner celebrating the 2012 visit of the Duke and Duchess of Cambridge to the Honiara Hotel and Tommy's earlier meeting the queen. There were great pots of bougainvillea waiting to be planted, and he had just imported 3000 seedlings of a bitter South African plant that he claimed would ensure a long and illness-free life. We walked outside, and Tommy showed me his biggest and most ambitious art projects: a giant mermaid leaping out of the water of a lily-clad pool in pursuit of two dolphins, and a bikini-clad woman wearing a cowboy hat and sitting astride not one but two horses. We gazed at the sculptures in awe. And then I thought back to the old photos and the halcyon days of the 1980s when the Honiara Hotel was *the* place in town, before the newer, flashier establishments had appeared. If the beautiful young people had slowly drifted away, their memory remained, frozen in a fantasy of fibreglass and concrete, surrounded by flying dolphins.

'And now, if you'll excuse me, I have the Central Bank Christmas party to attend', said Sir Tommy.

*

The weather was perfect as our boat, the MV *Maetolau*, crossed the Indispensable Strait, which separated Guadalcanal from Malaita. A few strips of cirrus relieved the faded blue of the late afternoon sky, and the waters were completely flat. There was no gentle rocking; the soft hum of the engines propelled the vessel on in a meditative limbo, too loud for conversation and too soft for distraction. There was silence among the hundred or so travellers, who had quickly fallen asleep, sprawled in the shade across the deck. In the stilled ocean, the only sign of life were the flying fish that darted periodically from under the prow. There were no tickets. Everyone who wanted to travel got into the boat, and later in the journey a young man with a camouflage tank top and a bright-red bandana decorated with flickering flames, a sort of Solomon Islands Sylvester Stallone, came round requesting payment. Beyond this, there was little interaction. Every now again a waft of cigarette smoke floated up the stairs from under the 'No smoking' sign.

After five hours, we arrived in Auki, the Malaitan capital. On the wharf I ran into a student who told me he was studying at the Technical Institute of Malaita and asked if I would like to visit.

The next day I walked to the institute, housed in a crumbling building just out of the town centre. I found myself in the dusty gemology department, where I was introduced to the departmental head, who was also the department's only member. He had just graduated in geology from the University of the South Pacific in Fiji. His neatly pressed business shirt and professionalism contrasted with the surroundings, which spoke of long-term neglect and decay.

'We're an exciting new institute that was founded three years ago', he told me, beaming with youthful optimism, and for a second I believed him, before becoming aware again of the holes in the floor, the rusting second-hand equipment and the piles of out-of-date textbooks.

'Malaita is very unusual geologically', he added. 'We have many semiprecious gems: jasper, onyx, quartz, garnet. We believe the land was formed as a consequence of the induction of the Australasian tectonic plate during the Miocene period, about 110 million years ago, but this hypothesis is controversial.'

'So, if the geology is basically the same as Australia's ...' I said, slowly cottoning on.

'Yes!' he jumped in, picking up my train of thought before I did. 'There should be diamonds and opals out there somewhere; we just have to find them. And we would, except that we can't afford the bus fare.'

Instead, to fund the search for valuable gems, he had decided to start making jewellery to sell to tourists in the market. A New Zealand designer had arrived a few weeks before to help him with this and seemed to have had grand ambitions for jewellery-making. But there were no tourists, and those that might arrive at some future point, I suspected, were unlikely to want one of the Bulgari-esque excrescences in quartz and copper that the gemology department now produced. I asked to see more of the rock samples they had, but the person with the keys to the cupboard was away.

As our discussion progressed, the head of the health program appeared. It was early on a Tuesday afternoon, but there were no students to be seen. 'How many people are enrolled here?' I asked the administration and finance officer who was leaning in the doorway.

'I can't remember', he replied before hawking a bright, sanguineous stream of betel nut spit out of the office window.

'I think there are about sixty', said the health department head, who seemed a bit more entrepreneurial than the others. He was wearing a brilliant-white t-shirt, and had bulging muscles, a crew cut and flashing white teeth. In another context he'd have been a model advertising the lifestyle benefits of overpriced spinach juice or dubious vitamin supplements. Unusually, it turned out that my suspicions were correct. 'I specialise in *kastom* medicine', he said. He had been collecting herbal remedies from traditional healers across Malaita. 'I can cure diabetes and cancer and I'm working on a cure for HIV/AIDS.' When patients imbibed his cancer cure, their tumours usually went away in about three months, he assured me, although this depended a bit on how sick they were: sometimes it took only six weeks. It appeared that he had persuaded someone from Cuba to invest in the scheme, and they were bringing a machine to Malaita to make the herbal cure in pill form.

At first, I was inclined to tell him that it was completely unethical to make money out of the poor and the sick with the delusion that his dirty water treatment was going to cure them. But the idea of the 'young and exciting' technical institute, already reaching the apogee of decay after only a few years of operation, beating global biotech companies to find a cure for cancer in pill form was too irresistible to discourage and I wished them luck.

*

Later, at the market, I stopped under the low-hanging palm leaves shading a massed collection of betel nut stores and met Mary, a seller. Her hair stood on end, and her forehead and cheeks showed the faded marks of tribal tattooing. She had worked with various NGOs on programs to raise awareness about gender-based violence and invited me to her village that evening for a rehearsal of a play she was directing.

That night, I arrived at the village and stumbled through the darkness towards her house, which was under construction. There was a tin roof but the rest was only an open wooden frame outlining where the rooms would one day be. Mary was sitting by herself on a chair in a corner at the back of the frame, faintly illuminated by a blinking torch bulb, while her husband and one of her sons were in the framework of the room next door, smoking cigarettes together in the dark, their faces dimly lit by the glowing ends as they inhaled.

Mary had called together her drama group for a rehearsal and she was soon joined by some teenagers silently lining the outer frame of the house. At a clap from Mary, the teenagers stood, and she suddenly barked orders at them. Apparently, this was to be a play about the causes and consequences of domestic violence and was based, she told me, on the biblical story of the prodigal son. Following Mary's shouts and commands, the rehearsal began and a young man begged money from his 'father'. He then proceeded to a 'nightclub', where he started boozing and smoking. Mary continued to give directorial shouts: 'You're drunk! Stagger more!' All the teenagers were ordered to 'have another cigarette!' to create the smoke-filled, dingy club feel necessary for the play. Having established that the young man was acting suitably inebriated, Mary shouted, 'Girls, more, and music louder!' Several young women proceeded to ply the young gent with attractive company, more booze and cigarettes, taking all his money in the process. Drunk and cashless, the youth returned to his father, who gave him a hug and said it didn't matter.

Mary turned to me with a smile of satisfaction, pleased with her directorial efforts and the response of the village players. She had also made a tidy profit by selling cigarettes and betel nuts to the performers during the rehearsal while demanding, in the name of art, that they smoke more. As if the play was not enough to get the message across, Mary then grabbed a nearby guitar and started strumming and singing at full throttle, barely aware of the awkward mumbling and lip-syncing of the teenage actors.

> The light of the city was so bright I lose control.
> I wasted my money living in the reckless life.
> Lord, if you listen to my cry please forgive me.
> Save me now – I'm coming home.

Clearly, the 'bright lights' in the song had not been inspired by the village, which was by that time pitch black, or by the Malaitan capital Auki, which closed its doors and went to bed at sunset.

'The bishop likes the song very much', Mary whispered to me with pride. 'We are performing it in front of him and the church on Sunday.'

I found it hard to know what to make of this morality play. It certainly had nothing to do with domestic violence. If anything, it suggested that the young women were responsible for the boy's downfall and was ultimately a recitation of temptation, sin and redemption that reinforced the church's patriarchal views of women. No wonder the bishop liked it so much or that the young women had sung their lines with such little enthusiasm.

I asked the teenagers if they liked acting, but none seemed confident enough to talk. After their performance they chewed betel nut and smoked cigarettes while staring at the floor. Finally, I asked how old they were, only to discover that they weren't teenagers at all but men and women in their mid-twenties, slightly reticent but still influenced by the preoccupations, and open profiteering, of their elders and the church.

*

Stephen, a psychiatric nurse I met buying betel nut on the main street of Auki one afternoon, had invited me to visit the wing of the hospital where he worked – one of only two specialised psychiatric institutions in the Pacific. Surrounded by flame trees and verdant lawns, the wing seemed initially very pleasant. Some of the patients were sitting outside beneath a tree under the relaxed supervision of a nurse.

'They have insight', Stephen told me, referring to the fact that they were aware of their own conditions and were cooperative in their treatments. As we stood talking, there was a sudden and insistent banging on a barred window close by, and one of the patients, who it appeared had been sleeping, signalled for us to shut up.

'No insight', said Stephen irritably, as we moved away from the window.

Inside, I was introduced to the registrar. 'Most of the people here are ill because of marijuana', he told me. I was about to ask what treatment the hospital offered, but he said he had an urgent meeting and pushed open a filthy door leading to the gents' toilet. I couldn't help noticing that the baseball cap he was wearing had 'DOPE' in Gothic capital letters across the front.

The chief psychiatrist was more forthcoming. He stood in a doorway, hovering between some reports on his table and the pull of the sun and the trees outdoors. 'We give them drugs, starting with a strong base load, and after a couple of days, when they've calmed down, we work out a course of antipsychotics. After a few weeks, when they've gained insight, we educate them about their illness and let them go. Most of the people here are repeats, and we don't have any of the newer drugs that reduce the major side effects', he said. The numbing effects of the medication, combined with lack of money and access to the drugs, meant that most of the patients were condemned to being driven back to the hospital when their supply of drugs ran out or they tired of its side effects and they had a relapse.

I asked about other forms of therapy and treatment. Was there any art, music, discussion or other outlets in addition to the antipsychotics? But Stephen and the chief psychiatrist looked at me blankly. 'Not much', said Stephen. He asked if I would like to meet some of the patients.

We walked down the hall to a large room. In it, four or five men were lying on the concrete floor in an attitude of deep boredom. The room was locked and we looked into the room from a corridor through a barred window.

'We've taken away the beds', Stephen informed me, 'because of bed bugs. We're waiting for the spray to arrive.'

In the corridor, opposite the window, was a television, being watched by several of the men through the bars while smoking cigarettes improvised from loose tobacco and rolled-up printer paper.

'They are let out every morning and every evening', Stephen told me, in an attempt to promote the institution's liberalism, but it only made me think even more of a prison.

The men in the room were suffering different levels of illness. One, Stephen told me, had almost finished his treatment and was about to go home, while others had only just been admitted and were clearly more disturbed. George, the man who was about to be released, was responsive, so we talked through the grille. He was looking forward to going home, although this wasn't his first time in the ward.

I spoke next to some trainee psychiatric nurses who had recently arrived from the Malaita branch of the Pacific Adventist University. 'We treat the whole person', they told me, 'focussing on their medical and spiritual needs, which we analyse through a process of spiritual diagnosis. We find that people get better more quickly if they are able to overcome their alienation from God.'

I asked what this spiritual treatment involved, but they struggled to explain what they actually did. There was much hiding behind the ambiguity of their newly learned professional language. Much was made of the need for diagnosis, understanding the needs of the patient and ensuring the complementarity of medical and spiritual treatment, but they could offer no examples of what this might entail. 'Singing', one of them ventured, finally, after I had broached the question from several different angles with no luck.

I decided to leave. As I did so, I suddenly paid proper attention to the television, which had been blaring away in the background. It was showing a film called *A Matter of Faith*, set in an anonymous college town somewhere in middle America. It presented a sterile world with white actors, white houses, clipped lawns and neat fences. All the men had crew cuts, square jaws and blue eyes. All the women were pretty and had long dark hair. All teeth shone with fluorescent whiteness.

The film's premise is that a Christian student's religious worldview is challenged when she enrols in a biology course at a secular university. 'One of the hardest things in a man's life is when he sends his little girl off to college', opines her devout father. She is drawn to the biology teacher, Professor Cayman, who has a 'neat routine where he shows we all came from apes'. Learning about Cayman, her father becomes irate when he discovers that 'the guy's an evolutionist and there's nothing in the whole course curriculum about biblical creation as even a plausible alternative'.

One of the protagonist's classmates, who is clued in to Cayman's neat trick and wants to save her from the biology professor's evolutionary ideas, asserts that 'apes come from apes and humans come from humans'.

For some minutes, I stood in the ward and watched the film unfold. George was glued to it, as was another man who gazed fixedly into the far corner clutching an extinguished cigarette. I asked George what he thought of the film.

'It's okay', he said, and there was silence between us for a moment as the drama continued. 'I don't have electricity in my village', he added.

It occurred to me that the neat, clean, all-white model universe of the film must seem like a visitation from Mars.

As I turned once more to leave, I found one of the student nurses behind me. 'We brought this film especially from the university. This is what we mean by spiritual treatment', he clarified, pleased that he had been able to answer my question.

On my way back to town, I decided to revisit the technical institute to see how their gem polishing was going. But not much was happening. The person who had the keys for the gem cupboard was still away, and no one knew when he'd be back. The field trip to search for diamond and opal riches had been indefinitely postponed. They had been lent a car with some fuel, which had initially solved the problem of not being able to afford the bus fare, but as they drove off on their field trip they found it wouldn't go uphill and so the gemology team remained stuck in town. Instead, the lecturer and his one student sat at a desk, the lecturer tapping at his computer while the student dozed over a yellowing copy of a thriller called *Bullets over Palestine*.

I left the institute and walked back down the street to the *Solomon Star* office. At the reception, I met Andrew, an Australian married to a Malaitan. He was very pleased with himself, having just overseen the translation of the Bible into Kwara'ae, a local language. He was visiting the local branch of the newspaper with some photos to commemorate the end of this massive exercise by a team of translators. In one photo, there was a cake that had been baked by his daughter. 'It says, "It is finished" in Kwara'ae – the last words of Jesus on the cross', he told me. 'Of course, we don't mean it literally', he added quickly, just in case. 'We're not here to start a church. Most people read the Bible or attend church services that are in English, but how much does this mean to them?'

I asked what version he was helping to translate, hoping he could recite some enigmatic translations into Pijin of some of the Old Testament.

But Andrew clearly read my thoughts. 'We've focussed on the New Testament', he said, disappointingly, before adding, 'Even then, it's the NIV.' I was uninitiated in ecclesiastical abbreviations, and he clarified that this meant the New International Version, the 'plain English' rendering.

But even the NIV hadn't quite managed to suppress the joy of the Pijin version. '*Yumi Dadi in heaven*' urges the faithful to turn over a '*niufala laef*' and follow the '*wei blong God evri dae*', quoted Andrew. It wasn't quite at the glorious level of the phrases invented by locals to send up visiting anthropologists, like those describing helicopters as '*Mix Master blong skae blong God*' or Prince Charles as '*Queenie numbawan bubu*', which caused academic paroxysms until the anthropologists realised they were being had. Their smart, satirical subjects understood their discipline better than they did.

'One of the translators has been recording the Kwara'ae version of the Bible', said Andrew, 'but he's been doing it all day and has run out of squawk, so I'm taking his prison class.'

This seemed too good an opportunity to miss, and so I left the newspaper offices and headed off to prison.

While the psychiatric ward had felt like a prison, the prison felt like a psychiatric ward. The prison seemed much more liberal than the ward, and while religious instruction was taught, so were literacy and craft skills. And there wasn't a Seventh Day Adventist to be seen. Andrew's religious instruction class was low key and undogmatic – more a chance for the inmates to practise Pijin literacy, reading comprehension and begin to think about the possibilities of post-prison life.

'I want to know what plan there is for my salvation', said one of the prisoners when I asked why he attended the class.

In response to my query as to their favourite story, one after another claimed it to be the prodigal son. In the context of an observant society, they seemed to derive some solace from the idea that, whatever they'd done to be locked up behind the razor wire, there was some scope for future social reacceptance.

I also learned that the person who usually led the Bible study group in the prison had just escaped, although little was said about this, so perhaps the prisoners had a more practical interest in the Word of the Lord.

'We visit them every week', said Andrew, 'and bring a bit of non-prison food for them to look forward to after the discussion.'

I leafed through the Pijin Bible stories and found that sections of it were illustrated. All the characters were white, and Jesus was depicted as an Anglo-Saxon with long blond hair and blue eyes.

While some of the reflection related to the chapter under discussion, '*Jon Baptaes tokabaotem Jisas*', a couple of the participants wanted to talk about sorcery and the possibility that they had been cursed by people who disapproved of their crimes. As the formal class finished, I asked Victor, the participant who had raised the issue of sorcery, more about it. He started telling me about sharks and how members of his community revered them and were able to call them. I had heard before of the shark callers, who were not unlike the Maori whale riders and were said to have special abilities to communicate with them. I wanted to ask him more about this but Andrew was there. Even in his open-minded and undogmatic Christianity, there was a 'before and after' – a 'dark, pagan world' that preceded the light of Christian thinking – which dispelled these traditions. 'That's getting spiritual', Andrew said, closing down the conversation. And so I was left wondering how to call to sharks.

*

'My name's Gunther. Come and sit here!' shouted a man, dressed only in a sarong, with a South African accent, walrus moustache and acres of flowing white chest hair. He was sitting in a sectioned-off area of the deck, under a sign that read 'Biergarten'. I hesitated. I hadn't been expecting washed-up beery expatriates. I continued to stand, and we had a strained conversation for a few minutes before he shouted, 'I'm deaf. Sit here.' I reluctantly acquiesced and sat on the adjacent deckchair in order to shout into Gunther's pileous ear.

Gunther, it turned out, was a German who had spent thirty-five years in the construction industry in Brisbane and whose mixture of clipped German and flattened Australian vowels made him sound like an Afrikaner. He had since spent twelve years, on and off, living on Malaita's artificial islands in the Langa Langa Lagoon, where he had used his construction skills to build the guesthouse on an island owned by his Malaitan wife, Rebekah.

'Locals couldn't build this', he asserted when I complemented him on the quality of the room I had been allocated.

It was difficult to resist the urge to point out that he was living on one of the ancient engineering marvels of the Pacific, a labyrinth of coral atolls all cut and built by hand, by the very locals he thought couldn't put up a wooden frame.

'All this bloody rain', he complained after an uneasy silence. 'It never used to be like this. Nothing's the same as it used to be. Climate change is stuffing everything up. We used to have seven metres of rain a year. Now it's more like ten.'

I said there had also recently been serious bushfires in Queensland.

'Let it burn', he shot back instantly. 'I don't like it there any more. I've been there more than thirty-five years, but they still won't give me a passport – bloody Australians. It used to be all right in the 1970s but not any more. They've stuffed it up: the corporates own everything, and there are too many immigrants.'

I got the sense that Gunther was slowly warming to his theme but, stuck in the deckchair next to him, it was going to be difficult to escape.

'Most places have gone to shit', he continued. 'Look at Fiji. There are three million tourists there every year. It's like the Gold Coast, although I've never actually been there. Wouldn't want to now.'

I asked if he was happy in Malaita.

'Yes', he replied, 'it's all right, but you can have too much of paradise. But what hope do I have at my age? My children won't look after me, but Rebekah will. Anyway, look at Namibia. Too many Chinese. This is the last frontier if you want to be alone.'

Abandoning Gunther, I went to a small platform overlooking the sea. There I found Rebekah, who was very different from her husband. At first, I gave Gunther the benefit of the doubt and assumed he was just professionally grumpy but had a heart of gold. But later, as I listened to him chastising Rebekah, complaining about the incapacity of the locals and listing perceived injustices, I came to the conclusion that he was a crank.

'You know', said Rebekah on the platform, out of Gunther's earshot, 'the Christians came along and they destroyed our memory. The old stories, the ancient lineages: they thought all these things belonged to the pagan past and tried to get rid of it. They made us wear their clothes and think in their way. We have lost so much.'

I asked if she considered herself a Christian.

'I use the word', she told me, 'but I don't believe, at least not anymore.'

Gunther's voice resonated from the other side of the guesthouse. 'Rebekah!' he shouted loudly and angrily. She went inside, at which point he started berating her about the preparations for dinner.

I suddenly felt the urge to be alone and certainly not in Gunther's company. While he was inside, I snuck off over the back wall of the guesthouse and into the adjacent mangrove swamp. Having taken a few muddy and uncertain steps, I found a stone path and followed as it cut its way through the dense overhang and spidery roots of the trees. After several hundred metres, the path forked, and I took the more overgrown and promising of the two directions, along a succession of raised rocky platforms. Soon, a number of beautiful thatched houses on stilts came into view, each on its own small, artificial land mass protruding out of the lagoon and connected to the path by a bridge of palms.

I came to a long, straight path covered with a light dusting of sand, making it soft underfoot, and lined with violet bromeliads. Here, to take shelter from a sudden downpour, I stood in the entrance of a thatched betel nut shop. I was joined there by some curious children, who introduced themselves magnificently as Arabella, Raphaella and Benedicta, and a serious young man called Remulus. While the girls played among the bromeliads, Remulus had a question for me: he wanted to know how different life was in Australia.

It was a hard comparison to convey to someone whose only experience of city life was Honiara and who came from a village where even the pathways were made to feel soft. I didn't want to give him the sense that local life, the 'simple life' as he called it, was in any way less desirable than Australia's urban environment. So I described the people, cars and skyscrapers, the endless roads and traffic jams.

He looked unconvinced by my account of urban congestion. 'We have everything here', he said. 'It is an easy life. There's our farm and the fish. But we have no money.' He had just returned from two years in Honiara working as a builder and wanted to study to be a primary school teacher but couldn't afford it. 'So last year I did a foundation course at a local seminary. I passed the exam and they have accepted me into a theological course for the next seven years to train to be a priest.'

I asked if this was what he wanted.

Without hesitating, he said no. 'But they will pay for my education', he added, caught between the devil and the deep blue sea.

I left Remulus to his grim decision-making and continued along through the bromeliads and down a muddy track past some vegetable gardens to the mouth of a small river. After crawling under low-hanging branches and across the black sand of the bank, I found a small clearing and had my own moment of existential indecision. Standing ankle deep in the estuarine water, I suddenly remembered there might be crocodiles lurking in the shallows. Instead of leaping back out, however, I reached for my phone and typed a query into the search engine in a moment of urban stupidity that I had just been warning Remulus about. 'Are there crocodiles in Malaita' I typed. But there was no internet connection. Looking down, I noticed in the sand several human footprints leading from the bank to the water, and recalled passing a small group of bathers who had come from this direction. So I dived in to the dark, slow-moving stream as it made its way towards the lagoon. The water was warm and then suddenly cold as I entered the middle of the stream. I swam against the current, watching gathering storm clouds and the occasional leap of a fish fleeing a lurking subaquatic predator.

After some time, I reached a fork in the river. I stopped swimming and floated on my back, looking up at the sky and the overhanging trees and drifting slowly with the current back down to the mouth.

As I emerged, I startled a family catching crabs with long bush knives. 'It's getting dark', said the mother. 'We'll give you lift back', and she dispatched her two small boys to fetch their dugout canoe for a ride home. As night fell, the canoe slipped quickly through the waters guided expertly by the boys. The sky was starless as we approached my island, but a school of squid beneath us fired astral flashes of phosphorescence through the dark of the lagoon.

13

BOUGAINVILLE:

AN ISLAND DESTINY

At the Destiny Guesthouse in Buka, the capital of Bougainville, there was a tug of war.

'He's new and I've arranged for my friends to show him around', said Ivy, a Papua New Guinean businesswoman who was also resident in the hotel.

But Mike, an Australian, wasn't listening and was already on the phone. He was on his way out. 'I came here to do some work for the UN', he said, 'but they weren't ready for me, so I'm going home. They're paying for it, not me.' Finally, ignoring me and Ivy, he got through on the phone. 'Hey, Cindy, I've got a little white man for you – *him stuka*', he added in Pijin – a good one. 'Look after him for me, Honey Bunny.'

Soon I could overhear Honey Bunny hatching plans about where I should reside and who I should visit. I decided to make a break for it to try to evade the competitive hospitality of Mike, Ivy and Honey Bunny, and as they argued I slipped out of the guesthouse through a side entrance and onto the main street.

But the wrestling match was just the beginning. 'Hello, my brother', said a man in a floppy camouflage hat and sunglasses that still bore the price tag on the lens. He told me that he, too, had just arrived, from another part of Papua New Guinea. 'I'm with the Christian Revival Crusade', he said, 'but I really want to go to Australia – Brisbane, Sydney, Adelaide – to preach the word of God. But particularly to the people of Adelaide. They need our help, brother, come join our crusade.' And once again, I was forced to escape, this time down a side alley.

I had been told to expect the unexpected. In a moment of blokey confidence, expat to expat, Mike had taken me sternly aside. 'It might feel safe, but you just don't know. They're volatile.' A moist cigarette clung between his ear and the sweat of his close-cropped skull. 'Ten years in in-country, and I still keep eyes in the back of my head', he had confided, the old hand guiding the newbie as he fixed me with a yellowing, alcoholic stare. If I knew to be alert to the potential physical dangers in Papua New Guinea, I had been totally unprepared to be mugged with generosity.

I stopped under a tree for a moment of shade. Next to it was a street stall and a wire fence that was hung with t-shirts in red, yellow and black Melanesian colours with a clenched fist next to the letters 'AROB' – Autonomous Region of Bougainville. At the entrance to a park opposite, a hand-painted sign in luminous-green lettering read 'One hundred and sixty days till the referendum'. Avoiding the gaze of the Christian Revival Crusade who had again come into view, I asked Jess, the stall owner, about the shirts and the sign, hoping to show 'my brother' that I was very busy doing something else.

'Business is good', she said and casually mentioned that the printed t-shirts cost around A$70. 'We get them made in Fiji and sent over. They're expensive but people are buying them.'

I asked which way she would be voting.

'I'm not from Bougainville, but I'm married to a local, so I won't vote', she told me bluntly. 'Anyway, the people here aren't ready for it. Just look around. Does this look like a capital to you? They think they can own the mine and have all the profits for themselves, but without PNG they can't do it or will have to sell it. In the meantime, we just try to make money from it either way. I can't afford a shop. I'm looking but it's too expensive, so I just work here under the tree. People still come, and if they want to buy expensive t-shirts, we will sell them.'

The coast was now clear, and I walked back to the main street, passing the bustling market with its betel nut sellers, and the colourful banana boats that ply the fast-running ocean passage between the island of Buka and the Bougainville mainland.

I was looking for a well-known local environmental activist and had a hunch that I might find her in the Department of Local Communities, where a number of civil society organisations were housed. But the doors were locked and the hall lights were out. One room appeared to have a light on, and a fading sign on the door announced that the '2016 S/M meeting' was taking place inside. I opened the door with some trepidation but to my relief found myself confronted by a blast of cold air from the air conditioner set to sixteen degrees and the warm, smiling face of Sione Atua, the director of the Bougainville Disability Forum. As if he was expecting me, Sione started showing me his organisation's annual 'action plan', which was written out on two small bits of torn notepaper and consisted of a number of squares in which were written a succession of code-like abbreviations and enigmatic phrases. Some of these were pitch-perfect replications of bureaucratic process. I learned that the organisation would be revising its policies and procedures, as well as initiating a consultative process leading to a new constitution. There would also, of course, be a meeting of executives. It was an impressive-sounding list and virtually all the disability forum could do, Sione told me, in the absence of any funding.

'The first thing we need', he said, 'is information. Except for me, we don't know who is disabled, how they are disabled, or where they live. We don't know if their disability is mental or physical. We don't know if they can't see or they can't walk.'

None of the staff of three – the director, the chair and the secretary – was paid. Sione told me that he went through the motions because, as a disabled person himself, he remained 'faithful to his people'. I noticed that the action plan was virtually identical to the previous year's action plan that he was using as scrap paper, except for an entry under the heading 'PNG Games'. It was completely unclear how his organisation supported anyone in any way. Sione sensed my interest and added proudly, 'We're planning to compete in boxing and running'.

*

Across the Buka passage is the small island of Sohano, which was the capital of Bougainville until 1975, when Australian rule in Papua New Guinea ended. The residences on Sohano are sharply differentiated: there are those at the top of the island and those at the bottom. On top of the rock, commanding a view of the Buka passage, stand the old colonial houses, with their stilts and hipped roofs and elegant lawns stretching out towards the sea. These are owned and lived in by the administrative upper orders of Bougainville, especially the judiciary. Several flights of well-maintained wooden steps leading from the beach up to a gabled gateway have signs which read 'for judges only'. Ancient trees covered in ferns and supporting immense canopies provide a vaulted green roof against the harsh North Solomons sun.

At the bottom of Sohano is a settlement, where I found Chief Tekuna, a dapper, sharp and funny man with 1970s sideburns, film-star looks and dark hair, a Polynesian from Bougainville's distant Mortlock Islands.

'Smile', I said as he posed for a photo, shirt unbuttoned, sideburns flashing and eyebrows raised like a 1970s Lothario.

'I am smiling', he replied. 'But I don't have any teeth.'

Gradually, as the sea claimed more of their islands and remote atoll life had grown increasingly difficult, the Mortlock Islanders migrated to Sohano, forming a displaced Polynesian settlement at the base of the rock.

'I'll go back to Mortlock to go under', Tekuna said, gesturing downwards.

'Or up?' I asked.

He laughed and shook his head. 'Definitely under', he said, before continuing:

I was the first to settle here. There were so many jobs – in government, on the mines, teaching if you had education. But not now. It is impossible for many young people to know what to do. Even on Mortlock, government recruiters used to turn up to try to get labour. My island has changed.

We can't even get there any more. There used to be a regular government ferry, but now the boat may or may not go every few months, and people end up being stranded in Buka. More people from Mortlock live here and in Port Moresby than live in Mortlock. There are only about a thousand left there now, mostly old. All the young ones have left, but that's where I'll go when I've retired here.

It has changed since I was young. Everyone lived there. We thought it was a big island, but now we've lost so much land. We can't grow anything in the way we used to, and there are almost no government services. But eventually, I will go back to my island and the sea will have my bones.

I asked Tekuna about the referendum and if he supported independence.

He equivocated for a moment. 'I think the referendum will be a disaster', he said. 'So many people from Mortlock live elsewhere in

PNG, so many other people have married here and live in Bougainville. What will happen to them?' Then he continued, 'Anyway, no one knows what it means. What actually is independence? And what is greater autonomy? No one has spelled this out.'

From nearby, his neighbour chipped in. 'We are a minority community. We believe we are close to Tongans and speak a language that is related to other Polynesian languages like Tongan and New Zealand Maori. But the government doesn't care about us; we're not their first priority.'

Tekuna interrupted, 'I've got to go to Buka for a doctor's appointment.' I commiserated, but he waved his hand to stop me. 'No, no', he said dismissively. 'I'm not unwell; I'm just trying to retire after forty years in the public works department, but they won't let me. I worked in HR so I know the system. I have to pay off three doctors to say I'm too ill to work, and I'll qualify for a pension. Today is doctor number one.'

I walked to the banana boat for the short ride back to Buka. On the way, I passed the local school buildings. Some were decaying and covered in student graffiti; others had recently been upgraded. A sign outside one classroom showed that Australian Aid helped to fund the refurbishment, and a graffito in sketchy red lettering under it read, 'Blood money, bad bones.'

*

On arriving back in Buka, I found a sense of commerce and activity. The Sunday torpor had worn off, and the sleepy backwater feel had been replaced by a more go-ahead spirit. The market bustled; the banana boat operators hustled; crowds walked the streets, stopping at the local stores. It could even have been a microscopic national capital in the making.

As I passed the market, a well-dressed businesswoman sporting sunglasses and gold earrings held out her hand and stopped me. 'Hi again! I'm Ivy', she said. 'Where did you run to yesterday?'

We began a conversation, but her phone kept ringing, and every few words were interrupted by another urgent caller.

'Yes', said Ivy into her device, 'oil nitrate. I can get that for you'. Moments later it was bêche-de-mer – 'No, keep drying them. The boat hasn't arrived yet. It should be here soon' – followed by a flurry of WhatsApp messages to keep her trading contacts happy. 'You know', she said, 'I think there are big opportunities in mud crab.'

As we stood there a passer-by made a largely indistinguishable remark about all the 'redskins' hanging around.

'I'm from a different part of Papua New Guinea', she explained with a resigned expression. 'Not as dark as people in Bougainville. And they call us "redskins". I always reply that I'm red on the outside and black on the inside.' Then she continued in an off-hand way while still checking her phone, 'By the way, that's a massacre site from the war.' She gestured towards an ordinary public park with a few betel-nut sellers. 'There's a mass grave under that tree', she said matter-of-factly referring to the brutal, decade-long conflict between Bougainville secessionists and the Papua New Guineans that began in 1988. It was unmarked although, not coincidentally, a large sign above the park read, '159 days to referendum'. But Ivy's concerns were more immediate.

'Business is tough', she continued. And she wasn't just making the inevitable merchant's complaints about red tape. 'Sometimes they don't want us redskins here. See that man over there?' She pointed to a man wearing militia fatigues, an old army hat, a red bandana and, on his right hand a single black fingerless glove studded with small metal spikes at the knuckles. Ivy told me he had been a soldier with the now-disbanded Bougainville Revolutionary Army and had subsequently been in prison for robbery, assault and rape. She continued, 'I had to deal with him for some supplies, and when it all went wrong, he sent me a text saying, "My last bullet is for you."'

As if hearing this, the man walked over. He didn't look at me but greeted Ivy with a few words. They bumped fists in a boxers' salute, adversarial one of respect.

So I meditate and spend time on my own. Maybe I'll disappear; maybe I'll migrate like the rest of my family to Australia. It's difficult to stay here, and I can't return home. They've burned down my house, built by my father, who was a product of the kiaps [the colonial era district officers]. He had a different mindset and just got things done. Everything has changed, and the church hasn't helped. We used to have sorcery – the sorcerer would sit to the right of the chief as an advisor and would mediate in case of disputes. There was no direct killing – it was done through the sorcerer, who maintained social control. The churches told us that this was wrong and introduced a new world view, but they failed to bring along a judiciary, a police force and other means of social control. It is violent now.

Ivy had her own story of violence. 'My former husband was a soldier in the PNG army, Delta Force, that was sent in to fight the BRA. He was part of the killing that happened here, and because of this we broke up. After the crisis I came to Bougainville to try to help the lives he had destroyed. My real interest here is early childhood education and that is what keeps me here. It is so important, and every time I think of leaving, I look in the mirror and I see those little black faces and I think, "Phonics".'

We walked down the street as dusk closed in. The Bougainville government had set up a large outdoor television and was playing films as part of a campaign to raise awareness about the upcoming referendum. But the content was bizarre. There were three shorts playing on repeat all day, every day, to a small and dwindling crowd. The first was propaganda produced by Bougainville Copper Limited (BCL) in the early 1970s about the Panguna copper mine. This was, at the time, the world's largest copper mine that produced immense profits for Australian-owned BCL and for the Papua New Guinea government, although very little of the money ended up back in Bougainville. It focussed on the heroic era of mining in Australia and showed great trucks bulldozing the landscape at a time when this was genuinely thought to be progress. The music was synthesised and triumphant – the sound of hard yakka, beer commercials and fast money – as the giant machines carved their way through the ancient rainforests to prosperity while big white men in hard hats operated heavy equipment.

The film cut to a small boy whose home had stood in the valley now demolished by the immense mine. On cue, he said, 'I like the bulldozers best: they have four gears forward and four gears backwards.'

'Only the women protest', said the deep-voiced narrator with more than a hint of condescension towards Bougainvillean traditions of matrilineal land ownership, 'and they want another environmental assessment. They get their token victory and the mine goes ahead anyway.'

'Do you know what you want to be when you grow up?' an Australian contractor asked the local boy.

'I don't know', answered the boy. 'I'm changing all the time, like my valley.'

I asked my neighbour what she thought of the film.

She was shocked by the environmental destruction. 'Look at all the trees', she said. A disoriented hawk circled, looking for its former home in the debris. 'The whole thing is so sad. It's all about the referendum. The government wants us to think about what it means. They see this as development, progress, economic opportunity. Maybe. But I think it's sad.'

'They seem to be using old Australian propaganda', I said, and she nodded vigorously. I asked if she thought the referendum would be successful.

'Yes. Ninety per cent will vote yes, and I will too', she replied.

'*Him strait*', said the young man sitting next to her – in Pijin, 'it's true.'

Nearby, a policeman visiting from Port Moresby was having difficulty with his phone. I recognised him as a fellow resident of the Destiny Guesthouse and he waved. 'Talk about independence', the policeman muttered to me under his breath. 'They can't even get the internet to work. You can forget the digital economy.'

The next film started playing. Gone was the Australiana of the 1970s; this was a film about a couple of travelling English musicians. 'That's not Bougainville', said Ivy after a few moments. Eventually we realised that it had been filmed in the Kalahari Desert: a different place and time, but with equal condescension to the Bougainville Copper Limited propaganda film.

If the almost nonexistent audience at the film didn't get the idea of the enormous amounts of money to be made from mining, perhaps they would be inspired to vote for independence.

As we walked on, we bumped into Marie, a friend of Ivy's, who worked with the Autonomous Bougainville Government. Along the way we encountered a large puddle.

'There needs to be a bridge here', Ivy joked as she skirted the muddy water.

'Perhaps there was a bridge proposal, but it ended up as an Incomplete Development Project', replied Marie, reeling off the jargon.

Not missing a beat, Ivy returned with 'Maybe we can get the Chinese to supply a non-concessional loan?'

It was funny but also true – a dress rehearsal of the international development jargon already being mastered by the soon-to-be-independent state's officials.

Ivy was heading for a bar where she had arranged to meet her friends Aidah and Liah, and she invited me along. The three women had first met in a safe house for victims of gender-based violence run by local Catholic nuns. This had provided a temporary roof, but the nuns had been harsh, abusive and violent themselves, so all three had run away from the 'support centre' and had then relied on each other for support. Although they had managed to escape marriages with violent men, they still had to be wary of sorcery allegations made by others who were envious of their relative success.

Both of Liah's parents had been severely injured in an assault. After she had left her husband, she had gone home to live with her parents but they then suffered another attack, this time from the neighbours. 'They hit my parents with a bush knife', she said, 'because someone said my mother was practising witchcraft. But really they see that we are getting ahead. I feel sick whenever I go back to the village. We try to get on with life, my mother has recovered but still has scars on her head and neck from the attack. But I know who did it, they still live there and they pretend nothing happened and I feel it in my heart.'

'In the past', said Aidah, whose father was a village chief, 'the sorcerer and the chief would work together and discuss how best to manage the spirit world, and this could involve different rituals, feasts, traditions and offerings. But now people have taken this into their own hands, and there is just violence against anyone who is accused.' The old way of managing conflicts had largely broken down. Now accusations based on sorcery could be made by anyone and this led to increasingly arbitrary violence, especially against women, as scores were settled, jealousies enacted and power inequalities brutally reinforced, fuelled by accusations of witchcraft.

Yet the three friends were defiant and were planning a joint business venture. 'Chinese New Year is coming', said Ivy. 'We need two thousand mud crabs to export to Hong Kong by next weekend.'

Underpinning their commercial plans was a simple aspiration: the women were planning to build their own homes. 'If we have small houses of our own, we will be safer', said Liah. 'We just need enough money for some palm leaves and timber, and we will be able to hide away and lead our own lives.'

'Perhaps', Ivy added after a pause, 'we can build a house from crab shells and become hermits and the nuns will never find us.'

It was late and dark, but the women refused to let me go back to the hotel alone. We walked through the shadowy backstreets of Buka, past numerous young men drinking in illegal beer bars selling warm bottles of South Pacific beer and brain-destroying home brew. They were preoccupied with their own entertainment and ignored us, but Ivy had met yet more female friends along the way. Together they closed ranks and I found myself in the middle of a protective phalanx of Bougainvillean women being escorted back to the Destiny Guesthouse.

*

Bougainville's recent history had all begun in Arawa, four hours along a bumpy road to the south. While struggling with a large clutch of pineapples and mangoes in the market, I met Gladys who offered to take me on a tour of the city. Arawa was the main town and commercial centre that serviced Bougainville's Panguna copper mine and the town had an eerie familiarity, despite being in the middle of Bougainville. Walking around with Gladys, I recognised its wide roads, orderly intersections and footpaths and neatly trimmed nature strips. I found myself in Section Ten, where the houses on stilts and the clipped lawns transported me back to a clear day in suburban Cairns or Brisbane. There was a Shell petrol station, a squash court, Coca-Cola advertisements, bank branches, and a faded white municipal building with the words, 'Celebrating ten years of independence, 1985'. It was an Australian town from the 1980s, decaying now, but frozen in time, capturing the moment when the war started and the nearby Panguna mine shut down.

As Gladys and I walked through Arawa, still scarred and abandoned from the conflict, she relived it in her mind as it was in its heyday: a well-run, lively municipality of well-paid mine workers, their families and the people who ran the businesses, schools and entertainment. This was no fly-in, fly-out operation; instead, miners and administrators lived and worked in the town and helped build a community. 'This was a marvellous supermarket', she recalled wistfully, as we came to a burned-out building and paused in the shade of its dilapidated awning. A few doors further on, Gladys pointed out the Johnson & Johnson Pharmacy, firmly shuttered and padlocked. At the small financial hub, there was a sign for 'Niugini Lloyds Bank', and at the peeling former municipal building, Gladys pointed out the Bank of the South Pacific, the name adorned with a coconut tree still visible on the walls. 'My mother used to work there', she said, her footsteps slowing as we passed. But something was on her mind, and as we came alongside an overgrown block with rusty wire fencing that had been her primary school, she started talking about the crisis. 'It was a terrible time', she repeated softly for a few moments, as if willing herself to remember. I had not asked her about it, but for her the past lived on indelibly.

'When the fighting started, I left school, and our family went back to the bush. We were scared, and we didn't want to be part of it, so we lived in our village. We didn't have any guns, but we defended it with traditional fighting sticks. We didn't attack anyone; we just tried to make sure we were safe. But then my brother became ill with an infection. It got so bad that my parents decided they had to get him to a clinic in a PNG army–controlled area. So we surrendered. But this made the BRA mad.'

She could barely describe what had happened next. The Bougainville Revolutionary Army members had come into the village. 'They had guns, so we couldn't stop them, and they demanded to see my mother. They accused her of passing secrets to the PNG Defence Force. My brother and I tried to stop them, but they pulled her away and dragged her off into the bushes. I knew who they were and had known them before the conflict. I was so scared that they would also take me away and rape me, but I couldn't let them take my mother, so I screamed that I wanted my mother back.'

We stood in the gentle rain of the afternoon, alone in an empty street in a partly abandoned town, while Gladys cried. 'That night', she continued, 'my mother crawled back to our village, and I held her in my arms.' She had been brutally assaulted by the militia. While she had miraculously survived, her health never fully recovered, and she had died the previous year, still young.

'I rarely leave my house now', said Gladys, 'except to go to the market and buy betel nut, and often I just want to be alone.'

After the conflict, at the age of twenty, Gladys went back to secondary school and later started a university course in business studies in Papua New Guinea. But she became pregnant to an abusive partner and returned to Arawa without finishing her degree. 'So now I sit at home and look after my children', she said, 'and sometimes I do housework for some people in town. I see those people sometimes, the BRA people who did this to us, but I ignore them. They say hello and smile at me, but I hate them, and I can't look at them. They were supposed to be fighting for us, not treating us like animals. We are the same people.' She pinched hard on her forearm to indicate the jet-black skin pigment that is distinctive of Bougainville.

We walked on, and I asked if she thought the town was slowly returning to life.

'Not really', she said flatly. 'We have the referendum coming up, but I don't know what is going to happen. We cannot go back to the

231

violence; I am too tired. The BRA say they have disarmed, but they have their guns hidden somewhere in their homes. I have heard some of them talking about World War Three if they don't get their way. Anyway, you don't need guns to kill.'

We stopped again for a moment on the empty footpath, listening to the rain.

'Come', she said eventually. 'Let's walk.'

*

While walking around the old commercial centre of Arawa, I also met Augustine. Now in his fifties, he had held a good job in the municipal administration before the conflict. I had met him outside another abandoned building in the town square, where he was leaning against a railing, dressed, even now, for the office. 'I have a problem with my children', said Augustine, as he sat in his office above the long-defunct North Solomons Photo Service. It was raining hard outside, and the office was dark and had no electricity. In a corner, two toilets sat side by side, the cubicle walls long gone, lending a soiled air to the office where Augustine was trying to start an organisation providing adult education and literacy classes. He worked at a small metal table in a shaft of light, and on the shelves around him were some old books, a spineless, yellowing New Testament and some reports, untouchable with age and grime.

Even in his current office he maintained a professional air. He boasted to me that he had overseen the introduction of the town's first traffic lights. 'We were second only to Port Moresby.' Pointing out of the window to an overgrown field where a game of touch rugby was taking place, he added, 'Arawa is supposed to be like Sydney. All the town planners used to call the highway the "Harbour Bridge", and next to that is "Parramatta."' On the town's edge, there used to be a golf course designed by Greg Norman. 'You see, this town isn't what it used to be. When I was growing up we had the best education in PNG. Bougainville students are clever, always came first in their school exams. We had Australian teachers, and the standards were very high. There were Europeans too in our schools.'

I asked if the Europeans had led separate, segregated lives, like in so many other mining contexts, but he said no.

'We were all together, it was very friendly, and there weren't too many distinctions, although the school authorities found that white women were attracted to local men and tried to put a stop to it by separating them when they got to secondary school', he said with a wry smile. 'But now it is different. We have a lost generation.' With this, he suddenly became distracted. I could hear some rummaging around in the dark behind my back, and Augustine kept looking anxiously past my shoulder. 'It's my son', he said at last, and I asked if I could meet him.

'This is my son, Don', said Augustine, summoning him from the back of the office so we could be introduced. We shook hands.

Whereas Augustine retained the professional, educated respectability of a man working in municipal government, his son was distracted and moved about nervously. He had Augustine's gentle, intelligent looks, but they were at odds with his tough militia style. He was wearing a red bandana – the symbol of affiliation to the Bougainville Revolutionary Army – and cut-down fatigues. He looked like a militia member. After a cursory nod, he lit a cigarette, blew smoke into the air above us as if marking his space and then, without a word, lurched – part swagger, part stumble – in a twitching, zigzagging manner, towards the door. We were clearly not of interest to him.

The slight tension and air of concern that had come over Augustine with Don's appearance were replaced with determination once he had left. 'He never went to school after the crisis', he said.

'He looks like it, but he is far too young to have ever been part of the BRA. In fact, our village stayed out of it, and we tried to provide education to people during that time. Anything we could think of, really – carpentry, building, making baskets – so that, despite the crisis, our young people would still know something. I named him Don after my Australian teacher at school who encouraged me to do business studies and taught me merchandising.'

I asked if Don could read.

Augustine reflected for a moment. 'Not really', he said. 'A few words and sentences, but not really. So many young people are like this. They think they are the BRA, but really they are not, and there are no jobs for them. There is marijuana and home brew, and so my organisation will try to teach these young people what they missed out learning.' Undefeated, he raised his hand and gestured at the mouldy office, the exposed lavatories and disintegrating reports. 'My team will work from here', he said.

*

Late that evening, I left Augustine's office. It had stopped raining and the night was cool. A few market stalls remained open, sheltering in the trunk and under the canopy of two immense fig trees. It was tempting to go back to the hotel, but there was one final person I wanted to meet: Ishmael, a local musician and peace activist, and I went to his house where the light was still on and asked to speak with him. A well-built man emerged in the half-light. He had a brisk and vigorous manner, and one arm, although still strong, was withered slightly; he held it at an angle across his powerful upper body. Part of this arm was missing and had healed in a fearful knot of muscle and sinew below the sleeve-line of his t-shirt, which bore the slogan 'Nothing is impossible' across his expansive chest. 'A close encounter with a grenade launcher', he stated, matter-of-factly, picking up my glance at the scar. 'I used to be a fighter', he added, unnecessarily. If the young men of Arawa sought to imitate his style, they were failing completely. There were no bandanas, camouflage or other insignia of mock militia. But equally there was little doubt that he had led a unit in the Bougainville Revolutionary Army. After a few moments' reflection, Ishmael remembered:

It was emotional for me when we gave up our weapons. I didn't become a peace activist immediately, and I didn't start wanting reconciliation, but gradually I reached this position through a series of small, cumulative decisions. When we signed the peace agreement, some commanders still wanted to keep fighting. But I follow nature. I read the signs and try to feel what is in the air. It seemed that our time for fighting was over. Francis Ona wanted to continue, but when we signed the peace agreement, one of the pillars of the agreement was a referendum on independence. I didn't want to give up my gun; I was a fighter and our unit had success. I wasn't tired of war, but I thought that what we needed to do with guns had been achieved.

Thinking of Augustine and his son, Don, I repeated concerns that there was a lost generation who had grown up with the war but were too young to remember or have been activists in a political cause.

'What do you mean?' he responded combatively. 'My children are okay. It is really up to the parents and how they bring up their children. The main thing is that this is our land and our future now, so I don't know what you mean by lost. In the end, we won the war, and now we need a strong vote in favour of independence. We fighters have done our part. I have put down my gun, and it will be a wasted opportunity if the people of Bougainville don't support

235

us in the referendum. If they don't, they will have let themselves down. We need ninety-five per cent of the vote in favour to show the government that we are united.'

I asked about his music.

'We play reggae now, mainly', he replied. 'We were inspired by the liberation movements of the Caribbean.' His song titles included 'United', 'One people', 'Justice', 'Independence', and I wondered if he wrote anything that was not about politics. 'They are all political', he said, then sang a few bars – a rich, deep melody arising from his barrel chest. '"There are tears in my eyes, my country. I cry for you. There are tears in my eyes." That's from "Bougainvillea nights"', he said, exposing the revolutionary army's softer side.

As I walked back to the hotel, I came across a giant television screen like the one in Buka, blaring out into the night. It was raining again, and in the abandoned marketplace an academic conference that had taken place some years earlier in Port Moresby was being beamed to an audience of none in the name of 'referendum awareness'. An international legal academic was mid-exposition, 'Of course there are several sets and subsets of referenda, of which I shall discuss only the most pertinent', he said, waving his pale arms against the dark mountains that loomed behind the Panguna mine.

*

Fifteen minutes out of Arawa, we came to a checkpoint. I was travelling with Blaise Ona, a traditional landowner and grandson of Francis Ona, a former leader of the Bougainville Revolutionary Army, and we had come to visit the site of the copper mine and his family's ancestral homeland, Panguna. The mine was also the safe haven from which Blaise's grandfather sheltered from Papua New Guinea's defence forces and it was still protected by loyal ex-BRA fighters. The checkpoint marked the entrance to territory once controlled by Ona. 'We are entering a no-go area', said Blaise, 'but my grandfather was a man of peace. He fought against soldiers and only against people with guns. Here, he wanted a checkpoint, not a road block. There is a difference.' In other contexts, a roadblock might suggest lawlessness, but not in Bougainville. 'The checkpoint means it's our land', said Blaise. 'Government control ends here.'

Alex, a former BRA fighter, came to the car. He wore a scarf draped over a Chuck Norris t-shirt, along with a red bandana that marked his BRA affiliation. He asked for a fee and then produced a receipt book and wrote down my name and address and the amount paid. They were not rebels but landowners, on their own land, and the receipts gave a small but important signal to all visitors of their claim to legitimacy.

'Francis did not want to fight', Blaise told me. 'But he defended his land, his tradition and the environment.'

Alex felt similarly. 'I think mining is over', he said as he handed me the receipt. 'We need to focus on agriculture now, before all the land is destroyed. You white people live by money, but we live by land. You can live on it, but you can't exchange it.' Before the crisis, Alex had been a supervisor at a limestone quarry, skilled in using and overseeing mining equipment and managing men. Like Augustine, he had retained his sense of professionalism. His Australian-accented English was perfect, his manner friendly yet brisk and businesslike. Had he not been at a checkpoint wearing a militia scarf, we could have been in a construction office somewhere, discussing a difficult project. 'I went back to the bush and survived there', he told me. 'I was offered mining jobs elsewhere, in Western Australia and at Ok Tedi, but I stayed on to fight with my people. My son is now thirty, but because of the crisis he has no education. He is a different generation, a lost generation. They look tough, with their beards and hair and army clothes, but they never fought. If there is no independence, there will never be peace in Bougainville.'

When we drove through the checkpoint the road suddenly deteriorated, and Blaise swerved his van left and right to avoid the potholes. Soon, we came to some derelict concrete outhouses marking the beginnings of what was once Panguna mine. Abandoned truck tyres, gradually disintegrating, lay by the side of the road, along with unidentifiable wrecks of rusting machinery. Blaise slowed and swerved. Nestled deep in the hillside I saw a row of boxes four storeys high that resembled stacked shipping containers. These had originally been built for miners but were now occupied by local landowners and their families, who had slowly returned to the vast ruin that was once their valley. Some of the boxes were rusting, while others were hung with washing. Cloud had descended into the deep greens and emeralds of the valley's rainforest-encrusted ridge.

We drove on, eventually coming to a section of the road that made a good viewing point, and Blaise stopped the van. We looked down into the massive cut starting just below the ridge line and spiralling down the valley in even gradations to the floor of the mine. In places along the sides, oxidised copper stained the cut green and a murky lake had formed in the narrow point at the bottom. Far, far below there were some houses. Some moving specs turned out to be a family with a couple of small children walking slowly back up to the top of the ridge.

'They still prospect here, especially after it rains', said Blaise. 'There is gold here. That was the problem. It claimed to be a copper mine, but the company, Bougainville Copper Limited, never declared all the gold, silver, cadmium and zinc they found. They just drove it to the wharf in Arawa and put it on ships to Australia, the US and Europe. The PNG government got less than one per cent of the profits from copper, and nothing came to us, the landowners, in Panguna.'

I asked if he had studied geology.

'No', he replied. 'I was a child when the crisis started. I stopped school at grade six and never went back. But I worry about that family we just saw. The children do not go to school; they try to find gold. But BCL used mercury, nitrate and cyanide – poisons and heavy metals that are still in the ground. They drink the water and eventually get sick.'

We stopped talking for a moment, and I could hear the rush of a small waterfall across the valley echoing against the bare, exposed sides of the pit. Some birds were chirping, and in the distance a couple of eagles circled, looking for prey.

'How do you feel, coming back and looking at what has become of the mine and the valley?' I enquired when we were moving again.

Blaise pondered for a second. 'Good', he said. 'It is peaceful now, and it is ours.' He stopped the van briefly next to a Japanese anti-aircraft gun from World War Two, pointing in perpetuity at a distant ridge.

I expected him – as Francis Ona's grandson, coming from the place at the heart of the Bougainville conflict – to show the same resolve as Alex and Ishmael in supporting independence. I put the question to him, nonetheless, but Blaise was more reflective.

'I think people will vote for it, but I don't see how independence is possible', he said. 'How will we make the mine work?' he asked. 'How will we support the economic development of our people? Our government can't even maintain the roads.' After a while, he added, 'I think our people are like African people.'

I was unsure what he meant but Blaise continued after a short pause.

'I think they live a simple life in the bush, and so do we.' His vision was one of small-scale coexistence. 'Look at people here', he said. 'They grow bananas and coconuts now, and if they have nothing, they can still survive with a small agricultural project. They pan for gold and find enough for them to go to the shop and have some money. We don't need this any more', he said, gesturing at the gouged, dissected, brutalised valley of his ancestors.

Blaise took me to an abandoned workshop where broken mining equipment used to be repaired. Here, he introduced me to Stephen and Chris, who had returned to their valley and had become the de facto caretakers of a workshop: a vast metal frame with a few twisted and rusting hulks of equipment that even the scrap-metal dealers who scoured the site refused to take. Their families were living in adjacent sheds made from corrugated iron and scraps of metal from the mine.

'Everyone will vote for independence', said Chris, the larger and more vocal of the two. 'We fought for it. I have seen everything that happened during the crisis and I know nobody will vote against independence. Under BCL and when we were part of Papua New Guinea, we needed to fight for our environment. Just look what they did here and elsewhere in PNG. But once we are independent, we'll open it all up – copper, gold, limestone – and get the mine started again, but this time for us.' His brief concern for the environment had vanished before the prospect of large amounts of cash. He was perhaps typical of a younger generation. Dressed in camouflage, albeit with an 'I love PNG' t-shirt, he looked the part and talked up independence.

How old he was when the crisis started?

'Six', he replied. He was affected by it but was not part of it and had a style and stridency that did not come naturally to the members of the older generation who actually fought.

'What do you think we should do with this building?' Stephen asked me.

Confronted with an enormous, collapsing metal structure in the middle of an open-cut mine, I couldn't bring anything particular to mind, so I returned the question.

Chris had the answer. 'This will become our export hub', he said with deep certainty. 'But no Chinese. I hate the Chinese', he continued, out of the blue. Given the role of Australia in the mine and in the Bougainville conflict, I asked what he thought of Australians. 'They're okay', he said. 'They're not Chinese. They just want to suck everything out of the ground and sell it. They don't care about anything.'

Blaise and I drove back along the road towards the checkpoint. The car ascended a ridge into a fine, cold mist that was refreshing after the sun and aridity of the mine. We stopped for a moment on the ridge before going down the potholed road, back through the no-go zone and into the government-controlled areas beyond the checkpoint. There was a clearing in the mist and suddenly a view of the dense forest in the valley below, with shadowy peaks just visible through a distant cloud. From our high point, we looked across the valleys of Bougainville and, as the clouds returned once more with the fading light, restricting our field of vision, I turned to get back into the car. Blaise hesitated.

'Look', he said, pointing down, 'there's a black orchid.'

14

KIRIBATI AND THE CURSE

OF THE GIANT CLAM

'We must offer a gift to ensure you are welcome and that you are protected', said my host, the custodian of the Cursing Place, who led me to a clearing in the coconut trees where a ring of stones surrounded a giant clam shell. I stood back as he bowed before the clam and approached it reverentially, announced the purpose of our visit and who I was, then requested the clam spirit's protection.

'You will be okay now', the custodian reassured me. He produced from his pocket a lime-green packet of Gallaher's Irish Mint Cream Cake chewing tobacco. After a lifetime of masticating reflectively at the bottom of the ocean it seemed that the ancient and irascible clam had developed salty old tastes. 'It likes chewing tobacco', averred the custodian, 'although I sometimes get away with giving it a packet of Rothmans, myself.'

Respectfully, I approached the clam, eyeing its grim jaws and large white teeth. The custodian, who had been walking next to me, suddenly advanced, stooping quickly to deposit a moist brown lump of tobacco into the clam's jaws before closing them with a snap.

Safe to explore the island, I took a photo of the clam, which now looked somehow less threatening and appeared, as far as I could tell, to have adopted a content and self-satisfied air. Then I left the Cursing Place to spend the day walking by the lagoon.

I had come to North Tarawa in the Republic of Kiribati to see a different side of the country. I had been in the south – one of the most populated stretches of the planet and a place of dense urbanisation – and wanted to get a sense of a more traditional island life. South Tarawa had become so polluted that even the hermit crabs had taken to finding abandoned bottle caps, rather than shells, in which to make their moveable homes. Nancy Phelan, an Australian author, travelled to Kiribati in the 1950s. Her book *Atoll Holiday* is an account of the country as it was before nuclear tests, climate change and independence, when just getting there took several weeks by boat. In the early 1990s, she revisited, but things had changed, especially in South Tarawa, as she reflected in *Pieces of Heaven*:

The climate was different, the time of year, the getting there. Instead of peaceful weeks at sea and a magical coming ashore, there was a flight with Air Nauru and arrival at Bonriki airport, tired, apprehensive, dreading the thought of action ...

I felt like a ghost as I walked along the once immaculate beach. The tide was out and odd bits of garbage were strewn across the water line. The shallows were murky, a greyish lagoon reflected a colourless sky. Corrugated iron was everywhere, hot ugly metal that flared in the sun and turned a once cool cave into an oven. Was Bairiki turning into a Santiago *callampa*, a Casablanca *bidonville*?

Later, as Phelan flew over Kiribati, she noted, 'Below are the phantom islands; white continents roll past above a blue sea. The

Pacific still waits, holding back, biding its time. Scientists and others talk calmly of rising temperatures, rising sea levels, low islands being submerged, the resettling of atoll people. Could these beautiful little islands one day disappear, their story end as it began, with nothingness, only the silent presence that broods over the empty wastes?' Was life better before or after independence, she wondered. 'It is Kiribati now', came the reply.

I had not known Kiribati before independence and urbanisation, so on my second visit to the country in 2019, ten years after my first, I was less surprised by what I found on South Tarawa. Some things had even improved. A causeway had been completed and no longer looked like the wreckage of adaptation projects from decades past. This also gave a greater sense of security, despite the narrowness of the atolls. The fatally invisible speed humps that quickly reduced all cars to rusting carcasses, as a result of impact damage, had been removed. The main road now had generous, shady, tree-lined footpaths on either side that were a pleasure to walk along and were cool during the day and on the drive in from the airport, and the lagoon was a liquid lapis lazuli that took the breath away. Still, Betio, the commercial hub at the southern tip of South Tarawa, looked even more overcrowded, built up and haphazardly constructed from tin and bits of old car wreck than it had a decade ago. The beaches had become filthier, and the great World War Two Japanese guns and coastal defences that had been installed to ward off the Americans seventy years earlier were rusted, uncared for and surrounded by rubbish and faeces.

*

One evening on South Tarawa, I was invited quite randomly by a friend to an event marking the departure from Kiribati, after sixty-five years, of a Catholic nun. Suffering from motor neurone disease and unable to speak, she was being repatriated to Australia for greater medical care in her declining days. The ceremony took on a raucous tone as if to make up for her lack of voice. Young nuns kicked the habit and sang and danced in commiseration and celebration. 'It's okay; it's custom', one said as they jettisoned their drab robes, put on the magnificent grass skirts and floral headdresses of Kiribati tradition and danced with the precisely calibrated abandon born of the years of musical training with which all young I-Kiribati children are raised.

Confused as to who I was, yet generous and hospitable, the nuns led me to a seat at the front with the dignitaries and I found myself sitting with a representative of the Australian government from Canberra to one side and the local bishop to the other.

'Not many visitors here', said the government representative between songs, when I told him I was a tourist.

I responded that I couldn't imagine why. If not the overcrowded South Tarawa, with its car graveyards, shanty towns and dirty beaches, then the rest of the country surely had the atoll paradises, wondrous beaches and local cultures that would attract tourists in their hordes?

'Not really', he said, as the frenetic dancing of the nuns recommenced.

'At least it's quite easy to get here from Australia and New Zealand', I said.

'Nup', replied the representative.

'Cheap flights with Air Solomons?'

'Hardly.'

'Great fishing, sublime climate …?'

There was an official snort. And still the grass-skirted sisters sang their high hosannas. 'I've had more high-profile missions, you know', the visiting official confessed between beats, and I sensed his lack of enthusiasm for the tourist sites of Kiribati might be related to his career trajectory, as he listed a series of apparently more desirable postings. 'What we have done, though', he finally conceded, 'is to build a climate-proof road.'

Back at the hotel, after the celebrations, I sat on the verandah overlooking the lagoon. The other guest was an air traffic controller from Tuvalu who was visiting Kiribati for an airport security course. This was run by two Singaporeans more used to one of the world's busiest airports than Bonriki International, with its two flights a week. He was looking particularly happy and relaxed, and was sitting on the veranda in a singlet, holding a beer.

'Cheers', he said, with great satisfaction. 'One of my relatives has just died.'

It wasn't immediately apparent why he was so cheerful at the news of this death, but at first I put it down to cultural differences.

'I was strategising which day of the course to miss – you have to be there at the beginning and the end, when they give out the certificates. So I thought I'd miss Thursday – in the middle, no one will notice. But with the death, everything changes. I can miss the whole thing. Thank you, Aunty!'

He chugged some more beer.

*

Everywhere I went, I asked, after a while, about climate change. Under former president Anote Tong, Kiribati led the world in campaigning and raising awareness of the issue. And with a maximum high point of 3 metres and a few tiny strips of atoll landmass in some places just a few metres wide, it is among the countries most vulnerable to sea level rise. Tong had bought land in Fiji and openly discussed the long-term viability of the country. 'Migration with dignity' was the official pledge, and education was seen as the means by which this could be achieved, ensuring that people would have skills, jobs, and careers that would support them as they resettled.

But Tong was no longer in power, and his successor, an evangelical Christian, opted more for adaptation and denial. 'Noah's pledge' once more entered the frame of reference for climate change: there will be no second flood. Caught in a bind between science and God, a former minister for the environment explained to me that, while he believed climate change was happening and water levels were rising, he also believed that the waters would go around Kiribati, leaving the atolls untouched – a phenomenon he illustrated with a wave of his hand around a large coconut.

'Oh, the alarm', said another former member of parliament, rolling her eyes, when I asked about climate change and the future. For all the talk of the islands suddenly disappearing under water, people were still getting on with their daily lives. The international media image of a helpless people drowning had become annoying and detracted from the way in which a proud and independent people were trying to adapt to changing circumstances. With the construction of new roads and causeways between the atolls, it was pointed out to me, the landmass of Tarawa had actually increased substantially. Although, this also revealed how marginal that landmass had been to begin with, a few roads could make such a dramatic difference.

At the country's national archives, I spoke with the librarian, who had a different view. 'It's in the genealogy', she said. She laid out maps of Kiribati genealogy leading back to the mythical founder, Nareau the Creator, a spider who slept in the eternal vortex of space and woke when he dreamed that someone was calling his name. Nareau ultimately created the atolls of Kiribati using his own dismembered limbs as the land. 'You see', said the librarian, 'Nareau the Creator could never destroy something that he himself had created. He would never destroy himself. Our past proves that we will survive into the future.'

But causes and symptoms seemed to have become confused, and I felt that Kiribati's people had, in a way, been badly served by some of the climate messages. They are not just going to sink out of sight one day; instead, the effects of climate change were already present in daily life, without the drama of a cyclone or a war or some sudden onset catastrophe. It was, I suspect, more like going bankrupt: slowly at first and then all of a sudden. Mass urbanisation – entirely new to Tarawa – was underpinned by a changing climate. So too were the protracted dry periods, during which the lack of rainfall meant already stressed water reserves had come under increased pressure.

At the time of my visit, much of South Tarawa was practising water rationing, with families queuing with plastic buckets at water lines buried in the atoll for the few hours in every day or two when the water supply was switched on. The reliance on imports, diets changing to canned food and horrific problems with diabetes and heart disease were the consequences of this 'slow' phase of social and economic change in response to a changing climate. Daily life rarely seemed dramatic, but climate change was upon the people of Tarawa and would, I thought, only become more obvious once the new causeways and roads began to crack and break up – as would inevitably occur – from the remorseless pressure of the sea. Before the latest round of climate infrastructure investment, Kiribati had already been the place to go to see the wreckage of adaptation past, as once 'climate-proof' roads, causeways and sea walls built to help the nation adapt to climate change fell apart.

On an unstable mound of rubble half way towards the airport, I stopped under a sign. 'Highest Point in Kiribati' it read, at all of three metres high. Even with the most optimistic assessment of warming temperatures and likely sea-level rise, great strain will continue to be put on this nation of atolls.

And despite the assurances that all was well, the pictures forming in people's imaginations suggested a less confident outlook. Emele, an archivist who worked at the national library, told me that she had inherited from her father a traditional role of interpreter of dreams in her community. Usually, the dreams people described to her were about human relationships – jealousies, competition, aspirations and anxieties. But there had been a change, and something unusual had recently been creeping into the local subconscious. Anxiety dreams, which typically involved waking up in fright at the perception of a sudden fall, were now about the sudden need to climb to get to higher ground.

*

I decided I needed to explore beyond South Tarawa to get a sense of Kiribati as it might have been before the majority of its population moved to the capital. So early one morning I arrived at the dock and for several hours watched the bustle as I waited for the boat to North Tarawa. Plywood outriggers loaded and unloaded in the artificial harbour. It was not clear which boat was going where, but here and there a grizzled captain clutching a plastic bucket and battered school exercise book started selling tickets, and crowds gathered around each one, heads bent in together, to have their names entered into the book and to secure their passage.

Some young men in an open-sided shed a few metres away were still drinking from the night before. As the heat intensified and the long hours began to take their toll, a fight broke out, much to the entertainment of the crowd. For some time a tag team of young drinkers attacked each other, but they caused little damage other than occasionally bumping into people in the crowd who were engrossed by the spectacle. Afterwards, not satisfied by the actual combat, the would-be combatants stood around breathing heavily, looking fierce and glaring at any members of the public who made eye contact.

It started to rain.

The police arrived, but they were there to meet a dead body that had been brought over on one of the boats. It was picked up and slung into the back of a truck, the translucent feet, a paler shade of death, sticking up over the edge.

Eventually, my boat was called. My name went into the exercise book and I established a perch on an outrigger. There was a last-minute flurry as passengers already aboard sent orders back for a final round of packaged noodles, and then we began the slow chug across the turquoise waters of the lagoon. After a sustained period of crunching and slurping, the children fell asleep to the gentle swaying of the boat. Their mothers took the opportunity to light up sweet pandanus cigarettes and drew long draughts of smoke as they looked out across the lagoon and enjoyed a few moments' respite. After an hour of so of the meditative drone of the engine, I was deposited on a beach in North Tarawa next to house on stilts over the water where I was to spend the night.

The following morning, I woke to a marvel. It was low tide and the lagoon had disappeared entirely. There was rain in the air, and the day was overcast and misty. The sand seemed to stretch to the horizon. In the diffused light, distant angular figures like dark stick insects were setting up fishing nets in the sand for the returning tide. I spent the day talking with local villagers who invited me into their homes with offers of shade and coconuts.

One man I encountered told me about his school days, before independence. 'You know, the British used to be here, so I speak English well. But it is not the same for the young people. They struggle to talk and are often shy in English.'

What was it like, I wondered, before independence?

'We used to have a white man – a governor – and he had a very big hat. We were called the Gilbert Islands then, but it is Kiribati now', he said, reflecting his pride at his own self-governing nation. Kiribati was no longer ruled by anyone else.

Another older man I met had once been a district officer, working in the government service. As the empire in the Pacific had finally come to an end, I-Kiribati had been given more senior jobs in the administration, which had previously been reserved for Europeans. 'But still', said the man, 'they were very strict and hierarchical. No native could be higher than a white man, and they had very strong opinions about how things should be done.'

Had it been a relief when the colonial system ended?

'Yes', he replied. 'We could be ourselves. We had some money from phosphate mining, and this is now worth more than a billion dollars as our national investment fund. We also renegotiated fishing rights and this helps our revenues. More importantly, our culture is strong.'

We drank from fresh young coconuts in the shade and listened to the wind rustling through the palms.

Throughout the day I captured these moments with my camera: the old man reminiscing, the early morning moonscape of the drained lagoon, the clam in the Cursing Place with its taste for chewing tobacco. But the clam had other ideas. I had dinner in a *maneaba*, a coral and coconut structure being used as an eatery. Afterwards I walked in the pitch darkness down to the beach, to the crooked walkway made of roughly hewn palm trunks that led over the water of the lagoon to my hut. I had just downloaded all my photos onto my computer and deleted them from my camera in readiness for the next day's discoveries. Holding the computer securely under my arm, I walked confidently – as I had already done several times that day – along the central plank. Buffeted by a sudden gust of wind, however, I stepped off the main plank and landed on another plank, which was unstable. It wobbled, opening up an alarming drop below. Instinctively, my arm shot out as a counter-balance. But in doing this, I lost hold of the computer, which flew through the night like a metal frisbee, glinting in the moonlight before dropping into the ocean. As I clambered back along the walkway to retrieve it, I noticed that the structure had become steady once more: none of the planks wobbled and all were solidly in place.

'It was the clam', one of the villagers told me. 'It didn't want you to take the pictures. You made an offering, so this was the compromise: you keep your camera but lose the computer.'

Strangely, although my computer had died, most of the photos somehow remained on my camera, except those of the clam. And there was a photo I didn't remember taking: a green-coloured packet of Gallaher's Irish Mint Cream Cake chewing tobacco glowing in the afternoon sun.

CANOES AGAINST THE CURRENT – PAST AND PRESENT IN A FUTURE OCEAN

AMONG THE ISLANDS AND ATOLLS OF THE PACIFIC OCEAN

The moment I inadvertently threw my computer into the Kiribati lagoon, I knew the time had come to stop writing. It was over ten years since I had first set foot in the Pacific Islands with a trip to Port Moresby, and I had now visited eleven of the region's twelve independent states (Papua New Guinea, Micronesia, Fiji, Kiribati, Marshall Islands, Palau, Samoa, Solomon Islands, Tonga, Tuvalu, and Vanuatu) and three of its dependent territories (Cook Islands, New Caledonia and the Northern Mariana Islands), although not all have been written about here. The exception was Nauru, whose government was hostile to journalists and writers and charged $8000 for a visa in an ineffective attempt to prevent people from reporting on the country's Australian-funded asylum-seeker detention centre. The appalling conditions there are well documented in Mark Isaacs' important book, *The Undesirables: Inside Nauru.*

While my exposure to the region had started as an aid worker, I quickly became fascinated by Pacific societies in themselves, rather than through the prism of aid and development programs that I had worked on, important as these programs continue to be.

The more I travelled, the more there was to write about, as each country and each island and each atoll slowly began to reveal its stories, its presents, and its pasts in response to my enquiries. It was liberating to arrive in a new place with only the intention of asking questions about what seemed interesting. The islanders I met were astonishingly generous with their time and tolerant of my attempts to scratch the surface of their societies. In the Marshall Islands, a visit that was initially meant to last a few days turned into several weeks, and it could easily have have lasted longer, had I not forced myself to catch a flight home. I met an American former Peace Corps Volunteer who had arrived in Majuro, the capital, in the early 1980s. Initially, this had been for a year or so, but he had lingered on for what was to become much of his adult life. I could see the same thing happening to me. Despite the problems that these distant islands faced, there was always something magical about the Pacific, a paradoxical expansiveness of small societies that held the world in a cluster of atolls. The subtle differences between cultures became more apparent to me the more I looked, and I found myself diving deeper and deeper into what anthropologist Francis Hezel has described as 'the new shape of old island cultures'. And there was always another island.

I also felt that my visit to Kiribati marked a certain circularity. In the guesthouse where I stayed, I found an old copy of Nancy Phelan's book *Atoll Holiday*, based on her 1958 visit. The guesthouse, whose three rooms faced onto the lagoon, was a delight and provided a book-crammed respite from days spent walking in the hot sun. At night, it caught the cool breeze off the lagoon and was a perfect vantage point from which to admire the constellations. I discovered that the guesthouse copy of *Atoll Holiday* had been inscribed by Nancy Phelan herself. 'To Dick and Peggy', her hosts in Kiribati, it said on title page, and she hoped that they would not be offended by how they had been depicted. Sixty years later, I showed this find to my hosts, Richard and his wife Beta, as they plied me with the local coconut toddy and answered my questions with great good humour. 'Those are my parents', said Richard, who had been born on North Tarawa and whose father had spent his career working in the colonial administration. Richard also made a brief appearance in the book as a 'flaxen haired child'. Perhaps mischievously, I said that I was following in Nancy Phelan's footsteps and asked how he and Beta would like to be depicted.

Somehow, despite the overwhelming influences of urbanisation, climate change, great power politics and nuclear testing, inter alia, that are in many ways the subjects of this book, there is much that perseveres in Pacific life. Return journeys, even ones across the generations, can bring back similar encounters. 'Don't worry', said Richard as I expressed sadness at leaving Kiribati, 'life is long', and memories, stories and cultural traditions in the region, like the currents of its large ocean states, are longer and stronger still.

But things are changing, and low-lying islands states face an uncertain future. The Pacific is, as traditional navigator Alson Kelen told me, 'where the nuclear age meets the climate change age'. Now the site of global contestation, the Pacific's island societies are at once an example and a warning. The vast currents of that great ocean are not as immutable as they once were. As the island choirs gather, once more to stand their ground, we must listen to their drumming and their song.

Select bibliography

Campbell, Ian, *A History of the Pacific*, University of California Press, Berkeley, 1989.

Dorney, Sean, *The Embarrassed Colonialist*, Penguin, Melbourne, 2016.

Evans, Julian, *Transit of Venus*, Eland, London, 1992.

Fischer, Steven Roger, *A History of the Pacific Islands*, Palgrave Macmillan, Basingstoke, 2002.

Hezel, Francis, *The New Shape of Old Island Cultures*, University of Hawai'i Press, Honolulu, 2001.

Grimble, Arthur, *A Pattern of Islands*, Eland, London, 2011.

Jeffery, Laura, *Niuatoputapu: Story of a Tsunami*, Tonga Books, Nuku'alofa, 2010.

Jetñil-Kijiner, Kathy, *Iep Jaltok: Poems from a Marshallese Daughter*, University of Arizona Press, Tucson, 2017.

Johnson, Giff, *Idyllic No More*, Giff Johnson, Majuro, 2015.

Laracy, Hugh et al. (ed.), *Tuvalu: A History*, University of the South Pacific, Suva, 1983.

Lawson, Stephanie, *Tradition Versus Democracy in the South Pacific*, Cambridge University Press, Cambridge, 1996.

Maclellan, Nic, & Chesneaux, Jean, *After Moruroa: France in the Pacific*, Ocean Press, Melbourne, 1998.

Maclellan, Nic, (ed.) *Louise Michel,* Ocean Press, Melbourne, 2004.

Michel, Louise, *The Red Virgin* (trans. Lowry, Bullitt, & Gunter, Elizabeth), University of Alabama Press, Tuscaloosa, 2003.

Phelan, Nancy, *Atoll Holiday*, Angus & Robertson, Sydney, 1958.

Phelan, Nancy, *Pieces of Heaven,* University of Queensland Press, St Lucia, 1997.

Prichard, Katharine Susannah, *Child of the Hurricane*, Angus & Robertson, Sydney, 1963.

Prichard, Tom Henry, 'In sapphire seas: the earl and the Dutchman – a story of Levuka', *Leader* (Melbourne), 20 August 1898, p. 32.

Prichard, Tom Henry, 'Half-hanged!', *Bulletin* (Sydney), 18 July 1896, p. 28.

Sahlins, Marshall, 'Poor man, rich man, big man, chief: political types in Melanesia and Polynesia', *Comparative Studies in Society and History*, vol. 5, no. 3 (April 1963), pp. 285–303.

Scott, Owen, *Deep Beyond the Reef,* Penguin Books, Auckland, 2006.

Acknowledgements

This book evolved over ten years of discussions and visits, and there are hundreds of people across the region to whom I am indebted.

In particular, I would like to thank Fran Berry, who initially commissioned the book, for her wonderful patience, enthusiasm and editorial suggestions throughout the writing process.

My friends and former colleagues in what was the Pacific Team at the Australian Red Cross have been a source of information and inspiration over the years: Mary Bateup, Zahra Bolouri, Kezia Brett, Kerryn Clarke, Paul Davenport, Joel Doutch, Kara Jenkinson, Petra McKay, Katrina Neville, Caragh Robinson, Kathleen Walsh, Donna Webb and Paula Fitzgerald.

In the Pacific, I am grateful for long conversations with many friends and former colleagues, and the generosity of people I talked with for this book: Wayner Louis, Sizue Yoma, Subesh Prasad, Hilary Hosia, Richard Newman, Senator Jeban Riklon, Alson Kelen, Marcella Sakaio, Abacca Anjain-Madison, Kelly Lorennij, Charles Reklai Mitchell, Clement Manuri, Cameron Ngatulu, Sir Tommy Chan, Sione Taumoefolau, Finau Heuifanga Limuloa, Tataua Pese, Augustine Garae, Ryan Smith, Neil Bauman, Fine Tu'itupou-Arnold, Charles Wapinien, John Hosea, Augustine Villiari, Blaise Ona, Llane Munau,

Ishmael Toroama, George Oli, Stephen Oli, Agnes English, Sione Atua, Richard Turpin, Beta Tewareka Tentoa, Hilary Hosia, Toube Aberaam, Aidah Kenneth and Gladys.

In Australia, I am equally indebted to the following people who have shared their remarkable knowledge of the region and literary insights: Tilman Ruff, John Cox, Patrick Dunn, Clara Gladstone, Jill Bamforth, Roger Bamforth, Julianne Schultz, John Tague, Vern Field and Gordon Peake. At Hardie Grant, thanks are also due to Arwen Summers, Loran McDougall and Penny Mansley.

In Port Moresby, Charles Wapinien showed me around and was a wonderful source of knowledge and information. He introduced me to the 007 Gang of Burns Peak, Port Moresby. The gang invited me into their community and generously shared their stories with me, and I would like to express my enormous gratitude to them. At their request, and in the hope that this book does not fall into the hands of the Port Moresby constabulary, their names are listed here: Antony Jerry Mandin, Joel Yagoma, John Francise (Jnr), Elaijah Maikolo, Alex Alico, Osan Porakali, Michael Maikolo, Tony Peter, Alu Bee, Lawrence John, Peter Levi, Tamity Mandin, Shadrack Jamal.

Tom Bamforth is an aid worker and writer. He has worked in humanitarian response and international development since 2005 when he was caught in the Pakistan earthquake while on an archeological tour of the North West Frontier Province, and he has worked and travelled extensively in the Pacific since 2008. His writing has appeared in *Granta, Griffith Review, Meanjin, Island, The Age,* and *Guardian.* He is the author of *Deep Field: Dispatches from the Frontlines of Aid Relief* (Hardie Grant 2014).

www.tombamforth.com